Grade Aid

for

Butcher, Mineka, and Hooley

Abnormal Psychology
Core Concepts

prepared by

Nicholas Greco IV
College of Lake County, Grayslake, Illinois

PEARSON

Boston   New York   San Francisco
Mexico City   Montreal   Toronto   London   Madrid   Munich   Paris
Hong Kong   Singapore   Tokyo   Cape Town   Sydney

TABLE OF CONTENTS

Preface

PREFACE

HOW TO USE THIS GRADE AID

This book is a tool that will help you to understand the concepts presented in the textbook. It is meant to give you a comprehensive, yet concise overview of the important aspects of each chapter.

The various sections of the Grade Aid are designed to give you a variety of learning experiences, will reinforce many key terms and ideas from the text, and most importantly provide you with invaluable test-taking practice. The answers to the questions and exercises are provided in the back of each chapter. Additionally, page numbers are given for each question or exercise so that you may check your answers. When used together, the text and the Grade Aid should provide you with the necessary knowledge to master the material.

The following is a more detailed description of the sections provided in the Grade Aid.

BEFORE YOU READ

This section provides a brief overview and table of contents for each chapter. The main purpose is to introduce you to the chapter before you begin to answer the questions in the Grade Aid. The table of contents comes directly from the corresponding chapter in the textbook.

OBJECTIVES

These are the goals you should be able to achieve after reading the chapter. They can be used to gauge your mastery of the chapter material.

AS YOU READ

The exercises in this section are meant to provide you with a variety of ways to remember the material. Given that not all people learn the same way, this selection of exercises hopefully will provide something for everyone. These sections include:

• Key words: use this part to define the important words identified by the authors. The page number that the word appears on is provided so that you may check your work. These are not in the answer section of your book.

• Who's Who and What's What—Matching: A matching section gives you the opportunity to become familiar with some important people, places, things, and ideas which are presented in each chapter. Again, it allows you to test your memory for important aspects of the chapter.

• Short answers: Writing is an important part of any class. This exercise is designed to see how well you can put your thoughts onto paper in a concise manner. This also provides a great way for you to test your strengths and weaknesses.

• The Doctor Is In: If you are taking an abnormal psychology class, perhaps you have aspirations of becoming a therapist. This section gives you an opportunity to test your diagnostic skills. Scenarios of disorders represented in the chapter are given, and you are asked to act as a "therapist" by diagnosing and treating the patient. These exercises allow you to apply the material in a "real world" scenario, and thus reinforce the complex yet rewarding study of abnormal psychology.

AFTER YOU READ

This section contains three practice tests. They are designed to provide you with invaluable test-taking practice. Each practice test roughly divides the chapter into thirds—each test asking questions from a third of the text. Again, the page numbers are provided at the end of each question. Take these tests and see how well you do. Then go back and correct your answers. These tests help prepare you for the comprehensive test which follows.

COMPREHENSIVE PRACTICE TEST

There are three types of tests in this section, multiple choice, true/false, and essay. They cover the entire chapter and afford you an opportunity to see how well you understand the concepts. Because there are several testing methods provided, you will a good amount of practice before the actual exam.

USE IT OR LOSE IT

This section consists of critical thinking questions designed to help you apply what you have learned in the chapter. These questions take on the various controversies within abnormal psychology, both theoretically and ethically. Of note, there is no right or wrong answer, so you are free to express yourself.

WEB LINKS

A number of carefully selected web sites are provided for more information concerning topics covered in each chapter.

CRISS CROSS

Another tool provided is a crossword puzzle that uses key words from the chapter. This comes at the end of each Grade Aid chapter and is a way to see how well you have remembered the definitions to the key words.

Chapter 1: Abnormal Psychology Over Time

BEFORE YOU READ

A solid foundation is the key to understanding a complex subject. While abnormal psychology is an extremely fascinating area of psychology, it can also be quite a challenging one given the numerous terminologies, the various disease states, and the wide range of treatments available. Every day we are surrounded by advertisements or medical updates in the news discussing the latest research findings on the radio, newspaper, or television for mental disorders; you may have a family member or friend with a mental disorder, or you have seen a movie on substance abuse or a mental disorder.

As advertisements and medical updates may be vague and much too brief, television and movies tend to overdramatize mental disorders. Therefore, the intent of *Chapter 1: Abnormal Psychology Over Time*, is to provide you with a foundation for understanding how mental disorders are defined and classified, how commonly they occur in the real world, the history of abnormal behavior from ancient times to the present, contemporary perspectives on abnormal behavior, and how to use psychological research methods to expand your knowledge regarding abnormality. Equally important, you will be able to separate fact from fiction and reality from myth, and gain an appreciation for the complexity of this fascinating field of psychology. Mastering these key concepts will allow you to become more comfortable with the information as you read the other chapters in the text. Soon what was once thought of as complex material will be viewed as invaluable knowledge.

- **WHAT DO WE MEAN BY ABNORMAL BEHAVIOR?**
  Why Do We Need to Classify Mental Disorders?
  What Are the Disadvantages of Classification?
  The DSM-IV-TR Definition of Mental Disorder
  How Does Culture Affect What Is Considered Normal?
  Culture-Specific Disorders

- **HOW COMMON ARE MENTAL DISORDERS?**
  Prevalence and Incidence
  Prevalence Estimates for Mental Disorders

- **HISTORICAL VIEWS OF ABNORMAL BEHAVIOR**
  Demonology, Gods, and Magic
  Hippocrates's Early Medical Concepts
  Later Greek and Roman Thought
  Abnormality During the Middle Ages
  Resurgence of Scientific Questioning in Europe
  The Establishment of Early Asylums and Shrines
  Humanitarian Reform
  Mental Hospital Care in the 20th Century

- **CONTEMPORARY VIEWS OF ABNORMAL BEHAVIOR**

Biological Discoveries: Establishing the Link between the Brain and
Mental Disorder
The Development of a Classification System
Causation Views: Establishing the Psychological Basis of a Mental
Disorder
The Evolution of the Psychological Research Tradition: Experimental
Psychology

• RESEARCH APPROACHES IN ABNORMAL PSYCHOLOGY
Sources of Information
Forming Hypotheses about Behavior
Sampling and Generalization
Criterion and Comparison Groups
Studying the World as It Is: Observational Research Designs
Retrospective Versus Prospective Strategies
Manipulating Variables: Experimental Strategies in Abnormal Psychology
Single-Case Experimental Designs
Animal Research

• UNRESOLVED ISSUES
Are We All Becoming Mentally Ill?: The Expanding Horizons of Mental
Disorders

OBJECTIVES
After reading this chapter, you should be able to do the following:

1. Discuss the complexities of defining abnormal behavior.

2. Explain the advantages and disadvantages of classifying mental disorders.

3. Explain the DSM-IV-TR definition of mental disorders.

4. Identify how cultural issues can influence the definition of abnormal psychology.

5. Describe how and why abnormal behavior was often attributed to possession by a demon or god in ancient times and the use of exorcism as the primary treatment.

6. Describe the various contributions that Hippocrates and Galen have made to the nature and causes of abnormal behavior.

7. Describe mass madness and the treatments available during the Middle Ages.

8. Discuss the inhumane ways in which mental patients were treated in the "insane asylums" of Europe and the United States.

9. Describe the humanitarian reforms instigated by Philippe Pinel, William Tuke, Benjamin Rush, and Dorothea Dix regarding the treatment of mental patients.

10. Discuss mental health care in the 20th century, the advances and the setbacks.

11. Explain how the discovery of a biological basis for general paresis and a handful of other disorders (such as senile mental disorders, toxic mental disorders, and certain types of mental retardation) contributed to the development of a scientific approach to abnormal psychology, and the emergence of biologically based modern experimental approaches to science.

12. Discuss how Emil Kraepelin's classification system was ahead of its time and why it still remains an important contribution to the field of psychopathology.

13. Trace the important events in the development of psychoanalysis and the psychodynamic perspective.

14. Describe how the techniques of free association and dream analysis helped analysts and their patients.

15. List the major features of the behavioral perspective.

16. Discriminate between classical and operant conditioning.

17. Discuss the importance of the experimental method.

18. Compare and contrast research approaches to the study of abnormal psychology.

19. Discuss how researchers can control sources of bias in the study of abnormality.

20. Discuss the issue of generalizing from animal research to human behavior.

AS YOU READ
Answers can be found in the Answer Key at the end of the book.

KEY WORDS
Each of the words below is important in understanding the concepts presented in this chapter. Write the definition next to each word. The page numbers are provided in case you need to refer to the book.

Term	Page	Definition
ABAB design	28	
Abnormal behavior	8	
Acute	22	
Analogue studies	28	
Asylums	13	

Behavioral perspective	21	
Behaviorism	21	
Case study	22	
Catharsis	19	
Chronic	22	
Classical conditioning	21	
Comorbidity	10	
Comparison or control group	25	
Criterion group	25	
Deinstitutionalization	16	
Dependent variable	26	
Direct observation	23	
Dream analysis	20	
Epidemiology	8	
Exorcism	12	
Experimental research	26	
Family aggregation	2	
Free association	20	
Incidence	9	
Independent variable	26	
Labeling	6	
Lifetime prevalence	9	
Mass madness	21	
Mental hygiene movement	15	
Mesmerism	19	
Moral management	15	
Nancy School	19	
Negative correlation	26	
Nomenclature	5	
Observational research	25	
One-year prevalence	9	
Operant conditioning	22	
Point prevalence	9	
Positive correlation	26	
Prevalence	8	
Prospective strategy	26	
Psychoanalysis	18	
Psychoanalytic perspective	18	
Retrospective strategy	26	
Sampling	24	
Self-report data	23	
Single-case research	26	

design		
Stereotyping	5	
Stigma	5	
Unconscious	19	

MATCHING
An Historical Who's Who in the Mental Health Field
Match each of the following people with her/his accomplishment or theory.

_____ Hippocrates *(460–377 B.C.)*
_____ Galen *(130–200 A.D.)*
_____ Avicenna *(980–1037)*
_____ Robert Burton *(1576–1640)*
_____ Paracelsus *(1490–1541)*
_____ Johann Weyer *(1515–1588)*
_____ Philippe Pinel *(1745–1826)*
_____ William Tuke *(1732–1822)*
_____ Benjamin Rush *(1745–1813)*
_____ Dorothea Dix *(1802–1887)*
_____ Emil Kraepelin (1856–1926)
_____ Franz Anton Mesmer *(1734–1815)*
_____ Sigmund Freud *(1856–1939)*
_____ Wilhelm Wundt *(1832–1920)*
_____ J. McKeen Cattell *(1860–1944)*
_____ Lightner Witmer *(1867–1956)*
_____ William Healy *(1869–1963)*
_____ Ivan Pavlov *(1849–1936)*
_____ John B. Watson *(1878–1958)*
_____ E. L. Thorndike *(1874–1949)*
_____ B. F. Skinner *(1904–1990)*

Descriptions and Achievements

A. American psychologist who adopted Wundt's methods and studied individual differences in mental processing.
B. American teacher who founded the mental hygiene movement in the United States.
C. Austrian physician who conducted early investigations into hypnosis as a medical treatment.
D. Islamic Arabian-born physician who adopted principles of humane treatment for the mentally disturbed at a time when Western approaches to mental illness were the opposite.
E. American psychologist who established the Chicago Juvenile Psychopathic Institute.
F. English Quaker who established the York Retreat, where mental patients lived in humane surroundings.
G. Swiss physician who rejected demonology as a cause of abnormal behavior.

H. Greek physician who believed that mental disease was the result of natural causes and brain pathology, rather than demonology.
I. American psychologist who established the first psychological clinic in the United States, focusing on problems of mentally deficient children.
J. French physician who pioneered the use of moral management in La Bicétre and La Salpétriére hospitals in France.
K. Known as the father of behaviorism, he changed the focus of psychology to the study of overt behavior rather than the study of theoretical mentalistic constructs.
L. Oxford scholar who wrote *Anatomy of Melancholia* in 1621.
M. The founder of the school of psychological therapy known as psychoanalysis.
N. Greek physician and advocate of the Hippocratic tradition who contributed much to our understanding of the nervous system.
O. German psychiatrist who developed the first diagnostic system.
P. German scientist who established the first experimental psychology laboratory in 1879.
Q. American physician and founder of American psychiatry.
R. Russian physiologist who published classical studies in the psychology of learning.
S. Developed concept of instrumental conditioning.
T. Formulated the concept of operant conditioning.
U. German physician who argued against demonology and was ostracized by his peers and the Church for his progressive views.

SHORT ANSWERS
Provide brief answers to the following questions.
1. Why do we need to classify mental disorders? (p. 5)

2. What are the drawbacks to classification? (p. 5)

3. Describe the current DSM-IV-TR definition of mental disorders. (p. 6)

4. How does culture define what is normal versus what is abnormal? (p. 7)

5. Discuss the difference between *prevalence* and *incidence*. (pp. 8–9)

6. Discuss humanitarian reform, highlighting moral management and the mental hygiene movement. (pp. 14–16)

7. Discuss mental health care in the 20th century. (pp. 16–17)

8. Describe the beginnings of psychoanalysis and the importance to the field of psychology. (pp. 18–20)

9. Briefly discuss Watson and Skinner's contributions on American Psychology. (pp. 21–22)

10. Discuss the strengths and limitations associated with using an experimental approach to study mental illness. (p. 26)

11. When might a single-case experimental design yield useful clinical information? (p. 26)

THE DOCTOR IS IN...PSYCHIATRIC HELP—5¢

1. You are working with Dorothea Dix and advocating for humane treatment for the mentally ill. You have just visited a local mental institution. In your journal entry, you write two paragraphs describing the conditions you have seen. (p.15)

2. It is the Victorian Era, and you are concerned about your wife who is presenting with symptoms of hysteria. What might Dr. Freud's treatment entail? (p. 18)

3. You are developing a new medication treatment for depression. Your previous research findings have demonstrated that the drug XYZ is effective in lab animals and safe in healthy humans; however, you must conduct a 300 patient study using 100 mg of drug XYZ with individuals suffering from depression in order to receive approval from the FDA. Describe how you would set up this experiment. Be specific regarding independent and dependent variables. (pp. 26–28)

CHAPTER 1: CORE CONCEPTS

AFTER YOU READ

PRACTICE TESTS
Take the following three multiple-choice tests to see how much you have comprehended from the chapter. Each represents roughly one third of the chapter. As you study the chapter, use these to check your progress.

Practice Test 1

1. Jane, her sister Susan, and their mother, Ruth, all suffer from depression and anxiety disorders. This is what we would describe as (p. 2)
      a. family aggregation.
      b. parental aggregation.
      c. maternal aggregation.
      d. similar aggregation.

2. The removal of _____ as a mental disorder from the DSM is an example of how the definition of *abnormal* or *deviant* may change over time. (p. 3)
      a. depression
      b. pedophilia
      c. homosexuality
      d. voyeurism

3. A classification system, like the DSM, provides us with necessary (p. 5)
      a. structure.
      b. focus.
      c. nomenclature.
      d. numenclature.

4. John can't hold a job, we don't expect him to get married, and he has bipolar disorder. This is an example of (p. 5)
      a. stereotyping.
      b. labeling.
      c. stigmas.
      d. All of the above

5. The most recent edition of the DSM is (p. 6)
      a. DSM-IV.
      b. DSM-IV-TR.
      c. DSM-IV-CR.
      d. DSM-IV-R.

6. Taijin Kyofusho is a form of anxiety disorder and is quite prevalent in (p. 8)
    a. Japan.
    b. Australia.
    c. Africa.
    d. China.

7. Ataque de Nervios is an example of a psychopathology that is specific to which culture? (p. 8)
    a. Middle Eastern
    b. African
    c. Asian
    d. Hispanic

8. Behavioral that deviates from the norms of society is called (p. 8)
    a. prosocial behavior.
    b. normal behavior.
    c. abnormal behavior.
    d. normal teenage behavior.

9. This is the study of the distribution of diseases, disorders, or health-related behaviors in a given population. (p. 8)
    a. etiology
    b. biology
    c. epidemiology
    d. pathology

10. Enrique presents to the E.R. with low mood, poor appetite, heightened irritability, and complaints of "feeling like I am going to die." As the psychiatry resident finishes her interview, she writes down a working diagnosis of major depressive disorder and panic disorder. This is an example of (p.10)
    a. incidence.
    b. comorbidity.
    c. comortality.
    d. prevalence.

Practice Test 2

1. He classified all mental disorders into three general categories—mania, melancholia, and phrenitis. (p. 11)
    a. Avicenna
    b. Hippocrates
    c. Galen
    d. Pluto

2. This Greek Physician took a scientific approach to the field, dividing the causes of psychological disorders into physical and mental categories. (p. 12)
    a. Avicenna
    b. Hippocrates
    c. Galen
    d. Pluto

3. This trend emerged in the Middle Ages in an effort to understand abnormal behavior and involved the widespread occurrence of group behavior disorders that were apparently cases of hysteria. (p. 12)
    a. lycanthropy
    b. tarantism
    c. mass madness
    d. None of the above

4. A radical approach to the treatment of mental illnesses was this symbolic act to drive out the devil. (p. 12)
    a. exorcism
    b. bloodletting
    c. trephining
    d. a and b

5. Beginning in the 16th century, these special institutions were meant solely for the care of the mentally ill. (p. 13)
    a. hospitals
    b. wards
    c. asylums
    d. None of the above

6. His unchaining of the mentally ill in French asylums demonstrated that humane treatment of the mentally ill was possible. (p. 15)
    a. William Tuke
    b. Henry IV
    c. Philippe Pinel
    d. Patrice Pinel

7. The York Retreat is a pleasant country house where mental patients lived, worked, and rested. It is still in existence today and was began by (p. 15)
    a. Benjamin Rush.
    b. Benjamin Franklin.
    c. Dorothea Dix.
    d. William Tuke.

8. A tireless reformer who championed the causes of the mentally ill and was a driving force in humane treatment. (p. 15)
    a. Benjamin Rush
    b. Benjamin Franklin
    c. Dorothea Dix
    d. William Tuke

9. In 1946, this government organization began and provided active support for research and training through psychiatric residencies and clinical psychology training programs. (p. 16)
    a. NIH
    b. NIMH
    c. NMHA
    d. FDA

10. This movement created great difficulties for many psychologically disturbed persons and for many communities as well. (p. 16)
    a. Institutionalization
    b. Deinstitutionalization
    c. Reinstitutionalization
    d. Preinstitutionalization

Practice Test 3

1. He played a dominant role in the early development of the biological viewpoint and developed a classification system that is the forerunner of the DSM. (p. 18)
    a. Emil Kraepelin
    b. Benjamin Rush
    c. Sigmund Freud
    d. John B. Watson

2. This comprehensive theory of psychopathology that emphasized the inner dynamics of unconscious motives is known as the (p. 18)
    a. physioanalytic perspective.
    b. psychoanalytic perspective.
    c. behavioral perspective.
    d. unconscious perspective.

3. Jake felt better after his emotional release, better known as (p. 19)
    a. free association.
    b. catharsis.
    c. dream analysis.
    d. transference.

4. This perspective is organized around a central theme: the role of learning in human behavior. (p. 21)
 a. classical perspective
 b. psychoanalytic perspective
 c. behavioral perspective
 d. unconscious perspective

5. Ivan Pavlov (1849–1936) is noted for his work with dogs in which he demonstrated what was to become known as (p. 21)
 a. operant conditioning.
 b. generalization.
 c. classical conditioning.
 d. a and c

6. Instrumental conditioning was later renamed operant conditioning by (p. 22)
 a. Skinner.
 b. Watson.
 c. Pavlov.
 d. Freud.

7. Dr. Miller studied Linda's post-traumatic stress disorder over a period of 10 years. Dr. Miller was using this method. (p. 22)
 a. direct observation
 b. survey
 c. case study
 d. self-report

8. It is impossible to test a new treatment on everyone in the United States with depression, so researchers typically use a representative and random (p. 24)
 a. sample.
 b. population.
 c. Both a and b
 d. None of the above

9. The local university is conducting a study to identify persons who have a higher-than-average likelihood of developing depression given their family history and to then focus on them before the disorder begins. This type of study would be (p. 26)
 a. prospective.
 b. retrospective.
 c. introspective.
 d. technospective.

10. This is the most basic experimental design in single-case research. (p. 28)
- a. ABAC
- b. ACAC
- c. ABAB
- d. ADAD

COMPREHENSIVE PRACTICE TEST
The following tests are designed to give you an idea of how well you understood the entire chapter. There are three different types of tests: multiple choice, true/false, and essay.

Multiple Choice

1. A classification system for mental disorders is advantageous because it gives us a way to (p. 5)
- a. structure information.
- b. advance research.
- c. create treatment plans.
- d. All of the above

2. Disadvantages of a classification system are (p. 5)
- a. stereotyping.
- b. stigma.
- c. labeling.
- d. All of the above

3. The number of active cases of an illness in a population during any given period of time is referred to as (p. 9)
- a. incidences.
- b. epidemiology.
- c. clinically significant.
- d. prevalence.

4. The number of new cases that occur over a period of time is referred to as (p. 9)
- a. incidences.
- b. epidemiology.
- c. clinically significant.
- d. prevalence.

5. Hippocrates said that mental illness could be classified into three general categories: (p. 11)
- a. spiritual, demonic, and exorcised.
- b. paranoid, depressed, and schizophrenic.
- c. blood, phlegm, and bile.
- d. mania, melancholia, and phrenitis.

6. If you were living in the last half of the Middle Ages in Europe and saw groups of people jumping and dancing, you would think this was (p. 12)
    a. mass madness.
    b. normal madness.
    c. group madness.
    d. Middle Age madness.

7. Treatment of the mentally disturbed during the Middle Ages consisted of such things as prayer, holy water, visits to holy places, and this symbolic act to drive out demonic possession. (p. 12)
    a. blood Letting
    b. exorcism
    c. trephining
    d. dancing

8. This method of treatment focused on the patient's social, individual, and occupational needs. (p. 14)
    a. humane management
    b. general management
    c. moral management
    d. hygienic management

9. This movement closed psychiatric hospitals and reduced the population of the mentally ill in the state and county mental hospitals. (p. 16)
    a. Institutionalization
    b. Deinstitutionalization
    c. Reinstitutionalization
    d. Preinstitutionalization

10. The portion of the mind that contains experiences of which a person is unaware is said to be the (p. 19)
    a. preconscious.
    b. collective unconscious.
    c. unconscious.
    d. conscious.

11. He reasoned that if psychology were to become a true science, it would have to abandon the subjectivity of inner sensations and other mental events. (p. 21)
    a. E. L. Thorndike
    b. John Watson
    c. B. F. Skinner
    d. Sigmund Freud

12. Symptoms short in duration are_____, while symptoms long in duration are
_____. (p. 22)
      a. acute, chronic
      b. chronic, acute
      c. chronic, chronic
      d. acute, acute

13. While John is waiting in his doctor's office, he is asked to fill out a questionnaire on his mood. This questionnaire is referred to as (a) (p. 23)
      a. self-report data.
      b. direct observation.
      c. case study.
      d. analogue study.

14. In Dr. Hill's research design, there is no manipulation of variables. She looked at people who already had suffered a trauma and compared these groups to those who had not. This research design would be (p. 25)
      a. observational.
      b. experimental.
      c. a case study .
      d. a survey.

15. Despite two failed experiments, the company was determined to demonstrate the efficacy of drug Z on depression. In the new trial, the dose of drug Z was increased to 20 mg in order to demonstrate a 25% decrease in depressive symptoms. The independent variable would be (p. 26)
      a. drug Z.
      b. a 25% decrease in depressive symptoms.
      c. Both a and b
      d. None of the above

True/False

1. T / F The DSM-IV-TR stands for the Diagnostic and Statistical Manual of Mental Disorders Fourth Edition Text Revision. (p. 6)

2. T / F Abnormal behavior is behavior that originates from the norms of the society in which it is enacted. (p. 8)

3. T / F Comorbidity seems to be especially low in people who have severe forms of mental disorders. (p. 10)

4. T / F Hippocrates is often referred to as the father of modern medicine. (p. 11)

5. T / F The four essential fluids of the body are blood, phlegm, bile, and black bile. (p. 11)

6. T / F Greek physicians followed the principle of opposite by opposite in their treatment. (p. 12)

7. T / F Philippe Pinel helped to establish the York Retreat with William Tuke. (p. 14)

8. T / F Dorothea Dix helped to lead the deinstitutionalization movement in America. (p. 15)

9. T / F Sigmund Freud was the first psychologist to set up an experimental psychology laboratory. (p. 20)

10. T / F Classical conditioning is a form of learning in which a neutral stimulus is paired repeatedly with an unconditioned stimulus that naturally elicits an unconditioned behavior. (p. 21)

11. T / F In Skinner's view, behavior is shaped when something reinforces a particular activity of an organism. (p. 22)

12. T / F When things vary in a direct, corresponding manner, this is known as negative correlation. (p. 26)

13. T / F If there is an inverse correlation, this is known as a positive correlation. (p. 26)

14. T / F Experimental research always involves testing hypotheses by manipulating variables across groups. (p. 26)

15. T / F The most basic experimental designs in single-case research is called the ABBA design. (p. 28

Essay Questions

1. Discuss the advantages and disadvantages of classification. (pp. 5–6)

2. Describe abnormality using the DSM and Wakefield's definition. (pp. 6–7)

3. Discuss the Mental Hygiene Movement and the role Dorothea Dix played in it. (pp. 15–16)

4. Explain the pros and cons of mental health care in the 20th century. (pp. 16–17)

5. Discuss psychoanalysis versus behaviorism. (pp. 18–22)

6. Explain the advantages and disadvantages of case studies, self-reports, and direct observations. (pp. 22–24)

WHEN YOU HAVE FINISHED

WEB LINKS TO ITEMS OR CONCEPTS DISCUSSED IN CHAPTER 1
DSM-IV-TR
      http://dsmivtr.org/
This is the official site for the Diagnostic and Statistical Manual of Mental Disorders. Here you will find many points of interest as well as a link to the DSM-V Prelude Project.

The Healers of Ancient Greece
      http://www.nlm.nih.gov/hmd/greek/index.html
This site provides a wonderful overview of the practice of medicine in ancient Greece. In addition to Galen, Aristotle, and Hippocrates, there is a fascinating timeline of Greek contributions to medicine.

An In-depth Look at Galen
      http://www.udayton.edu/~hume/Galen/galen.htm
Considered by some to be one of the most important contributors to medicine, everything one would want to know about Galen is contained on this Web site.

Philippe Pinel
      http://www.whonamedit.com/doctor.cfm/1027.html
Philippe Pinel's system for the humane treatment of mental illness is well known and while appropriately highlighted, Pinel's fascinating life is given the attention it deserves.

Benjamin Rush
      http://etcweb.princeton.edu/CampusWWW/Companion/rush_benjamin.html
A well-written biographical representation of the designated "Father of American Psychiatry," this site describes how Dr. Rush was a highly regarded physician who advocated for the treatment of mental illness as a disease.

Dorothea Dix
      http://www.greatwomen.org/women.php?action=viewone&id=48
A biography of this great woman is posted here.

Sigmund Freud

      http://plaza.interport.net/nypsan/freudarc.html

This site is devoted to Sigmund Freud with links to other Freud sites.

National Institutes of Mental Health

      http://www.nimh.nih.gov

The National Institute of Mental Health is the U.S. government agency devoted to research about the causes and treatment for mental resources. This home page will lead you to all kinds of information about disorders, treatment, clinical trials, and careers.

USE IT OR LOSE IT

Provide an answer to the thought questions below, knowing that there is more than one way to respond. Possible answers are given in the Answer Key.

The number of pharmaceutical company commercials and advertisements is overwhelming, especially for antidepressant medications. Why do you think we do not see any commercials or advertisements for antipsychotic medications?

Why do Freud's theories continue to be taught, despite the biological focus on the treatment of mental illness and the fact that many of his ideas cannot be proven?

CRISSCROSS

Now that you know all there is to know about this chapter, here's your chance to put that knowledge to work.

Across
2. The proportion of active cases that can be identified during a given period
3. Sudden onset of a disorder, usually with intense symptoms
5. Study of the distribution of mental disorders
6. Method Freud used to study and treat patients
7. Long-standing or frequent disorder, often with progressing seriousness
8. Occurrence rate of a given disorder
10. The process of selecting a representative subgroup
13. A major portion of the mind containing a hidden mass of instincts, impulses, and memories
14. A school of psychology that formerly restricted itself primarily to study of overt behavior
15. Form of learning in which a response is reinforced

16. Basic form of learning using a neutral stimulus with an unconditioned stimulus repeatedly to eventually elicit a conditioned response

Down
1. Method for probing the unconscious by having patients talk freely about themselves
4. Movement to close mental hospitals and treat patients in the community
9. Identifying two or more disorders in a psychologically disordered individual
11. Theories of animal magnetism (hypnosis) developed by Anton Mesmer
12. Institutions meant solely for the care of the mentally ill

Puzzle created with Puzzlemaker at DiscoverySchool.com

ANSWERS TO TEST QUESTIONS – CHAPTER 1

MATCHING
__H__ Hippocrates *(460–377 B.C.)*
__N__ Galen *(130–200 A.D.)*
__D__ Avicenna *(980–1037)*
__L__ Robert Burton *(1576–1640)*
__G__ Paracelsus *(1490–1541)*
__U__ Johann Weyer *(1515–1588)*
__J__ Philippe Pinel *(1745–1826)*
__F__ William Tuke *(1732–1822)*
__Q__ Benjamin Rush *(1745–1813)*
__B__ Dorothea Dix *(1802–1887)*
__O__ Emil Kraeplin *(1856–1926)*
__C__ Franz Anton Mesmer *(1734–1815)*
__M__ Sigmund Freud *(1856–1939)*
__P__ Wilhelm Wundt *(1832–1920)*
__A__ J. McKeen Cattell *(1860–1944)*
__I__ Lightner Witmer *(1867–1956)*
__E__ William Healy *(1869–1963)*
__R__ Ivan Pavlov *(1849–1936)*
__K__ John B. Watson *(1878–1958)*
__S__ E. L. Thorndike *(1874–1949)*
__T__ B. F. Skinner *(1904–1990)*

SHORT ANSWERS
Your answer should contain the following points.

1. Most sciences use classification systems that provide a nomenclature used to structure and organize information in a helpful way. In the mental health field, definitions of pathology assist in defining the range of problems mental health professionals can address, and how their treatment should be reimbursed.

2. Classification may lead to stigma, stereotyping, and labeling. The person may be defined by their illness rather than seen as a person with an illness.

3. A clinically significant behavioral or psychological syndrome or pattern, associated with distress or disability. It is not simply a predictable and culturally sanctioned response to a particular event, and it is considered to reflect behavioral, psychological, or biological dysfunction in the individual.

4. Cultural beliefs define how behaviors are accepted, and therefore determine whether others see a behavior as normal or abnormal in that culture.

5. *Prevalence* refers to the number of active cases in a population during any given time period. *Incidence* refers to the number of new cases that occur over a given period of

time. Incidence rates are typically lower than prevalence rates because they exclude already existing cases.

6. Pinel's experimental treatment of kindness and consideration in which chains, noise, and filth were removed and were replaced by peace, order, and sunny rooms. The York Retreat by William Tuke provided a restful, kind, and religious atmosphere. Moral management was a wide-ranging method of treatment that focused on a patient's social, individual, and occupational needs. The mental hygiene movement advocated a method of treatment that focused almost exclusively on the physical well-being of hospitalized patients. Dorothea Dix was a champion of the poor and forgotten people in prisons and mental institutions. Through her efforts the plight of the mental ill was uncovered and conditions were improved through funding and allocation of resources.

7. Hospital stays were quite lengthy, and the mentally ill were destined to be hospitalized for many years. In 1946, the NIMH was formed, the Community Health Services Act of 1963 was passed, and reductions in the number of hospitalized mentally ill decreased substantially due to deinstitutionalization.

8. Psychoanalysis began with Sigmund Freud with the help of Josef Breuer. Freud coined such terms as *catharsis,* the *unconscious, free association,* and *dream analysis*. Freud's views have provided information and insights into various treatments and techniques despite the numerous flaws in his theories.

9. John Watson provided and advocated for a highly scientific focus to the field of psychology. He was not interested in nor felt the field should be concerned with Freud's mental processes. He believed that for psychology to become a true science, it would need to abandon subjectivity of inner sensations and other mental events and limit itself to what could be objectively observed. B. F. Skinner's operant conditioning is behavior that operates on the environment and can reinforce a particular activity of an organism.

10. Strengths: Straightforward set-up and design—proposed treatment given to one group of patients and withheld from another similar group of patients. If treated patients improve, compared to the untreated group, the treatment works. Treatment can then be given to the "waiting list" control group. Limitations: Withholding beneficial treatment for a period of time.

11. When you want to study the same person over time, under a variety of conditions (or interventions).

THE DOCTOR IS IN
1. Your response should include a detailed description of the conditions of the back wards, chains, shackles, patients, food, staff, etc. Discuss your feelings and what plans for improvement you would make.

2. Dr. Freud would attribute the cause to thought or experiences in the unconscious, possibly feelings of ill will toward her spouse. The treatment would entail hypnosis, dream analysis, free association, and emotional release through catharsis.

3. You should select patients from the population under study using the DSM-IV-TR definition of depression. They should be currently suffering from depression. You may want to set a time period for the study, such as 8 weeks. The independent variable would be 100 mg of drug XYZ. The dependent variable would be the improvement in depressive symptoms. For example, 100 mg drug XYZ is expected to produce a 25% decrease in depressive symptoms over an 8-week period.

PRACTICE TESTS

Q#	TEST 1	TEST 2	TEST 3
1	A	B	A
2	C	C	B
3	C	C	B
4	A	A	C
5	B	C	C
6	A	C	A
7	D	D	C
8	C	C	A
9	C	B	A
10	B	B	C

COMPREHENSIVE PRACTICE TEST

Q#	M/C	T/F
1	D	T
2	D	F
3	D	F
4	A	T
5	D	T
6	A	F
7	B	F
8	C	F
9	B	F
10	C	T
11	B	T
12	A	F
13	A	F
14	A	T
15	A	F

Essay Questions
Your answer should contain the following points.

1. Advantages and disadvantages include the following:
   a. Provides nomenclature.
   b. Allows us to study the different disorders and learn more about them.
   c. Helps to provide a basis for the development of a treatment plan.
   d. Can promote stigma, stereotypes, and labeling.

2. DSM definition:
   a. A clinically significant behavioral or psychological syndrome or pattern.
   b. Associated with distress or disability.
   c. It is not simply a predictable and culturally sanctioned response to a particular event.
   d. It is considered to reflect behavioral, psychological, or biological dysfunction in the individual.

   Wakefield's definition:
   a. Causes significant distress or disability.
   b. Is not merely an expectable response to a particular event.
   c. Is a manifestation of a mental dysfunction.

3. The mental hygiene movement advocated a method of treatment that focused almost exclusively on the physical well-being of hospitalized patients. Dorothea Dix was a champion of the poor and forgotten people in prisons and mental institutions. Through her efforts the plight of the mental ill was uncovered and conditions were improved through funding and allocation of resources.

4. Hospital stays were shortened, increased patient rights; however, deinstitutionalization and reduced funding for the mentally ill have left many homeless and without care.

5. Psychoanalysis focuses on subjectivity of inner sensations and other mental events whereas behaviorism focuses on what can be objectively observed.

6. The advantages of disadvantages would be the following:

Case studies are only relevant to the individual under study, and the conclusions cannot be applied to other individuals.

Direct observation involves observation of the sample we want to study, using a variable that is relevant to our interests. This is also limited to the sample we are observing.

Self-report data is quick, inexpensive, yet not always reliable as subjects may deliberately lie, misinterpret the question, or want to present themselves in a favorable or unfavorable light.

USE IT OR LOSE IT

While mental illness has become less of a taboo subject, this seems to apply only toward more socially acceptable illnesses such as anxiety and depression. Unfortunately, illnesses such as bipolar disorder and schizophrenia are widely misunderstood and not viewed with the same level of concern as that of depression and anxiety. Society still has a number of outdated views of serious mental illness, and it may be quite some time before we see a change. In addition, pharmaceutical companies tend to market their medications to mainstream outlets that have the resources to buy their product. They too have a stereotyped view of the consumer.

Freud is a household word—just mention psychology and one automatically says "Freud." However, many of Freud's theories have been rightfully questioned through the years because of the lack of empirical evidence and overall utility of his theories to the field. Despite the numerous flaws, his theories are discussed because he introduced a revolutionary concept during his time—the idea of the unconscious and its role in motivating behavior. There are a number of more influential members of the mental health field whose contributions are much more pronounced such as Emil Kraepelin, Carl Jung, and Benjamin Rush.

CRISSCROSS ANSWERS

Across
2. Prevalence
3. Acute
5. Epidemiology
6. Psychoanalysis
7. Chronic
8. Incidence
10. Sampling
13. Unconscious
14. Behaviorism
15. Operant conditioning
16. Classical conditioning

Down
1. Free association
4. Deinstitutionalization
9. Comorbidity
11. Mesmerism
12. Asylums

Chapter 2: Causal Factors and Viewpoints

BEFORE YOU READ

Chapter 1 provided a solid foundation for understanding abnormal psychology by defining important terminology, discussing notable historical elements and people, and providing a brief overview of the various research methods used. With that base of knowledge, this chapter examines a range of possible explanations for abnormal behavior by comparing the various biological causal factors, psychosocial viewpoints, and sociocultural factors. Biological and genetic factors are discussed alone and in relation to their interaction with environment experiences. Psychosocial viewpoints including Freud's psychodynamic approach, behavioral, and cognitive-behavioral models are explored. The impact of social interactions will be considered, since humans are social beings who are profoundly affected by the cultures in which they live, as well as by their early environmental experiences. Given the complexity of the human experience, it is probable that most abnormal behaviors are the result of complex, interactive factors, rather than a single cause.

- **CAUSES AND RISK FACTORS FOR ABNORMAL BEHAVIOR**
  Necessary, Sufficient, and Contributory Causes
  Diathesis-Stress Models

- **VIEWPOINTS FOR UNDERSTANDING ABNORMAL BEHAVIOR**

- **THE BIOLOGICAL VIEWPOINTS AND BIOLOGICAL CAUSAL FACTORS**
  Neurotransmitter and Hormonal Imbalances
  Genetic Vulnerabilities
  Temperament
  Brain Dysfunction and Neural Plasticity
  The Impact of the Biological Viewpoint

- **THE PSYCHOSOCIAL VIEWPOINTS**
  The Psychodynamic Perspectives
  The Behavioral Perspective
  The Cognitive-Behavioral Perspective

- **PSYCHOSOCIAL CAUSAL FACTORS**
  Early Deprivation or Trauma
  Inadequate Parenting Styles
  Marital Discord and Divorce
  Maladaptive Peer Relationships

- **THE SOCIOCULTURAL VIEWPOINT**
  Uncovering Sociocultural Factors through Cross-Cultural Studies

- **SOCIOCULTURAL CAUSAL FACTORS**
  The Sociocultural Environment

Harmful Societal Influences
Impact of the Sociocultural Viewpoint

• UNRESOLVED ISSUES
Theoretical Viewpoints and the Causes of Abnormal Behavior

OBJECTIVES
After reading this chapter, you should be able to do the following:

1. Discuss the different conceptual approaches to understanding the causes of abnormal behavior. These approaches will include (a) necessary, sufficient, and contributory causes and (b) the diathesis-stress models.

2. Summarize the biological theories of abnormal behavior including neurotransmitter/hormonal imbalances, genetic and constitutional influences, and physical damage to brain structures.

3. Outline the major psychosocial theoretical approaches to abnormal behavior including the psychodynamic, behavioral, and cognitive-behavioral perspectives.

4. Discuss the substantive contributions of the psychosocial factors of deviant cognitions (schema and self-schema), early deprivation or trauma (e.g., parental deprivation, institutionalization, abuse), inadequate parenting and pathogenic family structures, and problems with peer relationships.

5. Describe the sociocultural perspective and its contributions to understanding abnormal behavior.

6. Explain why simplistic explanations rarely account for the complexity of abnormal behaviors.

AS YOU READ
Answers can be found in the Answer Key at the end of the book.

KEY WORDS
Each of the words below is important in understanding the concepts presented in this chapter. Write the definition next to each word. The page numbers are provided in case you need to refer to the book.

Term	Page	Definition
Adoption method	41	
Association studies	42	
Attachment theory	49	
Attributions	54	
Behavior genetics	40	
Biopsychosocial	36	

viewpoint		
Castration anxiety	47	
Chromosomes	39	
Classical conditioning	50	
Cognitive-behavioral perspective	53	
Concordance rate	41	
Contributory causes	33	
Cortisol	39	
Developmental psychopathology	35	
Developmental systems approach	44	
Diathesis-stress models	34	
Discrimination	52	
Ego	46	
Ego psychology	48	
Ego-defense mechanisms	46	
Electra complex	48	
Etiology	33	
Extinction	51	
Family history (or pedigree) method	40	
Generalization	52	
Genes	39	
Genotype	40	
Genotype-environment correlation	40	
Genotype-environment interaction	40	
Hormones	37	
Hypothalamic-pituitary-adrenal cortical axis	39	
Id	46	
Instrumental (or operant conditioning)	51	
Interpersonal perspective	49	
Intrapsychic conflicts	46	
Libido	46	
Linkage analysis	42	
Necessary cause	33	
Neurotransmitters	37	
Object-relations theory	48	

Observational learning	52	
Oedipus complex	47	
Phenotype	40	
Pituitary gland	37	
Pleasure principle	46	
Primary process thinking	46	
Protective factors	34	
Psychosexual stages of development	46	
Reality principle	46	
Reinforcement	51	
Resilience	35	
Schema	53	
Secondary process thinking	46	
Self-schema	53	
Spontaneous recovery	51	
Sufficient cause	33	
Superego	46	
Synapse	37	
Temperament	42	
Twin method	41	

MATCHING
Who's Who?
Match each of the following people with her/his accomplishment or theory.

_____ Karen Horney
_____ Harry Stack Sullivan
_____ Erik Erikson
_____ Erich Fromm
_____ Alfred Adler

Theory
A. Believed that people are inherently social beings motivated primarily by the desire to belong to and participate in a group.
B. Focused on dispositions that people adopt in their interactions.
C. Vigorously rejected Freud's demeaning female psychology.
D. Broadened Freud's psychosexual stages into more socially oriented concepts.
E. Maintained that the term *personality* was best defined in terms of an individual's characteristic way of relating to others.

What's What?
Match each of the following terms with its definition.

_____ Discrimination
_____ Generalization
_____ Intermittent
_____ Reinforcement
_____ Avoidance conditioning

A. A person, previously bitten, avoids dogs.
B. An occasional win at gambling keeps the behavior going.
C. A person, beaten as a child by an authority figure, has an involuntary fear of anyone in authority.
D. A child performs a response that produced candy in the past.
E. A child learns that although red and green strawberries look somewhat similar, only the red ones taste good.

Match each of the following parenting styles with its description of the result from using this type of parenting.

Parenting Style
_____ Authoritative
_____ Authoritarian
_____ Permissive/indulgent
_____ Neglecting/uninvolved

Descriptions
    A. impulsive and aggressive; spoiled, selfish, inconsiderate, and demanding; exploit people for their own purposes
    B. disruptions in attachment in childhood; moodiness, low self-esteem, and conduct problems later in childhood; problems with peer relations and academic performance
    C. energetic and friendly, competent in dealing with others and the environment
    D. conflicted, irritable, moody; poor social and cognitive skills

SHORT ANSWERS
Provide brief answers to the following questions.

1. List the five methods used in behavior genetics to study the heritability of mental disorders and give description of each. (p. 41)

2. Define and give an example of each of the following defense mechanisms: (pp. 46–48)

a. sublimation

b. reaction formation

c. displacement

d. fixation

e. projection

f. rationalization

THE DOCTOR IS IN...PSYCHIATRIC HELP—5¢

Read the following scenarios and diagnose the client. Remember to look carefully at the criteria for the disorder before you make a decision as to the diagnosis. Make a list of other information you might need to help you understand the causal factors.

1. Roger comes to your office because he has recently been laid off from his job as a store manager. He is concerned because he has started to drink heavily as a result of this and finds himself feeling incredibly sad and depressed. His wife is supportive, but he is afraid she will get tired of dealing with his moods and leave. Although she says she won't, he is becoming preoccupied with the idea of her leaving him. He tells you that his father abused alcohol and that his mother ended up leaving when she couldn't take it any more. His father always drank, according to Roger, would get really down, and, on at least one occasion, talked about suicide. Roger doesn't want to become like his father but finds himself acting in similar ways. He is thinking that maybe he should just tell his wife to leave him, then move to another state, and start all over.

Look at Roger's situation from psychodynamic, behavioral, and cognitive-behavioral perspectives. What in Roger's story would you emphasize from each of these perspectives and how would you treat him? (pp. 46–55)

AFTER YOU READ

PRACTICE TESTS
Take the following three multiple-choice tests to see how much you have comprehended from the chapter. Each represents roughly one third of the chapter. As you study the chapter, use these to check your progress.

Practice Test 1

1. Disorders could be classified and diagnosed better if their causes could be better understood instead of relying on (p. 33)
       a. clusters of symptoms.
       b. clusters of test results.
       c. interview techniques.
       d. unconscious motivations.

2. Diabetic neuropathy cannot exist unless the person has diabetes. This is an example of (p. 33)
       a. a necessary cause.
       b. a sufficient cause.
       c. a contributory cause.
       d. a primary cause.

3. With his recent layoff and severe car accident, John's mental well-being were being taxed. His wife's filing for divorce put him over the edge. This would be referred to as (p. 33)
       a. a necessary cause.
       b. a sufficient cause.
       c. a noncontributory cause.
       d. a primary cause.

4. The diathesis is a relatively _____ necessary or contributory cause, but it is generally not sufficient to cause the disorder. (p. 34)
       a. proximal
       b. distal
       c. unimportant
       d. a and c

5. Tim's parents use drugs and his father is often abusive toward his mother. In spite of this, Tim is doing well in school and has made the football team. Tim's success is a form of (p. 35)
       a. good genes.
       b. good luck.
       c. resilience.
       d. diathesis.

6. Max was only thirteen years old and had been in ten foster homes since his mother abandoned him eight years ago. He never knew his father, and his grandparents had died only a year after taking custody of him when he was five. He was beginning to amass a criminal record. Luckily, his social worker was able to find his maternal uncle who took him under his wing and helped get him back on track. This uncle provided the stability, warmth, and support that Max never knew existed. Max's uncle provided a (p. 34)
>   a. protective factor.
>   b. relief to society.
>   c. proximal cause.
>   d. distal cause.

7. When Sharon went to school, she was taught the theory and practice of the psychoanalytical viewpoint. The methods she used in her practice reflected this viewpoint, and she believed totally in this perspective. At a conference, she was introduced to the cognitive-behavioral viewpoint and became intrigued by it. She went on to study this perspective and incorporate it into her practice. Sharon's new insights constituted a (p. 36)
>   a. breakthrough.
>   b. paradigm shift.
>   c. break from tradition.
>   d. cognitive shift.

8. Malfunction of the negative feedback system in the hypothalamic-pituitary-adrenal-cortical axis has been implicated in such psychopathologies as (p. 39)
>   a. post-traumatic stress disorder. (PTSD)
>   b. depression,
>   c. OCD.
>   d. a and b

9. The fact that a number of disorders, such as depression, schizophrenia, and alcoholism, show heredity as an important predisposing causal factor is consistent with which perspective? (p. 36)
>   a. biological
>   b. behavioral
>   c. cognitive
>   d. psychoanalytical

10. The observed structural and functional characteristics that result from an interaction of the person's total genetic endowment and the environment are referred to as a person's (p. 40)
>   a. phenotype.
>   b. genotype.
>   c. self.
>   d. linotype.

Practice Test 2

1. After Susan's head injury, her left hemisphere was able to adapt and take on some of the functions that the right hemisphere used to. This flexibility of the brain to make changes in organization and/or function in response to prenatal or postnatal experiences is called (p. 43)
        a. neural understanding.
        b. synaptic pruning.
        c. synaptogenesis.
        d. neural plasticity.

2. At what age can we identify approximately the five dimensions of temperament development that may affect our personality? (p. 42)
        a. one to two years
        b. two to three months
        c. six months to one year
        d. four to five years

3. The _____ acknowledges that genetic activity influences neural activity, which in turn influences behavior, which in turn influences the environment, and that these influences are bidirectional. (p. 44)
        a. brain activity approach
        b. neural regulatory approach
        c. developmental systems approach
        d. None of the above

4. Because biological treatments seem to have more immediate results than other available therapies, these have been seen as a possible (p. 44)
        a. cure-all.
        b. Band-Aid approach.
        c. short cut.
        d. snswer to all the problems with therapy.

5. By adopting a perspective, it influences (pp. 44– 54)
        a. our perceptions of maladaptive behavior.
        b. the types of evidence we look for.
        c. the way in which we interpret data.
        d. All of the above

6. This concept is prominent in the psychoanalytic viewpoint because it is an almost universal symptom of neurotic disorders. (p. 46)
        a. depression
        b. repression
        c. digression
        d. anxiety

7. It is in this stage that sexual motivations recede in importance as a child becomes preoccupied with developing skills and other activities. (p. 46)
    a. oral
    b. anal
    c. latency
    d. genital

8. This is the outgrowth of internalizing the taboos and moral values of society concerning what is right and wrong. (p. 46)
    a. ego
    b. superego
    c. id
    d. sid

9. His theory has become an enormously influential theory in child psychology and child psychiatry, as well as in adult psychopathology. (p. 49)
    a. Eric Fromm
    b. John Bowlby
    c. Erik Erikson
    d. Sigmund Freud

10. This perspective emphasizes the social and cultural forces rather than inner instincts as determinants of behavior. (p. 49)
    a. psychoanalytic
    b. social-cognitive
    c. interpersonal
    d. behavioral

Practice Test 3

1. Tommy recently became fearful of heights and would not go up the slide at the park. This seemed to be in response to seeing his father nearly fall off the ladder at home, and his father refusing to climb up again. This would best be an example of (p. 52)
    a. classical conditioning.
    b. observational learning.
    c. cognitive-behavioral learning.
    d. operant conditioning.

2. This perspective focuses on how thoughts and information processing can become distorted and lead to maladaptive emotions and behavior. (p. 54)
    a. psychodynamic perspective
    b. behavioral perspective
    c. cognitive-behavioral perspective
    d. empirical perspective

3. Susan failed her midterm on Calculus and blamed everyone and everything around her except her own poor study habits. This is an example of (p. 54)
      a. attribution.
      b. contribution.
      c. distribution.
      d. constitution.

4. He is considered the founder of cognitive therapy. (p. 54)
      a. B. F. Skinner
      b. F. Lee Bailey
      c. Aaron Beck
      d. Carl Rogers

5. Kevin's parents are very warm and very careful to set clear standards and limits on certain kinds of behaviors, while allowing considerable freedom with these limits. This is an example of (p. 59)
      a. authoritative parenting
      b. authoritarian parenting
      c. permissive/indulgent parenting
      d. neglectful/uninvolved parenting

6. Kate's parents are very high on control but low on warmth. They are not openly loving and put many demands on Kate to "be the best." She is often conflicted and irritable. This is an example of (p. 59)
      a. authoritative parenting.
      b. authoritarian parenting.
      c. permissive/indulgent parenting.
      d. neglectful/uninvolved parenting.

7. Ralph's parents are very high on warmth but low on discipline and control to the point that Ralph has been brought home by the police on two separate occasions. They have been lucky thus far since no charges have been pressed. Despite this behavior, Ralph did not suffer any consequences on either incident. This is an example of (p. 59)
      a. authoritative parenting.
      b. authoritarian parenting.
      c. permissive/indulgent parenting.
      d. neglectful/uninvolved parenting.

8. Jill, who is twenty years old, is popular with many people and is comfortable in all settings. Jill has a good deal of (p. 62)
      a. luck.
      b. intuition.
      c. social competence.
      d. social ineptitude.

9. Estimates are that approximately _____ of the homeless are affected by mental illness. (p. 66)
      a. one half
      b. one quarter
      c. three quarters
      d. one third

10. In our society, the lower the SES, the higher the incidence of (p. 64)
      a. therapy.
      b. intervention of some sort.
      c. mental disorder.
      d. a and b

COMPREHENSIVE PRACTICE TEST
The following tests are designed to give you an idea of how well you understood the entire chapter. There are three different types of tests: multiple choice, true/false, and essay.

<u>Multiple Choices</u>

1. John suffers from post-traumatic stress disorder (PTSD), which was caused by the severe trauma of being held captive for two years as a prisoner of war. The severe trauma represents (p. 33)
      a. a necessary cause.
      b. a sufficient cause.
      c. a contributory cause.
      d. a primary cause.

2. Tami was becoming increasingly hopeless as her job search lingered on into its fifth month. Her friends were worried she would become depressed. Her hopelessness could be seen as (p. 33)
      a. a necessary cause.
      b. a sufficient cause.
      c. a contributory cause.
      d. a primary cause.

3. Tim's parents were cold and rejecting to him as a boy. As a teenager, Tim was shy and easily ashamed when girls rejected him. As an adult, Tim is prone to bouts of depression. This would be a good example of (p. 33)
      a. a necessary cause.
      b. a sufficient cause.
      c. a contributory cause.
      d. a primary cause.

4. The field of psychology that focuses on determining what is abnormal at any point in development by comparing and contrasting it with the normal and expected changes that occur in the course of development is (p. 35)
    a. cognitive-behavioral psychology.
    b. psychodevelopmental psychology.
    c. developmental psychopathology.
    d. cognitive-developmental psychology.

5. The belief that _____ in the brain can result in abnormal behavior is one of the basic tenets of the biological perspective today. (p. 36)
    a. diseases
    b. disorders of the central nervous system
    c. neurotransmitter imbalances
    d. None of the above

6. The specialized structure on the postsynaptic neuron at which the neurotransmitter exerts its effect is the (p. 37)
    a. synaptic cleft.
    b. synaptic vesicle.
    c. receptor site.
    d. enzyme.

7. After being released into the synaptic cleft, the neurotransmitter substance may be reabsorbed into the presynaptic axon button, a process called (p. 37)
    a. re-uptake.
    b. deactivation.
    c. recapture.
    d. active transport.

8. The _____ is referred to as the master gland of the body. (p. 37)
    a. adrenal gland
    b. hypothalamus
    c. endocrine gland
    d. pituitary gland

9. A person's total genetic endowment is referred to as her or his (p. 40)
    a. phenotype.
    b. genotype.
    c. self.
    d. linotype.

10. The family history method requires that an investigator observe a sample of relatives of each _____ (the subject, or carrier, of the trait or disorder in question), who then serves as the starting point. (p. 41)
    a. proband
    b. zygote

    c. risk person
    d. initiation point

11. The _____ perspective views human nature as basically "good." (p. 45)
    a. existential
    b. behavioral
    c. psychoanalytical
    d. humanistic

12. The _____ perspective places more emphasis on the irrational tendencies and the difficulties inherent in self-fulfillment—particularly in a modern, bureaucratic, and dehumanizing mass society. (p. 45)
    a. existential
    b. behavioral
    c. psychoanalytical
    d. humanistic

13. Celine is twenty-four years old and has a difficult time maintaining her weight. Freud would argue that Celine did not receive adequate gratification during this stage of development. (p. 46)
    a. anal stage
    b. oral stage
    c. genital stage
    d. phallic stage

14. The form of learning in which an individual learns to achieve a desired goal is (p. 51)
    a. classical conditioning.
    b. pperant conditioning.
    c. modeling.
    d. avoidance conditioning.

15. The behaviorist tradition has been criticized for its (p. 52)
    a. precision and objectivity.
    b. research orientation.
    c. failure to demonstrate effectiveness
    d. over-concern with symptoms.

16. The tendency to explain one's success as due to luck—as compared to hard work—is best categorized as an example of a specific (p. 54)
    a. attributional style.
    b. contributory effect.
    c. proximal schema.
    d. internal representation.

17. Instead of Freud's concept of fixation, Erikson proposed that parental deprivation might interfere with the development of (p. 56)
       a. high self-esteem.
       b. tolerance for stimulation.
       c. self-control.
       d. basic trust.

18. Evidence suggests that disordered _____ make a significant contribution to child and adolescent psychopathology, especially to problems such as depression, conduct disorder, delinquency, and attention deficit disorder. (p. 58)
       a. mothers
       b. brothers
       c. grandparents
       d. fathers

19. A(n) _____ parental style is likely to produce a child who is impulsive and aggressive, spoiled, selfish, inconsiderate, and demanding, and who will exploit people for her or his own purposes. (p. 59)
       a. authoritative
       b. authoritarian
       c. permissive/indulgent
       d. neglectful/uninvolved

20. Epidemiological studies that have linked psychopathology with social class are (p. 61)
       a. based on controlled experimentation.
       b. correlational in nature.
       c. establishing a clear-cut cause-and-effect relationship.
       d. good examples of analogue studies.

21. Amato and Keith (1991a, 1991b) found that the negative effects of divorce seemed to be decreasing, particularly since 1970, because _____ was decreasing. (p. 61)
       a. stigma
       b. the number of divorces
       c. the amount parents blamed each other
       d. availability of good legal advice

22. This is the best validated and most widely used test that has been adapted for use in many cultures. (p. 63)
       a. WAIS-III
       b. MMPI-4
       c. MMPI-2
       d. WRAT

CHAPTER 2: CORE CONCEPTS

23. Since Kleinman and Good consider cultural factors so important to understanding depressive disorders, they have urged the psychiatric community to do what? (p. 66)
   a. Incorporate it into all therapeutic treatment.
   b. Incorporate it into all educational programs.
   c. Incorporate another axis in the DSM.
   d. Create a new paradigm.

24. Your book mentions that, at present, the only unified perspective is called the (p. 68)
   a. unification viewpoint.
   b. cognitive viewpoint.
   c. cognitive-behavioral viewpoint.
   d. biopsychosocial viewpoint.

25. Dr. Smith combines many different approaches/techniques when assessing and working with clients. What is Dr. Smith's approach? (p. 67)
   a. confusing
   b. eclectic
   c. purist
   d. practical

True/False

1. T / F Protective factors are NOT necessarily positive experiences. (p. 34)

2. T / F Norepinephrine, serotonin, dopamine, and GABA are all neurotransmitters. (p. 37)

3. T / F Some forms of psychopathology have been linked to hormonal imbalances. (p. 37)

4. T / F A synapse is the site of communication between the axon of one neuron and the dendrites or cell body of another neuron and is a tiny filled space between neurons. (p. 37)

5. T / F The temperament of an infant has no profound effects on its developmental processes. (p. 42)

6. T / F The super ego mediates between the demands of the id and realities of the external world. (p. 46)

7. T / F There are four psychosexual stages of development: the oral, anal, phallic, and genital stages. (p. 46)

8. T / F Nondepressed people tend to have a self-serving bias in which they are more likely to make internal, stable, and global attributions for positive rather than negative events. (p. 54)

9. T / F Children deprived of needed resources normally supplied by parents or parental surrogates may be left with irreversible psychological scars. (p. 56)

10. T / F Authoritative parents are low on warmth, high on control, and often cold and demanding. (p. 59)

11. T / F There are four types of parenting styles, and research shows that the permissive parenting style is the most preferred. (p. 59)

12. T / F Candy is a loner and Brian is a bully. Each of them will probably have healthy mental health outcomes. (p. 62)

13. T / F In cultures such as Thailand, adults are highly tolerant of under-controlled behavior such as aggression, disobedience, and disrespectful acts in their children. (p. 63)

14. T / F Antisocial personality disorder is strongly related to socioeconomic status and occurs about three times as often in the lowest income category as in the highest income category. (p. 64)

15. T / F Prejudice against minority groups may play a role in explaining why these groups sometimes show increased prevalence of certain mental disorders. (p. 65)

Essay Questions

1. Compare and contrast the psychodynamic, behavioral, and cognitive-behavioral perspectives. (pp. 44–55)

2. Explain the four types of parenting styles that seem to be related to different developmental outcomes for children. (pp. 58–60)

3. What are the effects of divorce on parents and on children? (pp. 60–61)

WHEN YOU HAVE FINISHED

WEB LINKS TO ITEMS OR CONCEPTS DISCUSSED IN CHAPTER 2
Sigmund Freud
> http://users.rcn.com/brill/freudarc.html
> www.psychoanalysis.org

These sites provide for a deeper analysis of Freud's work.

A Jungian Perspective
> http://www.ship.edu/~cgboeree/jung.html

Carl Jung was Sigmund Freud's protégé; however, Jung's views clashed with Freud's and thus ended their collaboration. Jung was quite prolific and considered by some to be more influential and far-reaching than Freud's. See if you agree by visiting this site on the life and works of Carl Jung.

> http://www.cgjungny.org/

This is the official Carl Jung Web site with links to membership, lectures, summer study programs, and further reading.

Behaviorism Tutorial
> http://www.seop.leeds.ac.uk/entries/behaviorism/#6

This site gives a well-balanced view of the history and current perspectives of behaviorism. Interestingly, a discussion of antibehaviorism is provided.

All About Pavlov
http://www.ivanpavlov.com/
> You may become classically conditioned to return to this Web site to read the collection of lectures by Pavlov as well as his biography.

USE IT OR LOSE IT
Provide an answer to the thought question below, knowing that there is more than one way to respond. Possible answers are presented in the Answer Key.

Discuss how drugs and medications can affect the actions of neurotransmitters at the synapse.

CRISSCROSS

Now that you know all there is to know about this chapter, here's your chance to put that knowledge to work.

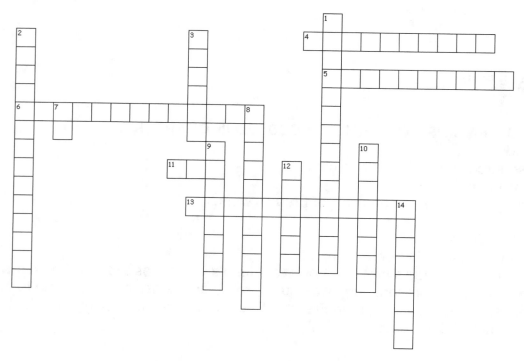

Across

4. The ability to adapt successfully
5. Gradual lessening of a conditioned response, when the UCS is omitted
6. Delivery of a reward or pleasant stimulus; aids in conditioning
11. Mediates between the demands of the id and the realities of the external world
13. The process of assigning causes to things that happen

Down

1. When one stimulus (or set of stimuli) can be evoked by another, similar stimuli
2. Distinguishing between similar stimuli and responding differently to these
3. One's frame of reference through the complexities of modern living
7. The source of instinctual drives
8. One's reactivity and characteristic ways of self-regulation
9. A stress hormone
10. Causal pattern of abnormal behavior
12. The basic emotional and psychic energy of life
14. The outgrowth of internalizing the taboos and moral values of society

Puzzle created with Puzzlemaker at DiscoverySchool.com

ANSWERS TO TEST QUESTIONS – CHAPTER TWO

WHO'S WHO
C. Karen Horney
E. Harry Stack Sullivan
D. Erik Erikson
B. Erich Fromm
A. Alfred Adler

E. Discrimination
C. Generalization
B. Intermittent
D. Reinforcement
A. Avoidance conditioning

C. Authoritative
D. Authoritarian
A. Permissive-indulgent
B. Neglecting-uninvolved

SHORT ANSWERS
Your answer should contain the following points.

1. The five methods used in behavior genetics to study the heritability of mental disorders are:
a. pedigree or family-history method—observation of samples of relatives of each proband case to see whether the incidence increases in proportion to the degree of hereditary relationship.
b. twin method—the study of monozygotic and dizygotic twins to look at concordance rates for mental disorders.
c. adoption method—the study of adopted offspring of parents with a mental disorder and those whose parents did not have a disorder to see if a disorder develops.
d. linkage analysis—studies that capitalize on currently known locations of chromosomes of genes for physical characteristics or biological processes to see if the same could apply for mental disorders.
e. association studies—studies of large groups of people with and without a disorder, followed by a comparison of the frequencies of certain genetic markers that are known to be located on particular chromosomes in the people with and without the disorder.

2.   a. sublimation
      b. reaction formation
      c. displacement
      d. fixation
      e. projection
      f. rationalization

THE DOCTOR IS IN

1. Psychodynamic: Emphasize the unconscious motives for Roger's behaviors—hurtful memories from his childhood about his mother and father. You might also say that his drinking is a result of the breakdown of his ego—an ego-defense mechanism.

Treatment: Use free association and dream analysis to become acquainted with the conscious and the unconscious. Also might want to include interpersonal therapy.

Behavioral: Look at Roger's behavior and the stimuli, and reinforcing conditions that control it. For instance, his drinking is getting him attention from his wife and because he is drinking so much it reinforces that he can't get a job. His drinking also reinforces his sadness and depression (alcohol is a depressant).

Treatment: Create a situation where alcohol is not a reinforcement but is substituted for something else that is positive, e.g., Roger and his wife walking together or looking through employment opportunities together. Attendance of AA meetings to continue to strengthen the behavior of not drinking.

Cognitive-behavioral: Look at Roger's basic information-processing mechanisms, his internal reinforcements, and how these are distorted. Explore his attributional style and the meaning he gives to his wife's behavior about leaving him and his thoughts of leaving her.

Treatment: Change thought patterns through logical reanalysis and by having Roger experiment with different behaviors or actions that would then be looked at in therapy.

PRACTICE TESTS

Q#	TEST 1	TEST 2	TEST 3
1	A	D	B
2	A	B	C
3	B	C	A
4	B	A	C
5	C	D	A
6	A	D	B
7	B	C	C
8	D	B	C
9	A	B	D
10	A	C	C

COMPREHENSIVE PRACTICE TEST

Q#	M/C	T/F
1	A	T
2	B	T
3	C	T
4	C	T
5	C	F
6	C	F

7	A	F
8	D	T
9	B	T
10	A	F
11	D	F
12	A	F
13	B	F
14	B	T
15	D	T
16	A	
17	D	
18	D	
19	C	
20	B	
21	A	
22	C	
23	C	
24	D	
25	B	

Essay Questions
Your answer should contain the following points.

1. A discussion of the id, ego, and superego, the defense mechanisms, the psychosexual stages of development, and the Oedipus and Electra complexes and how they relate to the individual's treatment.

The behavioral perspective should include a discussion of both operant conditioning and observational learning.

The cognitive-behavioral perspective should focus on not only the impact of Dr. Beck's cognitive therapy, but on how the basic tenets are the foundation of this model.

2. A detailed explanation of authoritative, authoritarian, permissive/indulgent, and neglectful/uninvolved parenting should be in your answer as well as the implications of such parenting for future growth of the individual.

3. The effects of divorce on parents include that it is a major source of psychopathology, physical illness, death, suicide, and homicide. The effects of divorce on children may include behavioral problems such as delinquency, effects on adaptive functioning, and lowered life satisfaction and goals.

USE IT OR LOSE IT

You should be able to discuss how the neurotransmitters transverse across the synapse and the importance of reuptake in the mechanisms of action for various drugs and medications.

CRISSCROSS ANSWERS

Across
4. Resilience
5. Extinction
6. Reinforcement
11. Ego
13. Attributions

Down
1. Generalization
2. Discrimination
3. Schema
7. Id
8. Temperament
9. Cortisol
10. Etiology
12. Libido
14. Superego

Chapter 3: Clinical Assessment, Diagnosis, and Treatment Approaches

BEFORE YOU READ

The accurate assessment and diagnosis of an individual is crucial for the development and implementation of appropriate treatments. Clinical assessment and diagnosis is much more than mere clusters of symptoms and regurgitation of facts. One must also be able to readily adapt their evaluation skills and be able to focus on the idiosyncratic nuances of the patient. While many of us are familiar with the saying "a textbook case", there is no textbook patient, and nor should your understanding be limited to only one assessment tool. Chapter 3 is devoted to a discussion of the goals, methods, and issues involved in clinical assessment, diagnosis, and treatment. These include the identification, description, and diagnosis of an individual's presenting symptoms. Clinical assessment depends on data from observation and interviews, as well as tests of physical, psychological, neuropsychological, and neurological function. This chapter describes what the different types of tests are, how these are constructed, how valid they are considered to be, and the types of information they provide. The use of the DSM system of classification commonly used in the United States is discussed in detail along with the practical and ethical implications of labeling people with a diagnosis.

This chapter also discusses the various therapeutic and pharmacological approaches available for the treatment of mental health issues. The efficacy and potential harm of these treatments as well as the selection of single or multiple (combination) treatments are discussed. While no single approach to psychotherapy has yet proven capable of handling the entire range of problems seen clinically, clinicians have a number of treatment options for which they can utilize. Consequently, the inclination to identify strongly with one approach or another is decreasing. Today, many therapists are familiar with a variety of techniques chosen from several therapeutic approaches and use these depending on the type of problems the client is having. The chapter closes with an interesting discussion on bias in the reporting of drug trials.

- **THE BASIC ELEMENTS IN ASSESSMENT**
  - The Relationship Between Assessment and Diagnosis
  - Taking a Social or Behavioral History

- **ASSESSMENT OF THE PHYSICAL ORGANISM**
  - The General Physical Examination
  - The Neurological Examination
  - The Neuropsychological Examination

- **PSYCHOSOCIAL ASSESSMENT**
  - Assessment Interviews
  - The Clinical Observation of Behavior
  - Psychological Tests
  - Advantages and Limitations of Objective Personality Tests

- **THE INTEGRATION OF ASSESSMENT DATA**
    Ethical Issues in Assessment

- **CLASSIFYING ABNORMAL BEHAVIOR**
    Reliability and Validity
    Formal Diagnostic Classification of Mental Disorders

- **AN OVERVIEW OF TREATMENT**

- **PHARMACOLOGICAL APPROACHES TO TREATMENT**
    Antipsychotic Drugs
    Antidepressant Drugs
    Anti-anxiety Drugs
    Lithium and Other Mood-Stabilizing Drugs
    Electroconvulsive Therapy
    Neurosurgery

- **PSYCHOLOGICAL APPROACHES TO TREATMENT**
    Behavior Therapy
    Cognitive and Cognitive-Behavioral Therapy
    Humanistic-Experiential Therapies
    Psychodynamic Therapies
    Martial and Family Therapy
    Eclecticism and Integration

- **MEASURING SUCCESS IN PSYCHOTHERAPY**
    Objectifying and Quantifying Change
    Would Change Occur Anyway?
    Can Therapy Be Harmful?

- **UNRESOLVED ISSUES**
    Is there a bias in the reporting of drug trials?

OBJECTIVES
After reading this chapter, you should be able to:

1. Describe the basic elements of clinical assessment, including:
a) its nature and purpose, b) the relationship between diagnosis and assessment, c) the types of information sought, and d) the different types of data of interest.

2. Summarize the various approaches to assessment of physical problems, including the general, physical, neurological, and neuropsychological examples.

3. List types of psychosocial assessments.

4. Discriminate between structured and unstructured interviews for the assessment of

psychosocial functioning, and evaluate the relative merits of each.

5. Discuss various approaches to the clinical observation of behavior and identify the advantages of each.

6. Explain the importance of rating scales in clinical observations.

7. Describe the major intelligence tests.

8. Discuss the advantages and disadvantages of projective personality tests.

9. Discuss the advantages and disadvantages of objective personality tests.

10. Summarize the process of integrating assessment data into a model for use in planning or changing treatment.

11. Explain the ethical issues involved in assessment.

12. Explain the purpose of classification systems for abnormal behavior.

13. Discuss reliability and validity as they relate to a classification system.

14. Explain the DSM classification of mental disorders.

15. Provide a general overview and understanding of psychotherapy.

16. Summarize the major psychopharmacological treatments currently in use (antipsychotics, antidepressants, antianxiety drugs, and lithium and other mood-stabilizers), discuss their history, major effects, side effects, modes of action, and effectiveness.

17. Describe early attempts at biological intervention, including coma and convulsive therapies and neurosurgery, and indicate which are currently believed to be effective.

18. Discuss the advantages of combining the biological and psychological forms of treatment.

19. List and describe the basic goals and techniques of the behavior therapies. Summarize recent developments in the behavior therapies, and evaluate their effectiveness in the treatment of maladaptive behavior.

20. List and describe the basic goals and techniques of the cognitive and the cognitive-behavioral therapies. Summarize recent developments, and evaluate their effectiveness in the treatment of maladaptive behavior.

21. List and describe the basic goals and techniques of the humanistic-experiential

therapies. Summarize recent developments in the humanistic-experiential therapies, and evaluate their effectiveness in the treatment of maladaptive behavior.

22. List and describe the basic goals and techniques of psychoanalysis, as well as developments in psychodynamic therapy since Freud. Evaluate the effectiveness of the psychodynamic approach to the treatment of maladaptive behavior.

23. Describe the basic goals and techniques of couples counseling, and family therapy. Summarize recent developments in these therapies, and evaluate their effectiveness in the treatment of maladaptive relationships.

24. Describe how success in psychotherapy is measured, how change is objectified, would change occur regardless of therapy, and discuss if therapy can be harmful.

AS YOU READ
Answers can be found in the Answer Key at the end of the book.

KEY WORDS
Each of the words below is important in understanding the concepts presented in this chapter. Write the definition next to each of the words.

Term	Page	
Acute	87	
Antianxiety drugs	93	
Antidepressant drugs	90	
Antipsychotic drugs	88	
Behavior therapy	97	
Chronic	87	
Client-centered therapy	101	
Cognitive/cognitive-behavioral therapy	99	
Computerized axial tomography (CAT scan)	73	
Counter-transference	104	
Dysrhythmia	73	
Electroconvulsive therapy (ECT)	95	
Electroencephalogram (EEG)	73	
Episodic	87	
Family therapy	106	
Free association	104	
Functional MRI (fMRI)	74	

Half-life	88	
Imaginal exposure	97	
Integrative behavioral couple therapy	106	
In vivo exposure	97	
Latent content	104	
Magnetic resonance imaging (MRI)	73	
Manifest content	104	
Marital therapy	106	
Mild	87	
Minnesota Multiphasic Personality Inventory (MMPI)	80	
Modeling	98	
Moderate	87	
Neuropsychological assessment	74	
Neurosurgery	96	
Objective tests	80	
Positron emission tomography (PET Scan)	73	
Presenting Problem	71	
Projective tests	119	
Psychodynamic therapy	103	
Psychopharmacology	88	
Psychotherapy	88	
Rating scales	116	
Rational emotive behavior therapy (REBT)	100	
Recurrent	87	
Reliability	84	
Resistance	104	
Response shaping	99	
Rorschach Test	78	
Self-monitoring	76	
Sentence completion test	79	
Severe	87	
Signs	85	
Structural family therapy	107	

Systematic desensitization	97	
Symptoms	85	
Tardive dyskinesia	89	
Thematic Apperception Test (TAT)	79	
Token economy	99	
Traditional behavioral Couple therapy	106	
Transference	104	
Validity	85	

MATCHING
Who's Who and What's What?
Match the following psychological tests with the appropriate description of each test's purpose.

Psychological Test

_____ Rorschach Test
_____ Thematic Apperception Test
_____ Minnesota Multiphasic Personality Inventory-2 (MMPI-2)
_____ WAIS-III
_____ WISC-IV
_____ Brief Psychiatric Rating Scale (BPRS)
_____ Sentence Completion Test

Purpose

A. Rating scale based on standardized interview
B. Intelligence scale for children
C. Intelligence scale for adults
D. Projective test using inkblots
E. Projective test using pictures
F. Structured personality test
G. Test that pinpoints topics that should be explored

Match the following individuals or terms with the appropriate description of each.

Psychological Test

_____ John Cade
_____ Albert Ellis
_____ Psychoactive
_____ Carl Rogers
_____ Ugo Cerletti and Lucio Bini
_____ Atypicals
_____ MAOI

_____ SNRI
_____ Aaron Beck
_____ Tardive Dyskinesia
_____ Agranulocytosis
_____ Antonio Moniz
_____ Ladislas von Meduna
_____ Depot neuroleptics
_____ Half-Life

Purpose
A. Another name for the second-generation antipsychotic drugs
B. A serotonin and norepinephrine reuptake inhibitor
C. An antidepressant which requires a tyramine controlled diet
D. Amount of time necessary for the level of active drug to be reduced by 50% in the body
E. Mind-altering
F. Antipsychotic medications administered in a long-acting injectable form
G. A movement abnormality that is a delayed result of taking antipsychotics.
H. Discovered that lithium salts were effective in treating manic disorders
I. Regarded as the modern originator of inducing convulsions to treat mental disorders
J. Italian physicians who after visiting a slaughter house and seeing electric shock used on animals, passed electric current through a patient's head, a method which became known as ECT
K. Introduced the frontal lobotomy in 1935
L. Founder of REBT
M. His cognitive therapy assumes that client's problems stem from illogical thinking
N. Founder of client-centered therapy
O. Potentially life-threatening condition of clozapine use

SHORT ANSWERS
Provide brief answers to the following questions.

1. Compare the functions, advantages, and disadvantages of the CAT, MRI, fMRI, and PET scans. (pp. 73-74)

2. Compare and contrast the projective versus the objective personality tests. (p. 119-127)

3. Explain the purpose of classifying abnormal behavior. (p.131)

4. Discuss the five axes of the DSM-IV-TR. (p. 134-135)

5. Discuss the problem of labeling. (p. 137)

6. Describe the three classes of antidepressants. (p. 611-614)

7. Discuss the advantages and disadvantages of Buspirone in treating anxiety. (p. 616)

8. Discuss the evolution of ECT. (p. 618-619)

9. Compared with some other forms of therapy, behavior therapy has some distinct advantages. Briefly explain. (p 621-623).

10. Briefly explain why the humanistic-experiential therapies have been criticized.

THE DOCTOR IS IN...PSYCHIATRIC HELP—5¢
Read the following scenarios and diagnose the client. Remember to look carefully at the criteria for the disorder before you make a decision as to the diagnosis. Make a list of other information you might need to help you understand the causal factors.

1. Tim, a 21-year-old man, has just been admitted to the hospital. He was found wandering the streets, talking to himself. It looks as if he has been homeless for some time. You are called in to do a clinical observation. What would you include in your observation of Tim? (p. 113-119)

2. You are seeing a new patient who has been referred to you by his primary-care doctor. Ben, a 29-year-old truck driver, went to his doctor thinking he was having a heart attack. When he drove across bridges, his heart would pound, his hands got sweaty, he would feel short of breath, and begin to hyperventilate. Several months ago, Ben was involved in an accident that left three people dead and several injured. Though it wasn't his fault (there had been heavy fog), he felt that as an experienced truck driver, he should have been able to prevent the accident. The symptoms began shortly after the accident and have lasted for six months. His primary doctor reports that Ben is not having any heart problems and is generally in good health.

What diagnosis would you give him on Axis I, II, and III? Why? (p. 134-135)

3. Bernice is a 47-year-old woman who recently lost her job in an auto factory. She is depressed and very concerned about how she is going to make ends meet when her unemployment insurance runs out. She married right out of high school and supported her husband through school by working in a factory. Her husband was killed in an auto accident seven years ago. She has two children, 22 and 15 years old. Bernice tells you that she is concerned about her drinking. Because her father was an alcoholic and her mother was always sad and withdrawn. She also still feels like a bad mother because she can't give her children all the things she sees other kids have, even though the children tell her they don't care.

After reading the above scenario, pretend that you are a therapist and decide what aspects of the scenario would be emphasized/important for each of the following approaches. Also, discuss one aspect of treatment from each approach you would use with Bernice.

Pharmacological Treatment:

Behavior Treatment:

Cognitive and Cognitive-Behavioral Treatment:

Humanistic—Experiential Treatment:

Psychodynamic Treatment:

AFTER YOU READ

PRACTICE TESTS
Take the following three multiple-choice tests to see how much you have comprehended from the chapter. Each represents roughly one-third of the chapter. As you study the chapter, use these to check your progress.

PRACTICE TEST NUMBER 1

1. Formal diagnosis is necessary after assessment for (p. 71)
      a. Insurance claims
      b. Planning treatment
      c. Deciding on which treatment facilities would be best for the client
      d. All of the above

2. When taking a social history, the clinician notes key dimensions that help her/him to understand the individual's problem. The key dimensions are (p. 71)
    a. Excesses, deficits, and appropriateness
    b. Excesses, desires, and dreams
    c. Behaviors, subconscious wishes, and fantasies
    d. Thought association and results of CAT scans

3. A significant divergence of normal brain patterns recorded on an EEG, which may be a result of some abnormality, is referred to as (p. 73)
    a. Dysthmia
    b. Dysrhythmia
    c. A brain tumor
    d. None of the above

4. Tommy washed to the hospital after being struck by a moving car while riding his bike. The ER physician suspects Tommy may have suffered a head injury and is concerned about bleeding on the brain. He orders a (p. 73)
    a. CAT scan
    b. BAT scan
    c. Rorschach
    d. C-Span

5. Mrs. Smith, 73, is experiencing some significant difficulty with cognitive activities and has lost some coordination. She is referred to a specialist who will test her cognitive, perceptual, and motor performance. This specialist is a (p. 74)
    a. Neuropsychologist
    b. Cognitive behaviorist
    c. Psychoanalyst
    d. Biologist

6. Walter's doctor believes he is suffering from schizophrenia; however he wants to rule out any organic causes and orders the following test. (p. 73)
    a. TAT
    b. MRI
    c. Brief Psychiatric Rating Scale
    d. MMPI

7. You have scheduled an assessment interview for a new client. You have chosen a standardized interview format that you hope will yield a clear picture of your client's situation. This will be a(n) _____ interview. (p. 76)
    a. Structured
    b. Unstructured
    c. Insightful
    d. Constructed

8. You have scheduled an assessment interview for another new client. There are several questions you want the client to answer, but you want to be free to explore responses in more depth. This format is considered a(n) _____ interview. (p. 76)
        a. Structured
        b. Unstructured
        c. Insightful
        d. Constructed

9. Tim has been admitted to the hospital, and you are about to administer several clinical observations using a rating scale. It is called the (p. 77)
        a. TAT
        b. WISC-IV
        c. BPRS
        d. MMPI-2

10. You are one of 40 investigators conducting a multi-million dollar research study on depression. The pharmaceutical company has selected this instrument for you to use to select your research subjects. (p. 77)
        a. TAT
        b. HRSD or HAM-D
        c. BPRS
        d. MMPI-2

PRACTICE TEST NUMBER 2

1. Which of the following is an example of an intelligence test? (p. 77)
        a. WISC-IV
        b. WAIS-III
        c. Standard-Binet Intelligence Scale
        d. All of the above

2. When Dr. Taylor asked the client to respond to an inkblot picture he was probably administering the _____ test. (p. 78)
        a. Thematic Apperception
        b. Rorschach
        c. Sentence-Completion
        d. Stanford-Binet

3. When Dr. Zimmer asked the client to make up a story based on the picture she was probably administering the _____ test. (p. 79)
        a. Thematic Apperception
        b. Rorschach
        c. Sentence completion
        d. Stanford-Binet

4. Dr. Jones gives her client the beginning of sentences and asks that she complete each one. This is known as the _____ test. (p. 79)
    a. Thematic Perception
    b. Rorschach
    c. Sentence completion
    d. Stanford-Binet

5. The MMPI consists of _____ clinical scales; each designed to measure tendencies to respond in psychologically deviant ways. (p. 80)
    a. 10
    b. 15
    c. 8
    d. The MMPI doesn't have clinical scales, because it is a projective test.

6. The degree to which a measuring device produces the same results each time it is used to measure the same thing is referred to as (p. 84)
    a. Reliability
    b. Validity
    c. Usability
    d. Consistency

7. The extent to which a measuring instrument actually measures what it is supposed to measure is referred to as (p. 85)
    a. Reliability
    b. Validity
    c. Usability
    d. Measurability

8. The psychiatric classification system widely used in Europe is the (p. 85)
    a. ICD-10
    b. DSM
    c. UCS
    d. TAT

9. The psychiatric classification system used in the United States is the (p. 85)
    a. ICD-10
    b. DSM
    c. UCS
    d. TAT

10. Which of the following people is the most obvious candidate for psychological treatment? (p. 88)
    a. Susan, whose husband left her
    b. Andre, who lost his job
    c. Carlos, whose wife just died from cancer
    d. All of the above

PRACTICE TEST NUMBER 3

1. The unique quality of antipsychotic drugs is their ability to (p. 88)
      a. Calm patients
      b. Put patients to sleep
      c. Reduce patients' anxiety
      d. Reduce the intensity of delusions and hallucinations

2. Virtually all of the antipsychotic drugs accomplish the same biochemical effect, which is (p. 88)
      a. Blocking dopamine receptors
      b. Blocking the production of noradrenalin
      c. Stimulating the production of endorphins
      d. Stimulating the production of glutamic acid

3. Tardive dyskinesia is a side effect of taking conventional (p. 89)
      a. Antipsychotic medication
      b. Antidepressant medication
      c. ECT
      d. None of the above

4. In 1988, this became the first SSRI to be released in the United States. (p. 90)
      a. Zoloft
      b. Haldol
      c. Prozac
      d. Paxil

5. The first antidepressant medications to be developed in the 1950s were (p. 92)
      a. SSRIs
      b. SNRIs
      c. MAO inhibitors
      d. Tricyclics

6. Benzodiazepines are used to treat (p. 93)
      a. Depression
      b. Anxiety
      c. Bipolar
      d. None of the above

7. Lithium compounds are used in the treatment of (p. 94)
      a. Anxiety
      b. Hyperactivity and specific learning disabilities
      c. Bipolar mood disorders
      d. Hallucinations and delusions

8. Which of the following caused an immediate decrease in the widespread use of psychosurgical procedures in this country? (p. 97)
    a. a 1951 law banning all such operations
    b. the advent of electroconvulsive therapy (ECT)
    c. the advent of the major antipsychotic drugs
    d. the unusually high mortality rate

9. Psychosurgery is sometimes used for patients with debilitating (p. 97)
    a. obsessive-compulsive disorders.
    b. severe self-mutilation.
    c. schizophrenia.
    d. a and b.

10. Generally, behavioral therapy has been found to be less useful for (p. 101)
    a. responses not initially in an individual's behavioral repertoire.
    b. the more pervasive and vaguely defined the client's problem is.
    c. older female patients.
    d. shy, withdrawn adolescents.

COMPREHENSIVE PRACTICE TEST
The following tests are designed to give you an idea of how well you understood the entire chapter. There are three different types of tests: multiple-choice, true-false, and essay.

MULTIPLE-CHOICE

1. _____ testing provides a clinician with behavioral information on how organic brain damage affects a person's functions. (p. 73)
    a. TAT
    b. Rorschach
    c. MMPI
    d. Neuropsychological

2. A classification system's usefulness depends upon its (pp. 84-85)
    a. Reliability
    b. Validity
    c. a and b
    d. None of the above

3. It became quite clear that there was history of abuse as the stories John made up about the pictures he was shown all represented verbal and physical abuse. John was given which test? (p. 79)
    a. TAT
    b. MMPI
    c. WAIS
    d. WISC

4. This objective personality test is one of the best studied, valid, and reliable measures available. (p. 81)
>   a. TAT
>   b. MMPI
>   c. WAIS
>   d. WISC

5. Sam's score on the depression assessment did not vary considerably from last week's assessment. We could say that the depression assessment has good (pp. 84-85)
>   a. Reliability
>   b. Validity
>   c. Normalcy
>   d. Construct Validity

6. Axis I of the DSM Multiaxial system focuses on (p. 85)
>   a. Mental Retardation
>   b. Personality Disorders
>   c. Psychosocial Stressors
>   d. Disorders of clinical attention such as depression and schizophrenia

7. The first three axes in the DSM system deal with (p. 85)
>   a. Psychosocial stresses
>   b. Global assessment of functioning
>   c. Assessing an individual's present clinical status
>   d. b and c

8. The fourth and fifth axes of the DSM-IV-TR deal with (p. 86)
>   a. Psychosocial stresses
>   b. Global assessment of functioning
>   c. Assessing an individual's present clinical status
>   d. a and b

9. Albert Ellis' _____ posits that a well-functioning individual behaves rationally and in tune with empirical reality. (p. 100)
>   a. Cognitive therapy
>   b. Rational emotive behavior therapy (REBT)
>   c. Classical psychotherapy
>   d. Response shaping

10. Cognitive and cognitive behavioral therapy are types of self-instructional training focused on (p. 100)
>   a. Avoidance training
>   b. Altering the self-statements an individual routinely makes in stress-producing situations
>   c. Reinforcers for socially appropriate behavior

d. All of the above

11. Therapists must constantly beware of developing mixed feelings toward the client, which is known as (p. 104)
    a. Negative affect analysis
    b. Psychosis psychoanalysis
    c. Counter-transference
    d. Cognitive transcounteranalysis

12. In integrative behavioral couple therapy (IBCT), _____ are integrated with change strategies to provide a form a therapy that is more tailored to individual characteristics and the needs of the couple. (p. 106)
    a. Acceptance strategies
    b. Fighting stances
    c. "Flight-or-fight" strategies
    d. Cognitive fu

13. Most family therapists believe that _____—not just the designated "client"—must be directly involved in the therapy if lasting improvement is to be achieved. (p. 106)
    a. A teacher
    b. The family dog
    c. The family
    d. A minister

14. The _____ are based on the assumption that we have the freedom and the responsibility to control our own behavior. (p. 101)
    a. Existential therapies
    b. Humanistic-experiential therapies
    c. Avoidance technology
    d. Democratic Party doctrines

15. The original version of Freud's psychoanalysis is practiced only rarely today, because it (p. 105)
    a. Is arduous
    b. Is costly in time, money, and emotional commitment
    c. May take several years before all major issues have been resolved
    d. All of the above

TRUE - FALSE

1. T / F In cases of severe disorders, decisions regarding treatment may be made about a client with his or her consent or consultation with family members. (p. 72)

2. T / F Assessment of an individual may involve coordinated use of physical, psychological, and environmental assessment procedures. (p. 72)

3. T / F Assigning a formal diagnostic classification is more important than having a clear understanding of the client's behavioral history. (p. 71)

4. T / F Rating scales, when used in clinical observation and self-reports, encourages reliability, objectivity, and allows the rater to indicate the presence, absence, or prominence of a behavior. (p. 77)

5. T / F Two general categories of psychological tests used for clinical practice are general medical exams and intelligence tests. (p. 77)

6. T / F The classification of mental disorders is intended to give direct insight into a person's problems. (p. 85)

7. T / F Alzheimer's dementia would be considered an acute condition. (p. 87)

8. T / F Mental retardation would be found on Axis III. (p. 85)

9. T / F Validity presupposes reliability. (p. 84)

10. T / F Acute mental disorders are relatively short in duration. (p. 87)

11. T / F Chronic mental disorders are relatively short in duration. (p. 87)

12. T / F Lithium is most useful for the treatment of anxiety. (p. 94)

13. T / F Atypical antipsychotics may effectively treat the positive and negative symptoms of schizophrenia. (p. 88)

14. T/ F SSRIs are chemically related to the older Tricyclic antidepressants. (p. 92)

15. T / F Benzodiazepines can be prescribed with ease as they are NOT, addictive. (p. 93)

16. T / F Electroconvulsive therapy is generally considered unsafe and is NOT used anymore in the United States. (p. 95)

17. T / F Behavior therapy involves the indirect and non-active treatment that recognizes the primacy of behavior, acknowledges the role of learning, and includes thorough assessment of evaluation. (p. 97)

18. T / F Two main themes in cognitive-behavioral therapy are the conviction that cognitive processes influence emotion, motivation, and behavior and the use of cognitive and behavior change techniques in a pragmatic manner. (p. 99)

19. T / F Gestalt Therapy emphasizes the unity of the mind and spirit, placing strong emphasis on the need to separate thought, feeling, and action. (p. 102)

20. T / F Transference involves the therapist reacting in accord with the client and having a mixture of feeling toward the client. (p. 104)

ESSAY QUESTIONS

1. Discuss in detail the MMPI-2. (pp. 80-83)

2. Please explain the following qualifying terms used in referring to mental disorders: acute, chronic, mild, moderate, severe, episodic, and recurrent. (p. 87)

3. Explain how ECT is administered, and contrast the public and therapeutic views of its use. (pp. 95-96)

4. Evaluate cognitive-behavioral therapies. (pp. 99-100)

5. Name and discuss the four basic techniques of Freud's psychoanalysis. (pp.103-105)

WEB LINKS TO ITEMS OR CONCEPTS DISCUSSED IN CHAPTER 3

The Rise and Fall of the Lobotomy

http://lobotomy.info/

A highly detailed history of the rise and fall of the lobotomy, complete with the after effects and motor functioning resulting from lobotomy.

The History of Lobotomies

http://www.psychosurgery.org/index.htm

This site not only provides historical perspectives on the use and abuse of this controversial psychosurgical technique, but also provides riveting oral histories from the friends and relatives of those who had undergone lobotomy.

Psychosurgical Discussions

http://www.psychosurgery.org/blog.html

Psychosurgery.org provides over 2 years of discussions regarding the pros and mainly cons of psychosurgery as well as various untold stories of patients who lives have been permanently affected in so many ways by psychosurgeries.

The History of ECT

http://www.psychiatrictimes.com/p040293.html

The Psychiatric Times provides relevant and timely articles within the field of mental health, and this article on the history of Electroconvulsive shock treatment is no exception.

DSM-IV-TR

http://dsmivtr.org/index.cfm

This is the official website for the DSM-IV-TR by the American Psychiatric Association.

DSM-V

http://www.dsm5.org/

This is the DSM-V Prelude Project Website. The DSM-V is scheduled to be published in 2011, and you can follow all of the progress and even submit suggestions.

Cultural Sensitivity

http://www.psychiatrictimes.com/p981221.html

This article by the Psychiatric Times examines the role and need for cultural sensitivity by psychiatrists.

Clinical Research Links

http://www.clinicaltrials.gov/

Clinical Trials.gov is a government-sponsored website that provides current information on both federally and privately supported clinical research trials in human volunteers across the country.

National Institutes of Mental Health

http://www.nimh.nih.gov/

The National Institutes of Mental Health homepage is the launch pad for everything on mental health and includes the latest clinical trials with links to ClinicalTrials.gov.

Various Assessments
http://mtdesk.com/lstpsych.shtml
This site provides a thorough list of the most widely used diagnostic and neuropsychological tests. Descriptions are provided for some of the tests.

Thematic Apperception Test (TAT)
http://www.minddisorders.com/Py-Z/Thematic-Apperception-Test.html
This site describes the Thematic Apperception Test, its purpose, precautions on its use, and the cultural, gender, and class issues.

MMPI-2
http://www.pearsonassessments.com/tests/mmpi_2.htm
This website presents many quick facts on the MMPI-2 which is one of the most validated and well-known personality tests. The contents, history, biographies of the authors, and an overview of the legitimate uses for it, as well as related tests are discussed.

Pearson Assessments
http://www.pearsonassessments.com/
Pearson Assessments is a leading provider of psychological assessments and scoring solutions for use in numerous professions. Such products include the MMPI-2, the Bender-Gestalt, and the BASC-2.

USE IT OR LOSE IT
Provide an answer to the thought question below, knowing that there is more than one way to respond. Possible answers are presented in the Answer Key.

Why do you suppose that some employers ask prospective employees to take the MMPI, and what they might be looking for?

Supposing one of your family members needed mental health care, what information would you need to pick a therapist?

CRISS-CROSS
Now that you know all there is to know about this chapter, here's your chance to put that knowledge to work.

CRISS-CROSS CLUES
Across
3. Extent to which a measuring instrument actually measures what it purports to measure

5. Sudden onset of a disorder

9. Learning skills by imitating

12. Assisting people with psychological problems to change

14. Structured tests used in psychological assessment

16. Confronting real (not imagined) feared stimuli

17. His cognitive therapy approach was originally developed for the treatment of depression

18. An unwillingness or inability to talk about certain things

19. Therapy that focuses on individual personality dynamics

20. Disorder patterns that tend to come and go

21. Long-standing or frequently recurring disorders

22. Procedure using psychological testing, observation, and interviews to develop a summary of a client's symptoms and problems

Down
1. Therapy designed for married couples

2. Also known as psychosurgery

4. Clients applying their attitudes and feelings toward their therapists

6. A disorder that tends to abate and to recur

7. Patient's subjective description of a physical or mental disorder

8. Passing an electric current through a patient's head
10. Albert Ellis rational emotive therapy
11. Degree to which a measuring device produces same results each time it is used
13. A measure of whether a drug does what it is supposed to do
15. Objective observations of a patient's physical or mental disorder by a diagnostician
17. a direct and active therapy acknowledging the role of learning

Puzzle created with Puzzlemaker at DiscoverySchool.com

ANSWERS TO TEST QUESTIONS – CHAPTER THREE

MATCHING
Psychological Test
D. Rorschach Test
E. Thematic Apperception Test
F. Minnesota Multiphasic Personality Inventory (MMPI)
C. WAIS-III
B. WISC-IV
A. Brief Psychiatric Rating Scale (BPRS)
G. Sentence Completion Test

___H___ John Cade
___I___ Albert Ellis
___E___ Psychoactive
___N___ Carl Rogers
___J___ Ugo Cerletti and Lucio Bini
___A___ Atypicals
___C___ MAOI
___B___ SNRI
___M___ Aaron Beck
___G___ Tardive Dyskinesia
___O___ Agranulocytosis
___K___ Antonio Moniz
___I___ Ladislas von Meduna
__F___ Depot neuroleptics
___D__ Half-Life

SHORT ANSWERS

Your answer should contain the following points.
1. a. CAT—Computerized Axial Tomography
Function: uses X-rays across patient's brain to produce images and locate abnormalities
Advantage: don't need surgery to look at brain abnormalities
Disadvantage: exposes patients to prolonged radiation; images not as clear

b. MRI—Magnetic Resonance Imaging
Function: measurement of variations in magnetic fields caused by varying amounts of water in various organs; to look at the anatomical structure of any cross-section of an organ
Advantage: less complicated than a CAT scan; very clear and able to give a look at all but the smallest brain abnormalities; noninvasive
Disadvantage: some patients claustrophobic in narrow cylinder

c. fMRI—function Magnetic Resonance Imaging

Function: used to measure brain activity; measures oxygenation (blood flow) of specific areas of brain tissue
Advantages: less expensive than PET scans; can map on-going psychological activity, e.g., sensations, images, and thoughts
Disadvantage: some minor problems with distraught psychiatric patients

d. PET—Postiron Emission Tomography
Function: shows how an organ is functioning by measuring metabolic processes
Advantages: images of metabolic activity allow for better diagnosis; can see problems that aren't just anatomical
Disadvantages: low fidelity pictures; better as a research technique than the clinical diagnostic procedure

2. The projective tests are unstructured in that they rely on various ambiguous stimuli such as inkblots or vague pictures, rather than on verbal questions. The objective tests, on the other hand, are structured, and they typically use questionnaires, self-report inventories, or rating scales in which questions or items are carefully phrased and alternative responses are specified as choices.

3. Classifying abnormal behavior:
a. provides clear communication
b. attempts to delineate meaningful side variations of maladaptive behavior
c. introduces order into discussion of the nature, causes, and treatment of abnormal behavior
d. allows communication about particular clusters of abnormal behavior
e. gathers statistics on how common are various disorders
f. meets needs of medical insurance companies

4. Axis I deals with clinical syndromes that may be the focus of clinical attention such as schizophrenia or depression. Axis II encompasses the personality disorders and mental retardation. Axis III involves general medical conditions. Axis IV deals with all the psychosocial and environmental problems. Axis V is the Global Assessment of Functioning.

5. Labeling can be a problem because
a. psychiatric diagnosis, as a label, applies to a category of socially disapproved, problematic behavior.
b. a label is too easily accepted as description of an individual, rather than a person's behavior.
c. individuals may accept the label and redefine themselves to play out that role
d. labeling can affect a person's morale, self-esteem, and relationships with others.

6. TCA or Tricyclic antidepressants operate to inhibit the reuptake of norepinephrine and serotonin once released into the synapse. The MAOIs or monoamine oxidase inhibitors were first discovered in the 1950s; they inhibit the activity of monoamine oxidase and a tyramine-controlled diet is necessary. The selective serotonin reuptake

inhibitors (SSRIs) are the second-generation class of antidepressants and carry fewer side effects than the two older classes. They are the most widely prescribed, relatively safer, and equally efficacious.

7. a. acts on serotonergic functioning
b. as effective as the benzodiazepines in treating GAD
c. low potential for abuse
d. no withdrawal effects
e. not as effective for those who had previously taken benzodiazepines
f. takes two to four weeks to take effect; therefore, not effective in acute situations

8. Ladislas von Meduna was the originator of inducing convulsions to relief symptoms associated with mental illlness. He used Metrazol to induce convulsions while Sakel in the 1930s used insulin. Cerletti and Bini were the originators of ECT in 1938. It is still used in the United States today with 100,000 patients treated with ECT each year.

9. a. treatment approach is precise
b. explicit learning principles is a sound basis
c. economy of time and costs is quite good

10. a. lack of highly systematized models of human behavior
b. lack of agreed-upon therapeutic procedures
c. vagueness about what is supposed to happen between client and therapist

THE DOCTOR IS IN

1. Included in the observation:
a. objective description of Tim's appearance and behavior
b. personal hygiene, emotional responses, depression, anxiety, aggression, hallucination, or delusions
c. You would also include a full medical workup including but not limited to a CAT scan and MRI.

2. • Axis I:
a. Post-traumatic stress disorder. Symptoms occurred after an accident and have lasted more than a month.
b. Panic or disorder (could also be phobia). Rapid heart beat, sweaty hands, shortness of breath in a specific situation.
• Axis II: None.
• Axis III: None.

3. Pharmacological Treatment:
Focus on possible genetic connection with depression and prescribe antidepressants

Behavior Treatment:

Bernice learned her behavior from her family and is modeling the behavior she learned. Have her focus on modeling the behavior of someone she admires and feels is successful and reinforcing behavior that might be beneficial, e.g., taking a few college classes, looking for a job, etc.

Cognitive and Cognitive-Behavioral Treatment:
Bernice's difficulties are a result of dysfunctional beliefs about herself and her situation. Use Ellis's REBT to restructure her belief system and self-evaluation, e.g., feeling like a bad mother in spite of her children saying otherwise.
Use Beck's cognitive therapy to challenge her illogical thinking about the present and the future, e.g., all she can ever do is factory work or stress-inoculation therapy, changing the way Bernice talks to herself about her current situation and how she is dealing with it.

Humanistic-Experiential Treatment:
Bernice's difficulties stem from problems with alienation, depersonalization, loneliness and failure to find meaning and genuine fulfillment. Using Rogerian therapy you would help Bernice learn to accept and be herself by establishing a psychological climate in which she can feel comfortable and accepted.

Psychodynamic Treatment:
Classical psychoanalysis—search for repressed memories, thoughts, fears, and conflicts stemming from Bernice's early psychosexual development that would have to do with her experiences and relationships with her father and mother.
Psychoanalytical oriented psychotherapy—attempt would be to help Bernice clarify distortions and gaps in the client's construction of the origins and consequences of her problem, thus challenging her "defenses."

Methods used:
Classical psychoanalysis—free association, resistance, transference, and dream analysis
Psychoanalytically oriented psychotherapy—active conversational style in which you would attempt to clarify distortions, such as her feelings about being family and if she is like her parents; schedule fewer sessions and face Bernice as you talk to her

PRACTICE TESTS

Q#	TEST 1	TEST 2	TEST 3
1	D	D	D
2	A	B	A
3	B	A	A
4	A	C	C
5	A	A	C
6	B	A	B
7	A	B	C
8	B	A	C

9	C	B	D
10	B	D	B

COMPREHENSIVE PRACTICE TEST

Q#	M/C	T/F
1	D	T
2	C	T
3	A	F
4	B	T
5	A	F
6	D	F
7	C	F
8	D	F
9	B	T
10	B	T
11	C	F
12	A	F
13	C	T
14	B	F
15	D	F
16		F
17		F
18		T
19		F
20		F

Essay Questions
Your answer should contain the following points.

1. The MMPI-2 is an objective test that contains ten clinical scales and includes a lie scale, infrequency scale, defensiveness scale, and response inconsistency scale. It is one of the most widely used and most validated scales in the field.

2. An acute condition is one that describes disorders of a short duration. A chronic condition is one in which the disorder is long-standing and permanent. Mild, moderate, and severe characterize the different points on a dimension of severity or seriousness. Episodic and recurrent are used to describe unstable disorder patterns that tend to come and go.

3. ECT is administered in two ways bilaterally or unilaterally while the patient is asleep as anesthetics and muscle relaxants are used to prevent injury. The general public views ECT as horrific and a primitive form of treatment given the number of procedures that were performed in the absence of muscle relaxants and anesthetics in the past. ECT is extremely effective for severely depressed and suicidal patients as well as treatment refractory patients.

4. Beck's cognitive treatment is a very popular and quite effective treatment that focuses on the thoughts and behaviors of the patient. This treatment is most effective when combined with psychopharmacological intervention. Evaluate cognitive-behavioral therapies. It may be most useful in helping basically healthy people to cope and is extremely beneficial in alleviating many types of disorders: depression, panic disorder, generalized anxiety disorder, bulimia.

5. a. Free association
• individual says whatever comes into her/his mind
b. Analysis of dreams
• procedure for uncovering unconscious material
c. Analysis of resistance
• the unwillingness or inability to talk about certain painful or threatening material
d. Analysis of transference
• client brings and unconsciously applies attitudes and feelings to her therapist

USE IT OR LOSE IT

Employers may use the MMPI to assist in determining whether prospective employees exhibit stable patterns of thought and emotion. They may also want to compare the responses to new hires with those of people they know to be successful in their field.

In order to pick an effective therapist for someone in your family you might want to ask about their specific degree, where they trained, their therapeutic philosophy, how much experience they have, and even personal factors such as gender and ethnicity. You may also want to check their professional licensure through your state's professional registry. Finally, you might want to find out whether their services are covered by your insurance policy!

CRISSCROSS ANSWERS

Across	Down
3. Validity	1. Marital
5. Acute	2. Neurosurgery
9. Modeling	4. Transference
12. Psychotherapy	6. Episodic
14. Objective tests	7. Symptoms
16. In vivo exposure	8. Electroconvulsive
17. Beck	10. REBT
18. Resistance	11. Reliability
19. Psychodynamic	13. Efficacy
20. Recurrent	15. Signs
21. Chronic	17. Behavior
22. Clinical assessment	

Chapter 4: Stress and Stress-Related Disorders

BEFORE YOU READ

Chapter 4 begins with a detailed discussion of stress, a topic of increasing concern as modern life becomes more complicated and pressured. The text discusses potential sources of stress, the factors that predispose people to stress and the biological and psychological aspects of stress responses. It is now clear that stress, and negative emotions including anger, anxiety, and depression, can predispose people to illness, and impact the severity of their illness and the course of their recovery. Conversely, we know that positive emotions such as hope and optimism can promote health, diminish the impact of illness, and even predict such things as recovery time following surgery. The implications of these relationships are explored in regard to cardiovascular disease. Clearly, a better understanding of how the brain and body work together to control illness, and of how psychological factors impact this relationship, will help us to identify those at risk for illness, and to treat those experiencing poor health. The definitions and symptoms of adjustment disorder, acute stress disorder, and post-traumatic stress disorder are explained in detail. Causal factors in post-traumatic stress are explored. Finally, prevention and treatment of stress disorders are discussed with a particular focus on psychotropic medication in the treatment of PTSD as an unresolved issues topic.

- **PSYCHOLOGICAL FACTORS IN HEALTH AND STRESS**
  What Is Stress?
  Factors Predisposing a Person to Stress

- **STRESS AND THE STRESS RESPONSE**
  Biological Costs of Stress
  Stress and the Immune System

- **LIFESTYLE FACTORS IN HEALTH AND ILLNESS**
  Cardiovascular Disease
  What Psychological Factors Are Implicated in Cardiovascular Disease?

- **COPING WITH STRESS**
  Task-Oriented Coping
  Defense-Oriented Coping
  Attitudes and Health

- **PSYCHOLOGICAL REACTIONS TO COMMON LIFE STRESSORS**

- **PSYCHOLOGICAL REACTIONS TO CATASTROPHIC EVENTS**
  Prevalence of PTSD in the General Population
  Causal Factors in Post-Traumatic Stress Disorder
  Long-Term Effects of Post-Traumatic Stress Disorder

- **PREVENTION AND TREATMENT OF STRESS DISORDERS**

Prevention of Stress Disorders
Treatment for Stress Disorders

• UNRESOLVED ISSUES
Psychotropic Medication in the Treatment of PTSD

OBJECTIVES
After reading this chapter, you should be able to do the following:

1. Define the concepts of stressor, stress, and coping; describe the basic categories of stressors; and discuss factors that increase or decrease a person's vulnerability to stress.

2. Explain how psychological problems can cause or affect medical problems, and how medical problems can cause or affect psychological problems.

3. Explain the role cortisol and other hormones play in stress reaction, and why extended contact can be problematic over the longer term.

4. Describe the function of the immune system, and the specialized roles of B-cells, T-cells, and macrophages.

5. Explain the interactions among the nervous system, the immune system, and behavior.

6. Explain what cytokines are and how they work.

7. Discuss damaging habits and lifestyles—such as smoking—and how they enhance risk for physical disease such as cardiovascular disease.

8. Explain the psychological factors involved and implicated in cardiovascular disease.

9. Discuss how one can cope with stress in life.

10. Characterize the DSM-IV-TR diagnosis of adjustment disorder.

11. List the diagnostic criteria for acute stress disorder and post-traumatic stress disorder (PTSD), and compare and contrast the two disorders.

12. Discuss the prevalence of PTSD in the general population and why this is not viewed as only a combat-related illness.

13. Discuss the causal factors of PTSD as well as the long-term effects.

14. Summarize the approaches that have been used to treat or to prevent stress disorders and evaluate their effectiveness.

15. Discuss the issue of using psychotropic medications to treat PTSD.

AS YOU READ
Answers can be found in the Answer Key at the end of the book.

KEY WORDS
Each of the words below is important in understanding the concepts presented in this chapter. Write the definition next to each word.

Term	Page	Definition
Acute stress disorder	127	
Adjustment disorder	127	
Allostatic load	118	
Antigens	120	
B-cell	120	
Behavioral medicine	114	
Coping strategies	115	
Cortisol	118	
Crisis	115	
Crisis intervention	116	
Cytokines	120	
Defense-oriented response	126	
Distress	115	
Essential hypertension	123	
Eustress	115	
General adaptation syndrome	118	
Health psychology	114	
HPA axis	118	
Hypertension	123	
Immuno-suppression	121	
Placebo effect	127	
Positive psychology	127	
Post-traumatic stress disorder (PTSD)	127	
Psychoneuro-	119	

immunology		
Stress	115	
Stress-inoculation training	132	
Stress tolerance	117	
Stressors	115	
Task-oriented response	126	
T-cell	120	
Type A behavior pattern	124	
Type D personality	124	

MATCHING
Who's Who and What's What
Match the following terms with their definitions.

Term

_____O_ Post-traumatic stress disorder
_____A_ Adjustment disorder
_____G_ Crisis
_____F_ Stress
_____C_ Stressor
_____H_ Eustress
_____B_ Stress tolerance
_____E_ Stress-inoculation training
_____L_ Psychoneuroimmunology
_____N_ Health psychology
_____J_ Behavioral medicine
_____I_ Positive psychology
_____M_ Type A behavior pattern
_____K_ Type B behavior pattern

Definition

    A. A maladaptive response within three months of a stressor
    B. One's ability to withstand stress
    C. An adjustment demand
    D. Severe psychological and physical symptoms as a reaction to unexpected environmental crises
    E. Preventative strategy, prepares people to meet stressful situations
    F. A by-product of poor or inadequate coping
    G. When a stressful situation exceeds one's adoptive capacities
    H. Positive stress

I. A focus on human traits and resources that might have direct implications for our physical and mental well-being
J. Broad interdisciplinary approach involving many disciplines
K. Relaxed, more laid-back, and less time-pressured people
L. The study of the interactions among behavior, the nervous system, and the immune system
M. Excessive competitive drive, extreme commitment to work, impatience or time urgency, and hostility
N. Subspecialty that deals with psychology's contributions to diagnosis, treatment, and prevention of psychological components of physical problems

SHORT ANSWERS
Provide brief answers to the following questions.

1. Describe what stress goes along with the difference between positive and negative stress. (p. 115)

2. Describe what Allostatic load is. (p. 118)

3. Selye (1956, 1976b) found that the body's reaction to sustained and excessive stress typically occurs in three major phases. Name and briefly explain each. (p. 118)

4. Explain immunosuppression and how long it may last. (p. 121)

5. What are the three diseases of the cardiovascular system? (p. 122)

6. Discuss the Type D personality type. (p. 124)

7. What is positive psychology? (p. 353)

8. Discuss the prevalence of PTSD in the general population. (p. 437)

THE DOCTOR IS IN...PSYCHIATRIC HELP—5¢
Read the following scenarios and diagnose the client. Remember to look carefully at the criteria for the disorder before you make a decision as to the diagnosis. Make a list of other information you might need to help you understand the causal factors.

1. Becky came to your office because she was sexually assaulted six months ago and is having difficulty. She tells you that she feels anxious and depressed. The rapist was an acquaintance of hers and she is questioning her ability to judge people. She is also having difficulty developing trust. Her self-esteem is really low and she is having problems concentrating at school because she keeps having thoughts about the rape. Becky has been having nightmares and has started to drink a lot to help her sleep. Her friends have been supportive, but they seem to be getting tired of her mood swings and angry outbursts. Becky feels like she is going crazy.

How would you diagnose Becky and why? What treatment would you recommend for her? (p.129)

AFTER YOU READ

PRACTICE TESTS
Take the following three multiple-choice tests to see how much you have comprehended from the chapter. Each represents roughly one third of the chapter. As you study the chapter, use these to check your progress.

Practice Test 1

1. The emphasis of _____ is on the role that psychological factors play in the occurrence, maintenance, and prevention of physical illness. (p. 114)
    a. health attitude
    b. behavioral medicine
    c. psychoneuroimmunology
    d. biofeedback

2. The term _____ is used to refer to times when a stressful situation approaches or exceeds the adaptive capacities of a person or group. (p. 115)
   a. *crisis*
   b. *traumatic*
   c. *frustrating*
   d. *acute*

3. A crisis or trauma may occur as a result of (p. 115)
   a. a disaster, such as a flood.
   b. a nasty divorce.
   c. an injury or disease.
   d. All of the above

4. The faster the changes, the greater the (p. 116)
   a. frustration.
   b. stress.
   c. excitement.
   d. LCU.

5. The term _____ refers to a person's ability to withstand stress without becoming seriously impaired. (p. 117)
   a. *frustration*
   b. *intervention*
   c. *stress tolerance*
   d. *vulnerability*

6. _____ can moderate the effects of stress on a person, and can even reduce illness and early death. (p. 117)
   a. Lack of support
   b. Positive social and family relationships
   c. Bureaucracy
   d. Understanding national politics

7. _____ can make a stressor more potent and weaken a person's capacity to cope with it. (p. 117)
   a. Lack of support
   b. Positive social and family relationships
   c. Bureaucracy
   d. Understanding national politics

8. Antigens in the blood stream are searched out and destroyed by (p. 120)
   a. B-cells.
   b. T-cells.
   c. macrophages.
   d. All of the above

9. Cortisol (p. 118)
    a. is necessary in an emergency, as it prepares the body for a fight or flight response.
    b. can damage brain cells, especially in the hippocampus, if not shut off.
    c. may cause an allergic reaction if allowed to accumulate,
    d. a and b

10. The immune system has been likened to a police force in that (p. 119)
    a. if it is too weak, it cannot function effectively, and the body succumbs to damage from invading viruses and bacteria.
    b. if it is too strong and not selective, it can turn on its own normal cells.
    c. it protects and serves.
    d. a and b

Practice Test 2

1. Which of the following is NOT a clinical manifestation of coronary heart disease? (p. 124)
    a. angio myopathy
    b. myocardial infarction
    c. angina pectoris
    d. disturbance of the heart's electrical conduction

2. High blood pressure is insidious and dangerous because it (p. 123)
    a. puts a strain on the heart and cardiovascular system.
    b. underactivates the heart and cardiovascular system.
    c. impedes breathing.
    d. None of the above

3. People who _____ have the lowest blood pressure. (p. 123)
    a. express their anger
    b. suppress their anger
    c. use their anger constructively
    d. Both a and b

4. Investigating patients who had had heart attacks, researchers found that clinically depressed patients were _____ more likely to die in the next six months than were their nondepressed counterparts. (p. 124)
    a. no
    b. two times
    c. five times
    d. forty-two times

5. A study that followed 1,500 men and women with no prior history of heart disease found that people who had suffered major depression were _____ more likely to have had a heart attack. (p. 124)
      a. one and one-half times
      b. two times
      c. four times
      d. not

6. People with low levels of emotional support (unmarried, small social network, lack of friends) are _____ likely to develop CHD, _____ likely to have another cardiac event, and _____ likely to die over the next five years. (p. 125)
      a. more, three times more, three times more
      b. less, not, not
      c. just as, twice as, more
      d. not, not, less

7. African Americans are at greater risk for high blood pressure because as a group (p. 123)
      a. they are less likely to exercise than other ethnic groups.
      b. their bodies process the enzyme Renin differently.
      c. heavy salt use is their dietary preference.
      d. All of the above

8. When confronting stress, a challenge is (p. 126)
      a. to meet the requirements of the stressor.
      b. to protect oneself from psychological damage and disorganization.
      c. to remain calm and in control.
      d. a and b

9. This may involve making changes in one's self, one's surroundings, or both, depending on the situation. (p. 126)
      a. task-oriented response
      b. life-oriented response
      c. work-oriented response
      d. stress-oriented response

10. When a person's feelings of adequacy are seriously threatened by a stressor, this tends to prevail. (p. 126)
      a. task-oriented response
      b. defense-oriented response
      c. detail-oriented response
      d. stress-oriented response

Practice Test 3

1. In the U.S., post-traumatic stress disorder (PTSD) appears to occur in about
_____ adults at some time in their lives, but the reported rates are lower in
national populations with fewer natural disasters and a lower crime rate. (p. 128)
  a. 1 in 12
  b. 1 in 100
  c. 1 in 1,000
  d. 1 in 1,000,000

2. There is a _____ ratio of female to male prevalence of PTSD, due largely to
the occurrence of assault against women. (p. 129)
  a. 1:1
  b. 2:1
  c. 1:2
  d. 10:1

3. The symptoms of PTSD may vary greatly depending on the (p. 129)
  a. nature and severity of the terrifying experience.
  b. degree of surprise.
  c. personality make-up of the person.
  d. All of the above

4. Regarding PTSD causal factors, (p. 130)
  a. personality seems to play a role.
  b. the nature of the event itself appears to account for most of the stress-
  response variance.
  c. there appears to be a greater likelihood of post-traumatic disorder among
  women than men.
  d. All of the above

5. A process of stress-inoculation training prepares people to tolerate an anticipated
threat by (p.132)
  a. providing information about the situation and ways people can deal with such
  dangers.
  b. providing self-statements that promote effective adaptation when rehearsed.
  c. having the person practice making such self-statements while being exposed
  .to stressors
  d. All of the above

6. The formal diagnosis of PTSD was not defined until (p.128)
  a. 1968.
  b. 1980.
  c. 1987.
  d. 2000.

7. Acute stress disorder can last for a minimum of _____ and a maximum of ____
____. (p. 129)
    a. 2 days, 2 weeks
    b. 2 days, 3 weeks
    c. 2 days, 4 weeks
    d. 2 days, 5 weeks

8. John was originally diagnosed with acute stress disorder after his horrific car accident. His doctor has changed the diagnosis to post-traumatic stress disorder as the symptoms have lasted beyond (p.129)
    a. 6 months.
    b. 3 months.
    c. 2 months.
    d. 1 month.

9. All new paramedics were required to attend a week long training that used cognitive-behavioral techniques to help them better manage the stressful and difficult situations they would be placed into. This training is called (p. 132)
    a. stress-isolation training.
    b. eustress-inoculation training.
    c. stress-inoculation training.
    d. distress-inoculation training.

10. These are helpful in alleviating PTSD symptoms of depression, intrusion, and avoidance. (p. 133)
    a. antidepressants
    b. hugs
    c. illicit substances
    d. distress-inoculation training

COMPREHENSIVE PRACTICE TEST
The following tests are designed to give you an idea of how well you understood the entire chapter. There are three different types of tests: multiple choice, true/false, and essay.

Multiple Choice

1. The term *stress* has typically been used to refer to the _____ placed on an organism, and the organism's internal biological and psychological responses to such demands. (p. 115)
    a. conflicts
    b. adjustive demands
    c. pressures
    d. crisis

2. The stress experienced during a wedding or graduation would be considered (p. 115)
    a. distress.
    b. eustress.
    c. wedstress.
    d. allstress.

3. The longer a stressor operates, the _____ its effects. (p. 115)
    a. more acute
    b. less frustrating
    c. more severe
    d. less severe

4. Encountering a number of stressors at the same time will make these _____ than when occurring separately. (p. 115)
    a. more acute
    b. less frustrating
    c. more severe
    d. less severe

5. While stress has not been found to cause specific physical diseases, it (p. 118)
    a. is becoming a key underlying theme in our understanding of the development and course of virtually all organic illness.
    b. may serve as a predisposing, precipitating, or reinforcing factor in the causal pattern.
    c. may interfere with the body's normal defensive forces or immunological system.
    d. All of the above

6. In humans, the stress glucocorticoid that is produced is called (p. 118)
    a. serotonin.
    b. ACTH.
    c. cortisol.
    d. metrasol.

7. Which of the following emotions is most closely related to coronary artery deterioration and development of heart disease? (p. 124)
    a. hostility
    b. competitiveness
    c. impatience
    d. impulsivity

8. In a two-year study of 34,000 male professionals with panic disorder, agoraphobia, and generalized anxiety, men with the highest levels of phobic anxiety were _____ likely to have a fatal heart attack and _____ likely to suffer sudden cardiac death than were men with the lowest levels. (p. 125)
      a. not, less
      b. three times more, six times more
      c. 1.414 times more, 1.732 times more
      d. 1.414 times less, 1.732 times less

9. Acute stress disorder occurs (p.129)
      a. at least four weeks after the traumatic event and lasts longer than four weeks.
      b. within four weeks and lasts from two days to four weeks.
      c. early and is long-lasting and late-arising.
      d. None of the above

10. Post-traumatic stress disorder differs from acute stress disorder in that it (p.129)
      a. lasts longer than four weeks.
      b. occurs within four weeks of the traumatic event and lasts from two days to four weeks.
      c. may be long-lasting or late-arising.
      d. a and c

11. _____ following a traumatic experience is considered important in preventing conditioned fear from establishing itself and becoming resistant to change. (p. 130)
      a. Obtaining medical attention
      b. Applying a tourniquet
      c. Prompt psychotherapy
      d. Getting back into a regular routine

12. According to the DSM-IV-TR, if the duration of PTSD symptoms is less than three months, this would be specified as (p.130)
      a. chronic.
      b. acute.
      c. moderate.
      d. a and c

13. According to the DSM-IV-TR, if the duration of PTSD symptoms is more than three months, this would be specified as (p. 130)
      a. chronic.
      b. acute.
      c. moderate.
      d. a and c

14. Jake was beaten, robbed, and left for dead. This happened three weeks ago. He has been having vivid dreams, nightmares, and cannot go anywhere without a friend. He refuses to talk about what happened and he sweats and shakes. According to DSM criteria, Jake would be diagnosed with (p. 129)

    a. PTSD.
    b. GAD.
    c. acute stress disorder.
    d. OCD.

15. Jenny was lucky to survive the hurricane in Florida last year after nearly drowning; at least that is what everyone tells her. She, however, has not been able to get her life "back on track." She is afraid to plan for the future, will not go near water, has not been able to hold down a job because the memories keep "popping back into my head." According to DSM criteria, Jenny would be diagnosed with (p. 130)

    a. PTSD.
    b. GAD.
    c. acute stress disorder.
    d. OCD.

TRUE/FALSE

1. T / F The ailments to which people are most vulnerable—whether physical, psychological, or both—are determined in no small part by who we are, where we live, and how we live. (p. 114)

2. T / F Eustress is positive stress. (p. 115)

3. T / F Distress is negative stress. (p. 115)

4. T / F Eustress tolerance is a person's ability to withstand stress without becoming seriously impaired. (p. 115)

5. T / F Positive social and family relationships CANNOT moderate the effects of stress on a person. (p. 116)

6. T / F Psychoneuroimmunology is the study of the interaction between the cardiovascular system and the immune system. (p. 119)

7. T / F Hypertension is having persisting systolic blood pressure of 140 or more and a diastolic blood pressure of 90 or higher. (p. 123)

8. T / F Essential hypertension is often symptomless until its effects show up as medical complications. (p. 123)

9. T / F Heart attack patients who are depressed at the time of their heart attacks or shortly afterward show a greatly increased risk for future coronary events and cardiac

deaths. (p. 124)

10. T / (F) Type D personality types are excessively competitive, are overly committed to their work, and are extremely hostile. (p. 124)

11. T / (F) Training and preparation can insulate persons from PTSD. This is why police officers never suffer from it. (p. 130)

12. (T) / F PTSD can result in the traumatic event being persistently re-experienced by the person, or, conversely, deliberate avoidance of any stimuli associated with the trauma, such as cars, if the event were a car crash. (p. 130)

13. (T) / F Everyone has a breaking point, and at sufficiently high levels of stress, the average person can be expected to develop some psychological difficulties following a traumatic event. (p. 131)

14. T / (F) Allison's rape one week ago has left her extremely traumatized. Her diagnosis would most likely be PTSD. (p. 129)

15. T / (F) Antidepressants are NOT useful for the treatment of PTSD. (p. 133)

Essay Questions

1. Explain how stress affects the immune system. (pp. 118–122)

2. Please describe the three diseases of the cardiovascular system. (pp. 122–125)

3. Please discuss the Type A and Type D personalities. (p. 124)

4. Compare and contrast acute stress disorder and PTSD. (pp. 129–130)

5. Discuss the treatments for stress disorders. (p. 133)

WHEN YOU HAVE FINISHED

WEB LINKS TO ITEMS OR CONCEPTS DISCUSSED IN CHAPTER 4

National Center for PTSD
http://www.ncptsd.va.gov/index.html
The National Center for PTSD is one of the most respected centers for training, research, and the treatment of PTSD, and their Web site is no exception. There are numerous articles, a section on PTSD assessments, facts on PTSD, and special topics listed in alphabetical order such as child abuse, cognitive emotional processing, and disasters.

NIMH
http://www.nimh.nih.gov/healthinformation/ptsdmenu.cfm
The NIMH posts up-to-date, relevant information on PTSD.

The American Academy of Experts in Traumatic Stress
http://www.aaets.org/
The American Academy of Experts in Traumatic Stress is one of the largest professional organizations devoted to trauma in the world and has an international membership. This Web site provides discussion forums, timely and relevant publications, discussion of various treatment modalities, and has board certification programs for professionals.

USE IT OR LOSE IT
Provide an answer to the thought question below, knowing that there is more than one way to respond. Possible answers are presented in the Answer Key.

Explain why stressing about an exam in this class could contribute to your developing a cold.

CHAPTER 4: CORE CONCEPTS

CRISSCROSS

Now that you know all there is to know about this chapter, here's your opportunity to put that knowledge to work.

Across

5. PTSD that occurs within four weeks of event; lasts more than two days, but not more than four weeks
7. positive stress
9. a leukocyte that matures in the thymus
11. chemical messengers in the blood that appear to be of crucial importance for health
12. a by-product of poor or inadequate coping
13. negative stress
14. a patient who believes a treatment is going to be effective and is likely to improve, even if the treatment has no effect
15. foreign bodies (viruses, bacteria, and others) in one's body
16. a field that deals with psychology's contributions to diagnosis, treatment, and prevention

Down

1. broad, interdisciplinary approach of physical disorders thought to have psychosocial factors as a partial cause
2. a compromising of the body's immune system to the possible detriment of one's health
3. study of interactions among behavior, the nervous system, and the immune system
4. disorder resulting from a major, severe stressor; may be short-term or long-lasting
6. hypertension for which there is no known cause
8. an ability to withstand stress
10. known as an adjustment demand
11. time when a stressful situation approaches or exceeds the adaptive capacities of a person or group

Puzzle created with Puzzlemaker at DiscoverySchool.com

ANSWERS TO TEST QUESTIONS – CHAPTER FOUR

MATCHING
Who's Who and What's What?

___D___	Post-traumatic stress disorder
___A___	adjustment disorder
___G___	crisis
___F___	stress
___C___	stressor
___H___	eustress
___B___	stress tolerance
___E___	stress-inoculation training
___L___	psychoneuroimmunology
___N___	health psychology
___J___	behavioral medicine
___I___	positive psychology
___M___	Type A behavior pattern
___K___	Type B behavior pattern

SHORT ANSWERS
Your answer should contain the following points.

1. Stress refers to both the adjustive demands placed on an organism and to the organism's internal biological and psychological responses to such demands. Positive stress can result from weddings; negative stress would be associated with a loss such as the death of a loved one.

2. Allostatic load is the biological cost of adapting to stress.

3. Selye found that the body's reaction to sustained and excessive stress typically occurs in three major phases.
a. Alarm reaction, in which the body's defensive forces are activated.
b. Stage of resistance, in which biological adaptation is at the maximum level.
c. Exhaustion, in which bodily resources are depleted and the organism loses its ability to resist.

4. Immunosuppression can be caused by short-term threats to our sense of well-being or by the death of a spouse. It can last briefly or for one to three years in some cases.

5. Hypertension, coronary artery disease, and stroke.

6. Type D personality types have a tendency to experience negative emotions and also to feel insecure and anxious.

7. This school of psychology focuses on human traits and resources that might have direct implications for our physical and mental well-being.

8. Resnick recently estimated that 5 to 6 percent of men and 10 to 12 percent of women in the United States have experienced PTSD at some time in their lives.

THE DOCTOR IS IN

Post-traumatic stress disorder: Symptoms have lasted longer than one month. She feels anxious and depressed, and is having difficulty concentrating due to intrusive thoughts regarding the rape. She is having mood swings and is starting to drink to keep the nightmares away. Treatment: Seek specialized rape crisis counseling services for short-term counseling. Services might include advocacy for Becky if she goes to court, possibly direct-exposure therapy if symptoms persist. Give her the number to the telephone hotline and possibly use psychotropic medications.

PRACTICE TESTS

Q#	TEST 1	TEST 2	TEST 3
1	B	A	A
2	A	A	B
3	D	C	D
4	B	C	D
5	C	C	D
6	B	A	B
7	A	D	C
8	D	D	D
9	D	A	C
10	D	B	A

COMPREHENSIVE PRACTICE TEST

Q#	M/C	T/F
1	B	T
2	B	T
3	C	T
4	C	F
5	D	F
6	C	F
7	A	T
8	B	T
9	B	T
10	D	F
11	C	F
12	B	T
13	A	T

14	C	F
15	A	F

Essay Questions
1. Stress affects the immune system by lowering resistance to infection and disease. A discussion of antigens, T-cells, B-cells, and cytokines should also be included in your answer.

2. Hypertension is having a persisting systolic blood pressure of 140 or more and a diastolic blood pressure of 90 or higher. Coronary artery disease is a potentially lethal blockage of the arteries that supply blood to the heart muscle or myocardium. Stroke is the result of the clogging of arteries and thus affects the arterial blood supply to the brain.

3. Type A personality types have an excessive competitive drive, extreme commitment to work, impatience or time urgency, and are prone to hostility. Type D personality types have a tendency to experience negative emotions and also to feel insecure and anxious.

4. Acute stress disorder lasts for a minimum of two days and a maximum of four weeks and occurs within four weeks of the traumatic event. PTSD is diagnosed when the duration of the disturbance lasts more than one month.

5. Treatments include psychotherapy, psychotropic medications, and short-term crisis therapy.

USE IT OR LOSE IT
Stress triggers the fight-or-flight response, which causes changes in hormonal and neurotransmitters that inhibit immunological responses. Since the body has limited energy sources, responses that enable an individual to escape danger are given precedence over immune responses. Consequently, experiencing a stressor may make the body more susceptible to infections and illnesses.

CRISSCROSS ANSWERS

Across
5. Acute stess
7. Eustress
9. T Cells
11. Cytokines
12. Stress
13. Distress
14. Placebo effect
15. Antigen
16. Health psychology

Down
1. Behavioral medicine
2. Immunosuppression
3. Psychoneuroimmunology
4. PTSD
6. Essential hypertension
8. Stress tolerance
10. Stressor

Chapter 5: Panic, Anxiety, and Their Disorders

BEFORE YOU READ

At one time or another we have all experienced some degree of worry, whether it be in our personal lives, at school, or at work. Most worries tend to be fleeting and temporary. However, when one's worry becomes constant and interferes with daily performance in social, occupational, or school functioning, then it is cause for concern. Anxiety disorders are the most common disorders and affect more than 23 million Americans a year. For those coping with an anxiety disorder, the worry, fear, and anxiety is overwhelming, and they may feel that they have no control over their lives. Chapter 5 provides a wonderful exploration into these common yet challenging disorders. You will learn there are many different types of anxiety disorders, from phobias (specific and social) to panic disorders, which can be so severe that people think they are having a heart attack. You will also be introduced to generalized anxiety and obsessive-compulsive disorders, their prevalence rates and causes, and the types of treatment to help people manage their anxiety. Finally, you will gain an appreciation for the symptom overlap among these disorders and the complexity of diagnosis.

- **THE FEAR AND ANXIETY RESPONSE PATTERNS**

- **OVERVIEW OF THE ANXIETY DISORDERS AND THEIR COMMONALITIES**

- **SPECIFIC PHOBIAS**
    Blood-Injection-Injury Phobia
    Age of Onset and Gender Differences in Specific Phobias
    Psychosocial Causal Factors
    Genetic and Temperamental Causal Factors
    Treating Specific Phobias

- **SOCIAL PHOBIAS**
    Interaction of Psychosocial and Biological Causal Factors
    Treating Social Phobias

- **PANIC DISORDER WITH AND WITHOUT AGORAPHOBIA**
    Panic Disorder
    Agoraphobia
    Prevalence, Gender, Comorbidity, and Age of Onset of Panic Disorder with and
        without Agoraphobia
    The Timing of a First Panic Attack
    Biological Causal Factors
    Behavioral and Cognitive Causal Factors
    Treating Panic Disorder and Agoraphobia

- **GENERALIZED ANXIETY DISORDER**
    General Characteristics
    Prevalence, Age of Onset, and Comorbidity

Psychosocial Causal Factors
Biological Causal Factors
Treating Generalized Anxiety Disorder

• OBSESSIVE-COMPULSIVE DISORDER
Prevalence, Age of Onset, and Comorbidity
Characteristics of OCD
Psychosocial Causal Factors
Biological Causal Factors
Treating Obsessive-Compulsive Disorder

• SOCIOCULTURAL CAUSAL FACTORS FOR ALL ANXIETY DISORDERS
Cultural Differences in Sources of Worry
Taijin Kyofusho

OBJECTIVES
After reading this chapter, you should be able to do the following:

1. Compare and evaluate the merits of Freud's use of the concept of anxiety in the etiology of the neuroses versus the descriptive approach used in DSM since 1980.

2. Distinguish between fear and anxiety.

3. Describe the major features of phobias.

4. Identify and differentiate different subtypes of phobia.

5. Explicate the major etiological hypotheses, and discuss the most effective treatment approaches.

6. List the diagnostic criteria for panic disorder, and compare and contrast panic attacks and other types of anxiety and explain the association with agoraphobia.

7. Summarize prevalence and age of onset.

8. Describe recent findings on biological, behavioral, and cognitive influence for anxiety proneness.

9. Summarize the evidence that anxiety sensitivity constitutes a diathesis for development of panic attacks.

10. Describe how safety behaviors and cognitive biases help to maintain panic.

11. Compare and contrast the major treatment approaches for panic disorder and agoraphobia.

12. Summarize the central features of generalized anxiety disorder.

13. Identify the central nervous system processes and structures associated with generalized anxiety disorder, and evaluate treatments for the disorder.

14. Describe the defining features of obsessive-compulsive disorder, summarize theories of etiology along with supporting evidence (or the lack thereof), and outline the treatment of OCD.

15. Provide several examples of sociocultural effects on anxiety disorders.

AS YOU READ
Answers can be found in the Answer Key at the end of the book.

KEY WORDS
Each of the words below is important in understanding the concepts presented in this Chapter. Write the definition next to each word.

Term	Page	Definition
Agoraphobia	150	
Amygdala	153	
Anxiety	139	
Anxiety disorders	138	
Anxiety sensitivity	155	
Blood-injection-injury phobia	142	
Compulsions	163	
Fear	139	
Generalized anxiety disorder (GAD)	158	
Interoceptive fears	157	
Neuroses	138	
Neurotic behavior	138	
Obsessions	163	
Obsessive-compulsive disorder (OCD)	163	
Panic	139	
Panic disorder	149	
Panic provocation agents	152	
Phobia	140	
Social phobia	146	
Specific phobia	141	

MATCHING
Who's Who and What's What?
Match the following terms with the appropriate description.

D	Phobia
G	Anxiety
F	Neuroses
I	Inflation effect
A	Vicarious conditioning
C	Nocturnal panic
E	Anxiety sensitivity
J	Anxious apprehension
M	CRH
L	Bed nucleus of the stria terminali
K	Taijin Kyofusho (TKS)
H	Aaron Beck
B	O. H. Mowrer

Definition
A. The transmission of a phobia from one person or animal to another by observing a person or animal behaving fearfully
B. Credited with devising a two-process theory of avoidance learning in OCD
C. Panic attack that occurs during sleep
D. Persistent and disproportionate fear of some specific object or situation that presents little or no actual danger
E. A trait-like belief that certain bodily symptoms may have harmful consequences
F. Psychological disorders that resulted when intrapsychic conflict produced significant anxiety
G. A complex blend of unpleasant emotions and cognitions
H. Cognitive psychologist who coined the phrase, "automatic thoughts," which are associated with panic triggers
I. When a person is exposed to a more intense traumatic experience (not paired with the conditioned stimulus) after a first traumatic experience, thus becoming more fearful of the conditioned stimulus
J. Future-oriented mood state in which a person attempts to be constantly ready to deal with negative upcoming events
K. Anxiety disorder found in Japan related to Western social phobia
L. Extension of the amygdala believed to be an important brain area mediating generalized anxiety
M. Anxiety producing hormone recently implicated as playing a role in GAD

SHORT ANSWERS
Provide brief answers to the following questions.

1. List the five subtypes of specific phobia and give examples of each. (p.142)

2. Discuss methods used to treat social phobias. (pp. 145–146)

3. You are a psychoanalyst and a client comes to see you with GAD. How would you explain the causal factors for this disorder? (p. 160)

4. Describe the different types of obsessive thoughts and compulsions. (p. 163)

THE DOCTOR IS IN...PSYCHIATRIC HELP—5¢
Read the following scenarios and diagnose the client. Remember to look carefully at the criteria for the disorder before you make a decision as to the diagnosis. Make a list of other information you might need to help you understand the causal factors.

1. Teresa comes to your office. Her primary care doctor, who could find nothing wrong with her, has referred her to you. She tells you she feels as if she is losing control and going crazy. She says that for the past two months, she has been unexpectedly having shortness of breath, heart palpitations, dizziness, and sweating. These experiences seem to come out of the blue and make her so afraid that she doesn't want to leave her house.

How would you diagnose her and what would your treatment plan be? (pp.138–156)

2. Ned visits your office at the urging of his family. Ned tells you he has been feeling anxious about the future and says he needs to be ready to deal with any negative thing that might come up—like his car breaking down or getting lost when trying to get to a new area. Both of these would affect his work, thus, his financial well-being, and, ultimately, his family. He tells you he can't seem to control the constant state of apprehension and always feels tense and over-aroused. He hasn't been sleeping well and has had difficulty concentrating at work. His family says he is constantly irritable and he has felt a lot of muscle tension, especially in his neck and shoulders.

How would you diagnose Ned and what would be the most effective treatment for him? (pp. 138–156)

3. In the past few months, Jean has been washing her hands 50 to 75 times a day. Her hands are now cracked and bleeding and she is unable to work. In addition to hand washing she has to constantly check her stove and door locks and she must do this in a particular way or she has to start all over again. She has come to see you because she is about to lose her marriage as a result of her behavior. Jean knows her behaviors are senseless and excessive but she can't control them.

How would you diagnosis Jean and what treatment plan would you create? (pp. 163–166)

After You Read

PRACTICE TESTS
Take the following three multiple-choice tests to see how much you have comprehended from the chapter. Each represents roughly one third of the chapter. As you study the chapter, use these to check your progress.

Practice Test 1

1. Who believed that neuroses were the result of intrapsychic conflict? (p. 138)
   a. Pavlov
   b. Ellis
   c. Freud
   d. Beck

2. The components of fear and panic are (p. 139)
   a. cognitive/subjective.
   b. physiological.
   c. behavioral.
   d. All of the above

3. Anxiety, unlike fear, is a complex blend of emotions and cognitions that is oriented to the (p. 139)
   a. object of fear.
   b. past experience.
   c. future.
   d. All of the above

4. Many human and animal experiments have established that the basic fear and anxiety response patterns are highly (p. 139)
    a. predictable.
    b. conditionable.
    c. inevitable.
    d. a and c

5. A reduction in phobic behavior tends to occur when a person _____ the feared situation. (p. 140)
    a. faces
    b. clarifies
    c. avoids
    d. understands

6. _____ is a phobia that, unlike most phobias, begins with an initial acceleration of blood pressure and heart rate, and is followed with a rapid decrease in both heart rate and blood pressure. (p. 142)
    a. Blood-injection-injury
    b. Agoraphobia
    c. Arachnophobia
    d. Social phobia

7. Which viewpoint explains phobias as a defense against anxiety? (p. 142)
    a. behavioral
    b. cognitive
    c. psychodynamic
    d. humanistic

8. By watching her older sister react in a fearful way to spiders, Keri learned to be afraid of spiders also. This is called (p. 143)
    a. aping conditioning.
    b. mimicking conditioning.
    c. vicarious conditioning.
    d. None of the above

9. John had dogs all his life and was quite comfortable being around dogs. After John was bitten by a dog, he did not develop a phobia. Why? (p.143)
    a. He didn't care.
    b. It didn't hurt.
    c. The dog didn't mean it.
    d. His experiences had immunized him.

10. Steve, who has an unreasonable fear of elevators, watches as his therapist goes up and down an elevator in a calm and nonchalant way. Later, he walks into the elevator with his therapist and goes up one floor. This is an example of (p.145)

a. participant modeling.
b. specific phobia modeling.
c. reality modeling.
d. None of the above

Practice Test 2

1. Social phobias usually begin in (p. 146)
    a. early childhood.
    b. midlife.
    c. adolescence or early adulthood.
    d. old age.

2. Phobias tend to develop in response to stimuli that (p.146)
    a. could actually be dangerous.
    b. are typically modern inventions.
    c. are depressing.
    d. are not actually dangerous.

3. Like other phobias, social phobias are often (p. 147)
    a. evolving.
    b. learned.
    c. easily ignored.
    d. None of the above

4. Unlike specific phobias, social phobia can sometimes be treated with (p. 148)
    a. cognitive therapy.
    b. behavioral therapy.
    c. medication.
    d. None of the above

5. What distinguishes panic attacks from other types of anxiety? (p. 149)
    a. brevity
    b. intensity
    c. physiological symptoms
    d. a and b

6. Panic attacks are about twice as prevalent in women as in men. This is thought to be a result of _____ factors. (p. 152)
    a. behavioral
    b. gender
    c. sociocultural
    d. unconscious

7. In family and twin studies, panic disorders have a _____ heritable component. (p. 152)

   a. high
   b. low
   c. moderate
   d. predictable

8. The _____ is the central area involved in what has been called a "fear network" with connections to lower (locus coeruleus) and higher (prefrontal cortex) areas of the brain. (p. 153)
   a. hippocampus
   b. amygdala
   c. limbic system
   d. All of the above

9. Beck and Emery (1985) and Clark (1986, 1988, 1997) proposed a model of panic that says clients are hypersensitive to their bodily sensations and prone to giving them the worst possible interpretations. What is this theory called? (p. 154)
   a. fear of fear theory
   b. comprehensive learning theory
   c. cognitive theory
   d. biological readiness theory

10. Ken often has an upset stomach. He is very anxious about this condition. Although Ken does not have any panic attacks, his preexisting high level of _____ makes him more prone to developing a panic disorder. (p. 155)
   a. awareness
   b. cognition
   c. a and b
   d. anxiety sensitivity

Practice Test 3

1. It is estimated that GAD is experienced by approximately _____ percent of the population in any one-year period and _____ percent at some point in their lives. (p. 159)
   a. 10; 70
   b. 2; 4.7
   c. 8; 11.2
   d. 3; 5.7

2. For people with GAD, worry (p. 160)
   a. has both positive and negative consequences.
   b. has minor and major consequences.
   c. has no known effect at this time.
   d. is irrelevant.

3. A(n) _____ is an overt repetitive behavior or more covert mental act. (p. 163)

a. compulsion
b. obsession
c. behavior
d. intuition

4. PET scan studies have shown that people with OCD have _____
levels in the caudate nucleus, the orbital frontal cortex, and the cingulated cortex.
(p. 167)
    a. normally active
    b. Normally inactive
    c. abnormally inactive
    d. abnormally Active

5. Biological causal factors are _____ implicated in the causes of OCD.
(p. 166)
    a. strongly
    b. mildly
    c. superficially
    d. somewhat

6. Which of the following drugs provide symptom relief from panic disorder with or
without agoraphobia yet may lead to physiological dependence? (p. 156)
    a. SSRIs
    b. minor tranquilizer
    c. fricyclic antidepressant
    d. monoamine oxidase inhibitor

7. Which of the following is NOT typically a part of cognitive-behavior therapy for panic
disorder? (p. 154)
    a. exposure to feared situations and/or feared bodily sensations
    b. deep muscle relaxation and breathing retraining
    c. identification and modification of logical errors and automatic thoughts
    d. carbon dioxide inhalation and/or lactate infusion

8. The benzodiazepines are minor tranquilizers that probably exert their effects through
stimulating the action of (p. 162)
    a. acetylcholine.
    b. GABA.
    c. serotonin.
    d. norepinephrine.

9. An impulse the person cannot seem to control is called a(n) (p. 163)
    a. compulsion.
    b. delusion.
    c. hallucination.

d. focal phobia.

10. The only disorder that shows virtually no difference in prevalence between men and women is (p. 164)
    a. OCD.
    b. social phobia.
    c. specific phobia.
    d. GAD.

COMPREHENSIVE PRACTICE TEST

The following tests are designed to give you an idea of how well you understood the entire chapter. There are three different types of tests: multiple-choice, true/false, and essay.

Multiple Choice

1. The term *neurosis* was dropped from the DSM–III in the year (p. 138)
    a. 1969.
    b. 1980.
    c. 1975.
    d. 1990.

2. The most common way of distinguishing between fear and anxiety is that fear involves a(n) (p. 139)
    a. increase in heart rate.
    b. unpleasant interstate of something dreadful going to happen.
    c. inability to specify a clear danger.
    d. obvious source of danger.

3. Paula has been feeling extremely anxious and experiencing physical responses, such as a racing heart and dizziness. In all likelihood she will first consult her (p. 150)
    a. primary care doctor.
    b. therapist.
    c. psychiatrist.
    d. dentist.

4. At the age of 21 months, Karen was a very timid and shy child. She hid behind her mother and rarely ventured over to play with other children in her playgroup. Based on the study done by Kagan and his colleagues, what can you predict about the risk of Karen developing multiple specific phobias by the age of seven or eight? It is (p. 144)
    a. about the same as other children in her playgroup.
    b. less than uninhibited children in general.
    c. higher because of temperamental factors.
    d. higher because her playgroup has more boys than girls.

5. The most common specific social phobia is fear of (p. 146)

a. public speaking.
b. crowds.
c. urinating in public restrooms.
d. public affection.

6. From an evolutionary perspective, social phobias are a by-product of (p. 147)
   a. dominance hierarchies.
   b. learning.
   c. observing.
   d. modeling.

7. Billy, who is 25 months old, is behaviorally inhibited. What can you predict, based on the Hayward et al and Kagan's research, will be the likelihood of Billy developing a social phobia by the age of 13? (p. 148)
   a. He has increased risk.
   b. He has no increased risk.
   c. He will develop a social phobia.
   d. None of the above

8. An early hypothesis about the origins of agoraphobia was that it was a (p. 154)
   a. fear of fear.
   b. fear of going shopping.
   c. fear of commitment.
   d. None of the above

9. Unlike other anxiety disorders that often have an acute onset, people with GAD report (p. 159)
   a. being anxious most of their lives.
   b. a slow and insidious onset.
   c. sudden onset.
   d. a and b

10. Something that may account for why people with GAD feel constantly tense and vigilant for possible threats is their relative lack of (p. 160)
   a. interest in their surroundings.
   b. understanding.
   c. safety signals.
   d. something to be really worried about.

11. GAD seems to share a common genetic diathesis with (p. 161)
   a. personality disorders.
   b. PTSD.
   c. major depressive disorder.
   d. eating disorders.

12. A(n) _____ is a persistent and recurrent intrusive thought, image, or impulse that is experienced as disturbing and inappropriate. (p. 163)
      a. compulsion
      b. obsession
      c. behavior
      d. GAD

13. OCD is characterized by (p. 164)
      a. anxiety.
      b. compulsions.
      c. the fear of being responsible for something horrible happening.
      d. All of the above

14. OCD may be characterized by excessively high levels of (p. 168)
      a. GABA.
      b. fluoxetine.
      c. serotonin.
      d. None of the above

15. More than _____ percent of people with OCD who come for treatment experience both obsessions and compulsions. (p. 164)
      a. 100
      b. 90
      c. 80
      d. 70

16. Joe cannot seem to relax at any time during the day. His shoulders are tight, he is irritable, he does not sleep well, and he cannot focus at work or at home. He knows something is wrong, but he cannot control his worries. This has been going on for more than half the year. Joe would most likely have which diagnosis? (p. 159)
      a. social phobia
      b. panic disorder
      c. OCD
      d. generalized anxiety disorder

17. Medications that affect this neurotransmitter seem to be the primary class of medication for OCD. (p. 169)
      a. GABA
      b. serotonin
      c. dopamine
      d. acetylcholine

CHAPTER 5: CORE CONCEPTS

TRUE/FALSE

1. T / F Fear or panic is a basic emotion that involves activation of the "flight or fight" response. (p. 139)

2. T / F Anxiety involves a positive mood, worry about the future, and the ability to predict the future threat. (p. 139)

3. T / F Per the DSM-IV-TR, the duration of specific phobia is at least three months. (p. 141)

4. T / F Life experiences influence a person's likelihood of developing a phobia. (p. 143)

5. T / F The best treatment for specific phobia is cognitive therapy. (p. 145)

6. T / F The treatment of choice for specific phobias is exposure therapy. (p. 145)

7. T / F The term *social anxiety disorder* is increasingly preferred by researchers and clinicians, instead of *social phobias*. (p. 146)

8. T / F Social phobics have a deep sense of control over events in their lives. (p. 142)

9. T / F Agoraphobia can occur in the absence of full-blown panic attacks. (p. 152)

10. T / F Seven to thirty percent of adults who have experienced panic attacks will go on to develop panic disorder. (p. 152)

11. T / F To meet DSM-IV-TR criteria for generalized anxiety disorder, the worry must occur more days than not for at least three months, and it must be experienced as difficult to control. (p. 158)

12. T / F People with panic disorder automatically pay attention to pleasant information in their environment. (p. 152)

13. T / F Most people with GAD manage to function in spite of their high levels of worry and anxiety. (p. 159)

14. T / F People with GAD have a history of experiencing many important events in their lives that they feel are predictable and controllable. (p. 159)

15. T / F The neurotransmitter GABA is now strongly implicated in generalized anxiety. (p. 153)

16. T / F OCD is different from other anxiety disorders in that there is a large gender difference in adults. (p. 164)

17. T / F When OCD clients were asked to suppress intrusive thoughts, they reported twice as many intrusive thoughts on those days as opposed to the days they were given no instructions. (p. 166)

Essay Questions

1. Discuss the DSM-IV-TR criteria for diagnosing generalized anxiety disorder (GAD). (pp. 158–159)

2. Give examples of cultural differences in sources of worry. (pp. 169–170)

3. Discuss the DSM-IV-TR criteria for diagnosing obsessive-compulsive disorder (OCD). (pp. 163–164)

WHEN YOU HAVE FINISHED

WEB LINKS TO ITEMS OR CONCEPTS DISCUSSED IN CHAPTER 5

NIMH Web Site on Anxiety Disorders
    http://www.nimh.nih.gov/healthinformation/anxietymenu.cfm
This is the Web site for the National Institute of Mental Health, and its presentation of the various symptoms, treatments, resources, and recent research involving the study of anxiety disorders.

American Psychological Association's Anxiety Web Page
    http://www.apa.org/topics/topicanxiety.html
The American Psychological Association hosts this Web page devoted entirely to anxiety disorders. There are terrific links to books, videos, journals, press releases, and the *Monitor on Psychology* that has cutting edge articles and information on various topics.

NIMH Web Site on GAD
    http://www.nimh.nih.gov/healthinformation/gadmenu.cfm

The National Institute of Mental Health has a Web site devoted entirely to generalized anxiety disorder, and this site serves as a solid foundation for furthering one's information on this complicated yet fascinating disorder.

National Mental Health Association Web Page on Generalized Anxiety Disorder
        http://www.nmha.org/infoctr/factsheets/31.cfm
The National Mental Health Association Web page on generalized anxiety disorder provides a good overview of facts, information, and resources.

Anxiety Network International Panic Disorder Web Site
        http://www.anxietynetwork.com/pdhome.html
The Web site provides numerous descriptions that those with panic disorder have faced and overcome. There are various Web links and a general sense of support for those with panic disorder.

Medline Web Site on Panic Disorder
        http://www.nlm.nih.gov/medlineplus/panicdisorder.html
The Medline Plus Web site on panic disorder provides trusted information on everything from treatment, research and clinical trials, the NIMH, statistics, and child and adolescent issues involving the disorder.

NIMH Web Site on GAD
        http://www.nlm.nih.gov/medlineplus/obsessivecompulsivedisorder.html
The Medline Plus Web site on obsessive-compulsive disorder provides the latest news on the disorder as well as topics on treatment, research and clinical trials, the NIMH, statistics, and child and adolescent issues involving the disorder.

OCD and Children
        http://www.kidshealth.org/kid/feeling/emotion/ocd.html
Kids Health is a unique Web site that was created by the Nemours Foundation's Center for Children's Health Media. The information is physician-approved and not jargon-laden so it is a good mix of accurate information in a mentally digestible format.

USE IT OR LOSE IT
Provide an answer to the thought question below, knowing that there is more than one way to respond. Possible answers are presented in the Answer Key.

Why do you think that people who have panic attacks frequently believe that they are having a heart attack?

CRISSCROSS

Now that you know all there is to know about this chapter, here's your opportunity to put that knowledge to work.

Across
4. Disturbing persistent, recurrent, intrusive thoughts, images, or impulses
5. The experienced emotion when the source of danger is not obvious
6. May involve fears of things (animals, water, heights, tunnels, spiders)
8. The exaggerated use of avoidance behaviors or defense mechanisms
9. A blend of emotions that is more oriented to the future and much more diffuse than fear

Down
1. Clearly excessive ritualistic overt repetitive behaviors
2. Involves fears of situations in which a person is exposed to the scrutiny of others
3. The experienced emotion when the source of danger is obvious
7. A collection of nuclei critical involved in the emotion of fear

Puzzle created with Puzzlemaker at DiscoverySchool.com

ANSWERS TO TEST QUESTIONS – CHAPTER 5

MATCHING
Who's Who and What's What
D. Phobia
G. Anxiety
F. Neuroses
I. Inflation effect
A. Vicarious conditioning
C. Nocturnal panic
E. Anxiety sensitivity
J. Anxious apprehension
M. CRH
L. Bed nucleus of the stria terminali
K. Taijin Kyofusho (TKS)
H. Aaron Beck
B. O. H. Mowrer

SHORT ANSWERS
Your answer should contain the following points.

1. The five subtypes of specific phobias including examples of each:
a. Animal—snakes, spiders
b. Natural environment—heights or water
c. Blood-injection-injury—sight of blood or injury
d. Situational—airplanes or elevators
e. Atypical—choking or vomiting

2. Methods used to treat social phobias:
a. Behavior therapy—prolonged exposure to social situations in graduated manner
b. Cognitive behavior therapy—identify underlying negative automatic thoughts; help change negative automatic thoughts through logical reanalysis—the challenging of the automatic thought
c. Medication—can also be treated with beta-blockers, antidepressants, and antianxiety drugs

3. a. Unconscious conflict between the ego and id impulses that are not being dealt with because the person's defense mechanisms have broken down or become overwhelmed
b. Perhaps defense mechanisms never developed
c. Inoperative defense mechanisms leave the person anxious nearly all of the time

4. Examples of obsessions and compulsions:

a. Obsessive thoughts—contamination fears, fears of harming self or others, lack of symmetry, pathological doubt, need for symmetry, sexual obsessions and religious or aggressive obsessions

b. Compulsions—five primary types: cleaning, checking, repeating, ordering/arranging, counting and primary obsessional slowness

THE DOCTOR IS IN

1. Teresa

Diagnosis: Panic disorder with agoraphobia

Treatment: A variety of treatment methods could be used.

• Medication: not as good but could prescribe benzodiazepines or antidepressants

• Cognitive-behavior therapy (see Developments in Practice)

You would

• teach Teresa about nature of anxiety and panic, and how to self-monitor her experiences

• teach her how to control her breathing

• help her identify her automatic thoughts during panic attacks

• teach her how to decatastrophize, e.g., expose her to feared situations and feared bodily sensations (interceptive fears)

2. Ned

Diagnosis: Generalized Anxiety Disorder

Treatment:

• Medication: possibly Buspirone or some antidepressants

• Cognitive-behavior therapy: training in applied muscle relaxation techniques and cognitive restructuring techniques aimed at reducing distorted cognitions, information processing biases, and catastrophizing about minor events. GAD is still one of the most difficult anxiety disorders to treat.

Benefits:

• superstitious avoidance of catastrophe

• actual avoidance of catastrophe

• avoidance of deeper emotional topics

• coping and preparation

• motivating device

3. Jean

Diagnosis: Obsessive-compulsive disorder

Treatment: Behavioral treatment involving a combination of exposure and compulsive response prevention is perhaps the most effective. SSRIs are a possibility, but there is a high relapse rate when the drugs are stopped. In severe intractable OCD, which has not responded to therapy or drugs, neurosurgical techniques may be considered.

PRACTICE TESTS

Q#	TEST 1	TEST 2	TEST 3
1	C	C	D
2	D	A	A
3	C	B	A
4	B	C	D
5	A	D	A
6	A	C	B
7	C	C	D
8	C	B	B
9	D	C	A
10	A	D	A

COMPREHENSIVE PRACTICE TEST

Q#	M/C	T/F
1	B	T
2	D	F
3	A	F
4	C	T
5	A	F
6	A	T
7	A	T
8	A	F
9	D	T
10	C	F
11	C	F
12	B	F
13	D	T
14	C	F
15	B	T
16	D	F
17	B	T

Essay Questions
Your answer should contain the following points.

1. Generalized anxiety disorder (GAD) is characterized by:
a. chronic excessive worry about a number of events or activities—formerly called free-floating anxiety
b. worry must occur more days than not for at least six months and be difficult to control
• cannot be associated with another concurrent Axis I disorder
• subjective experience of worry must be accompanied by at least three of the following symptoms: restlessness, being keyed up; sense of being easily fatigued; difficulty

concentrating or mind going blank; irritability; muscle tension; sleep disturbance

2. Examples of cultural differences in sources of worry:
a. Yoruba culture of Nigeria—three primary clusters of symptoms associated with generalized anxiety:
• worry focusing on creating and maintaining a large family and fertility
• dreams may indicate the person is bewitched
• bodily complaints—water in my brain, "ants creeping in my brain," etc.
b. China—Koro, fear of penis shrinking or nipples retracting
c. Japan—Taijin Kyofusho—concern about doing something that will embarrass or offend others

3. Obsessive-compulsive disorder (OCD) is characterized by:
a. recurrent and persistent thoughts, impulses, or images that are experienced at some time as intrusive and cause marked anxiety
b. thoughts, impulses, or images are not simply excessive worries about real life problems
c. person attempts to ignore or suppress or neutralize them with some other thought or action
d. person recognizes self as a product of his or her own mind.
e. repetitive behaviors or mental acts the person feels driven to perform
f. behaviors or mental acts are aimed at preventing or reducing distress or preventing some dreaded event or situation
g. person recognizes the obsessions or compulsions are excessive or unreasonable

USE IT OR LOSE IT

The symptoms of panic attacks can include rapid breathing, heartbeats, chest pain, and sweating, which can also accompany heart attacks. Since these symptoms can occur quite suddenly people may panic and believe that they are ill, and even dying.

CRISSCROSS ANSWERS
Across
4. Obsessions
5. Panic
6. Specific phobia
8. Neuroses
9. Anxiety

Down
1. Compulsions
2. Social phobia
3. Fear
7. Amygdala

Chapter 6: Mood Disorders and Suicide

BEFORE YOU READ

All of us have experienced both happy and sad moments in our lives with hopefully more happy moments than sad ones. This is a normal part of everyday life; however, these normal variations in emotion are not the same as the changes in mood and functioning that are seen in mood disorders. Depressed individuals typically will present with extraordinary sadness, low interest, sleep disturbances, and feelings of guilt and hopelessness, while those who experience a manic episode will present with a markedly elevated euphoric mood, rapid speech, and have a decreased need for sleep. Yet even within these categories there are significant differences in the severity and duration of these disorders. This chapter will explore the biological and psychosocial causes of mood disorders and the ways in which they can be differentiated. The types of treatments available for mood disorders will be explained, as well as their application and efficacy. Cultural differences in the experience and treatment of mood disorders will also be addressed. Lastly, you will learn that people who suffer from mood disorders are at risk for suicide. The final portion of this chapter discusses the risk factors for suicide, and what can be done to intervene or prevent suicidal attempts. At the end of this chapter, you should have a greater appreciation for the complexity and severity of these disorders, and the continued need for research into new and more effective treatments.

- **WHAT ARE MOOD DISORDERS?**
   The Prevalence of Mood Disorders

- **UNIPOLAR MOOD DISORDERS**
   Depressions That Are Not Mood Disorders
   Dysthymic Disorder
   Major Depressive Disorder

- **CAUSAL FACTORS IN UNIPOLAR MOOD DISORDERS**
   Biological Causal Factors
   Psychosocial Causal Factors

- **BIPOLAR DISORDERS**
   Cyclothymic Disorder
   Bipolar Disorders (I and II)

- **CAUSAL FACTORS IN BIPOLAR DISORDER**
   Biological Causal Factors
   Psychosocial Causal Factors

- **SOCIALCULTURAL FACTORS AFFECTING UNIPOLAR AND BIPOLAR DISORDERS**
   Cross-Cultural Differences in Depressive Symptoms
   Demographic Differences in the United States

- **TREATMENTS AND OUTCOMES**
  Pharmacotherapy
  Alternative Biological Treatments
  Psychotherapy

- **SUICIDE**
  The Clinical Picture and the Causal Pattern
  Suicide Prevention and Intervention

- **UNRESOVED ISSUES:**
  Is There a Right to Die?

OBJECTIVES

After reading this chapter, you should be able to do the following:

1. Define the characteristics of mood disorders.

2. Explain the prevalence of mood disorders.

3. Describe unipolar mood disorders.

4. Differentiate depressions that are not mood disorders from those that are.

5. Identify the mild to moderate depressive disorders.

6. Describe criteria for diagnosing major depressive disorder and its subtypes.

7. Discuss biological and psychosocial causal factors in unipolar and bipolar mood disorders.

8. Describe various types of bipolar disorders.

9. Explain how various sociocultural factors affect unipolar and bipolar disorders.

10. Assess treatments and outcomes of mood disorders.

11. Explain prevalence rates of suicide among people with mood disorders.

12. Describe who is likely to attempt suicide versus who is likely to complete suicide.

13. Describe the various motives for why someone takes his or her own life.

14. Explain the sociocultural and biological variables that affect suicide.

AS YOU READ
Answers can be found in the Answer Key at the end of the book.

KEY WORDS
Each of the words below is important in understanding the concepts presented in this chapter. Write the definition next to each word. The page numbers are provided in case you need to refer to the book.

Term	Page	Definition
Attributions	190	
Bipolar I disorder	195	
Bipolar disorder with a seasonal pattern	196	
Bipolar II disorder	196	
Chronic major depressive disorder	180	
Cyclothymic disorder	195	
Depression	174	
Depressogenic schemas	189	
Diathesis-stress theories	187	
Double depression	180	
Dysfunctional beliefs	189	
Dysthymic disorder	177	
Hypomanic episode	195	
Learned helplessness	190	
Major depressive disorder	177	
Major depressive episode	174	
Major depressive episode with atypical features	179	
Major depressive episode with	179	

melancholic features		
Mania	174	
Manic episode	175	
Mixed episode	195	
Mood disorders	174	
Negative automatic thoughts	189	
Negative cognitive Triad	189	
Pessimistic attributional style	191	
Rapid cycling	196	
Recurrence	180	
Relapse	180	
Seasonal affective disorder	181	
Severe major depressive episode with psychotic features	179	
Specifiers	179	
Suicide	206	
Unipolar disorder	174	

MATCHING
Who's Who and What's What
Match each of the following people with her/his accomplishment or theory.

Psychologist

C _____ Martin Seligman

E _____ Emile Durkheim

A _____ Aaron Beck

B _____ Sigmund Freud

E _____ Emil Kraepelin

D _____ Abramson et al., 1989

Accomplishment or Theory
A. Depressogenic schemas/negative automatic thoughts
B. "Mourning and Melancholia"
C. learned helplessness theory
D. hopelessness theory

E. introduced the term *manic-depressive insanity*

F. French sociologist who studied the sociocultural factors in suicide

SHORT ANSWERS
Provide brief answers to the following questions.

1. A friend of yours recently lost a grandparent. You have just finished studying mood disorders in your Abnormal Psychology class. What could you tell him about the normal response phases to the loss? (p. 176)

2. In the Brown and Harris 1978 study, what factors were associated with the women who experienced stressful life events but did not become depressed? (p. 187)

3. Discuss the ways interpersonal problems can play a causal role in depression and how depression affects others. (pp. 190–192)

THE DOCTOR IS IN...PSYCHIATRIC HELP—5¢
Read the following scenarios and diagnose the client. Remember to look carefully at the criteria for the disorder before you make a decision as to the diagnosis. Make a list of other information you might need to help you understand the causal factors.

1. Helen comes into your office asking for help. She is a 29-year-old woman, married with no children. She reports that she has been feeling sad for a long time—almost three years now. Although she does have periods of feeling normal, these don't last. Recently her husband has been making comments about how little she has been eating. Helen says that she has no energy and can't seem to sleep through the night. She is starting to think of herself as a worthless person for not being able to just snap out of it. How would you diagnose Helen? (pp. 177–179)

2. As a leading expert on adolescent suicide, you have been asked to give a talk on known risk factors. What would you include in your speech? (p. 207)

3. Winter is coming, and Miles is feeling incredibly sad. He moved to Minnesota three years ago to take a new job. He likes his job and finds it very rewarding. When he finally comes to see you, he reports that it takes a lot of effort for him to get out of bed. He tells you that the last two years were about the same. He tells you that he feels much better, even normal, when spring comes around. How would you diagnose Miles? (p. 181)

4. Ed was brought to the hospital by the police. His wife called them when he became aggressive. She had refused to give him a credit card. He had been awake for almost three days straight, working on a very big plan to buy a city and become the mayor. He had been spending money that they didn't have, and his wife was worried. When he was admitted to the hospital, he talked nonstop about needing a phone, because the deal was about to go through. He kept telling the hospital staff he was going to become famous and be able to save the city from ruin. After talking to his wife, you discover that not too long ago Ed had been very depressed. Before he became so "wild," as she put it, she thought that maybe he was getting better. How would you diagnose Ed? Why? (pp. 195–196)

AFTER YOU READ

PRACTICE TESTS
Take the following three multiple-choice tests to see how much you have comprehended from the chapter. Each represents roughly one third of the chapter. As you study the chapter, use these to check your progress.

Practice Test 1

1. The most common form of mood episode is (p. 174)
    a. a fugue.
    b. a manic episode.
    c. a dissociative disorder.
    d. a major depressive episode.

2. Mania is characterized by (p. 174)
    a. sadness and dejection.
    b. shame and confusion.
    c. excitement and euphoria.
    d. frustration and anxiety.

3. Depression is characterized by (p. 174)
    a. sadness and dejection.
    b. shame and confusion.
    c. excitement and euphoria.
    d. frustration and anxiety.

4. Mood disorders are differentiated by (p. 175)
    a. severity.
    b. frequency.
    c. duration.
    d. a and c

5. A person who has been diagnosed with dysthymia may experience normal mood periods that last (p. 177)
    a. a few days or weeks, up to a maximum of two months.
    b. six months or more.
    c. several days but no more than one month.
    d. None of the above

6. Sue meets the criteria for major depressive disorder. However, her therapist also notes some patterns of symptoms that she feels are important for understanding the disorder and treating Sue effectively. These additional patterns are called (p. 179)
    a. equalizers.
    b. identifiers.
    c. noteworthy

d. specifiers.

7. According to the DSM-IV-TR, to receive a diagnosis of major depressive episode, the person must be markedly depressed for most of the day most days for at least ___ weeks. (p. 175)
    a. 5
    b. 4
    c. 3
    d. 2

8. Twin studies have provided evidence that there may be a _____ genetic component to unipolar depression. (p. 181)
    a. significant
    b. minimal
    c. moderate
    d. overwhelming

9. In the 1960s and '70s, research focused on the following neurotransmitters and their effect on depression: (p. 182)
    a. norepinephrine, dopamine, and serotonin.
    b. serotonin and epinephrine.
    c. cortisol, norepinephrine, and DST.
    d. None of the above

10. Originally, diathesis-stress models assumed that diatheses were biological. Recently, depression researchers have begun to propose diatheses that are (p. 187)
    a. cognitive.
    b. social.
    c. subconscious.
    d. a and b

Practice Test 2

1. Jayne tended to think that either the worst or the best things would happen to her, never anything in-between. This is an example of (p. 189)
    a. dichotomous or all-or-none reasoning.
    b. selective abstraction.
    c. arbitrary inference.
    d. None of the above

2. The cognitive diatheses that have been studied for depression focus on _____ patterns of thinking. (p. 191)
    a. positive
    b. inconsistent
    c. negative
    d. a and b

3. Research has found that a person may have a vulnerability to depression if he/she experiences an early childhood loss of a parent and (p. 187)
    a. poor parental care.
    b. support of siblings.
    c. involvement with an extended family.
    d. All of the above

4. The psychodynamic approach to depression emphasizes the (p. 188)
    a. importance of dreams.
    b. importance of the id.
    c. importance of early loss (real or imagined).
    d. creation of defense mechanisms.

5. According to the behavioral theories of depression, people become depressed when their responses no longer produce positive reinforcement or when (p. 188)
    a. they learn depression is good.
    b. their rate of negative reinforcement increases.
    c. they generalize.
    d. None of the above

6. A psychological theory on why there are sex differences in unipolar depression proposes that women are more prone to experience (p. 192)
    a. a lack of control over negative life events.
    b. discrimination in the workplace.
    c. poverty.
    d. All of the above

7. In this disorder, the person does not experience the full-blown manic episodes but has experienced clear-cut hypomanic episodes. (p. 196)
    a. dysthymia
    b. cyclothymia
    c. bipolar I disorder
    d. bipolar disorder II

8. Who introduced the term *manic-depressive insanity* to describe a series of attacks of elation and depression? (p. 195)
    a. Freud
    b. Hippocrates
    c. Kraepelin
    d. Charcot

9. Bipolar mood disorder is distinguished from major depression by (p. 195)
    a. at least one episode of mania.
    b. disturbance of circadian rhythms.
    c. evidence of earlier cyclothymia.

d. evidence of earlier dysthymia.

10. The original learned helplessness theory refers to the depressed patient's perception that (p. 190)
    a. accustomed reinforcement is no longer forthcoming.
    b. they have no control over aversive events.
    c. reinforcement is inadequate.
    d. the world is a negative place.

Practice Test 3

1. This is a widely used mood stabilizer for bipolar disorder. (p. 203)
    a. Lithium
    b. Prozac
    c. Ativan
    d. Effexor

2. The highest rates of suicide occur between the ages of (p. 206)
    a. 20 and 25 years old
    b. 18 and 24 years old
    c. 18 and 25 years old
    d. 25 and 28 years old

3. While these antidepressants were quite effective, they have been replaced by newer antidepressants that do not have restrictions on foods rich in tyramine. (p. 202)
    a. SSRIs
    b. TCAs
    c. MAOIs
    d. benzodiazepines

4. Since about 1990, the type of antidepressants increasingly prescribed because of fewer side effects are (p. 202)
    a. tricyclics.
    b. selective serotonin re-uptake inhibitors (SSRIs).
    c. imipramine.
    d. ECT.

5. _____ is a brief form of treatment for unipolar depression that is highly structured and attempts to teach people to evaluate their beliefs and negative automatic thoughts. (p. 204)
    a. CBT
    b. ECT
    c. IPT
    d. None of the above

6. The treatment for unipolar depression that focuses on current relationships issues is called (p. 205)
    a. CBT.
    b. ECT.
    c. IPT.
    d. None of the above

7. Three main thrusts of suicide prevention efforts are the treatment of the person's mental disorders, working with high-risk groups, and (p. 210)
    a. cognitive therapy.
    b. family therapy.
    c. crisis intervention.
    d. psychotherapy.

8. All of the following are symptoms of the manic phase of bipolar mood disorder EXCEPT (p. 195)
    a. a notable increase in activity.
    b. euphoria.
    c. high levels of verbal output.
    d. deflated self-esteem.

9. In the 1995 Clark study, people who committed suicide (p. 210)
    a. did not tell others their intent.
    b. only talked about suicide in vague terms.
    c. talked clearly about suicide or death in the weeks or months prior to the attempt.
    d. told a mental health professional but not friends about their intentions.

10. Suicide is committed most often during the _____ phase of a depressive episode. (p. 206)
    a. early onset
    b. peak of depression
    c. late onset
    d. recovery

COMPREHENSIVE PRACTICE TEST

The following tests are designed to give you an idea of how well you understood the entire chapter. There are three different types of tests, multiple-choice, true/false, and essay.

Multiple Choice

1. Simultaneous symptoms of mania and depression are referred to as (p. 174)
    a. a trouble syndrome.
    b. an overwhelming episode.
    c. a mixed episode.
    d. a unipolar episode.

2. Which of the following is true? (p. 199)
    a. Low social support and stressful events independently predict depressive recurrences in bipolar events.
    b. Low social support but not stressful events predict depressive recurrences in bipolar events.
    c. Stressful events but not low social support predict recurrences in bipolar events.
    d. Low social support but not stressful events predict recurrences in bipolar events.

3. Which of the following mood disorders is most common and has actually increased in recent years? (p. 175)
    a. cyclothymia
    b. major depression
    c. dysthymia
    d. sdjustment disorder with depressed mood

4. Mild depression may be seen as "normal and adaptive" if (p. 176)
    a. it is brief and mild.
    b. it involves looking at issues that would normally be avoided.
    c. it keeps us from using energy to obtain futile goals.
    d. All of the above

5. A diagnosis of major depressive disorder CANNOT be made if the person has experienced (p. 175)
    a. hypersomnia.
    b. psychomotor agitation.
    c. hypomania.
    d. diminished ability to concentrate.

6. The DSM-IV-TR suggests that major depressive disorders should not be diagnosed following the loss of a loved one even if all symptoms are met for the first (p. 175)
    a. 2 months.
    b. 3 months.
    c. 4 months.
    d. 6 months.

7. Susan meets the criteria for major depression, but she also awakens early in the morning, has excessive guilt, and has lost twenty pounds in the past month due to her poor appetite. Additionally, she does not respond appropriately to happy events, like her daughter's graduation three weeks ago. The specifier that would describe this major depressive episode would be (p. 179)
    a. psychotic.
    b. seasonal.
    c. atypical.
    d. melancholic.

8. When major depression and dysthymia coexist in an individual, it is referred to as (p. 180)
     a. double dysthymia.
     b. double depression.
     c. two depressive disorders.
     d. comorbid depressive subtypes.

9. Because depressive episodes are time-limited, these are usually specified as (p. 180)
     a. starting and stopping.
     b. first and second.
     c. single and recurrent.
     d. a and b

10. A neurophysiological finding shows that damage to the _____ but not the _____anterior cortex often results in depression. (p. 184)
     a. right, left
     b. left, right
     c. frontal, middle
     d. middle, frontal

11. Circadian rhythms, which may play a causal role in depression, are controlled by strong and weak (p. 185)
     a. links.
     b. beats.
     c. oscillators.
     d. kentilators.

12. The typical treatment for seasonal affective disorder focuses on (p. 185)
     a. behavioral therapy.
     b. psychotherapy.
     c. RET.
     d. light therapy.

13. Gary has fallen further and further behind in his rent. His roommates are threatening to kick him out. This stressful life event is known as a(n) (p. 185)
     a. independent life event.
     b. dependent life event.
     c. secondary life event.
     d. primary life event.

14. Women who are at a genetic risk for depression will experience more (p. 186)
     a. good days than bad.
     b. exhaustion.
     c. stressful life events.
     d. None of the above

15. In the brains of depressed patients, abnormalities have been detected in the (p. 199)

      a. anterior cingulate cortex.

      b. hippocampus.

      c. amygdala.

      d. All of the above

16. Jennifer bought two expensive sport cars she could not afford, was flirting with every man she met, and had not slept in four days. She is most likely having (p. 175)

      a. a manic episode.

      b. a depressive episode.

      c. a panic attack.

      d. a dysthymic episode.

17. Depression rates are higher for women than for men by a ratio of (p. 176)

      a. 2:1.

      b. 3:1.

      c. 4:1.

      d. 5:1.

18. Rick has been depressed most of his life, with some periods of relief, but nothing that has lasted more than two months or even a couple of weeks at a time. He has poor appetite, low energy, and cannot concentrate. His diagnosis would most likely be (p. 177)

      a. cyclothymic disorder.

      b. dysthymic disorder.

      c. bipolar disorder.

      d. OCD

TRUE/FALSE

1. T / F Major depression is more common in men (21 percent lifetime prevalence rate) than women (13 percent lifetime prevalence rate). (p. 176)

2. T / F It is normal to feel depressed as a result of a recent loss or stress. (p. 176)

3. T / F There is no difference in the prevalence rates between men and women for bipolar disorder. (p. 176)

4. T / F People with dysthymia and major depression have periods of normal moods. (p. 177)

5. T / F People with double depression rarely have relapses. (p. 180)

6. T / F Seasonal affective disorders are an example of recurrent depressive episodes. (p. 181)

7. T / F Bipolar, but not unipolar depression runs in families. (p. 181)

8. T / F Hormones play a significant role in causing depression in women. (p. 192)

9. T / F Bipolar is distinguished from major depression by at least one episode of mania or a mixed episode. (p. 194)

10. T / F A recent survey documented that most people with depression don't receive treatment or receive inappropriate care. (p. 202)

11. T / F Tricyclics have been the antidepressants most commonly prescribed since about 1990. (p. 202)

12. T / F Discontinuing antidepressants when symptoms have remitted may cause relapse. (p. 203)

13. T / F Women are about three times as likely to attempt suicide as are men, but about four times more men than women die by suicide each year. (p. 206)

14. T / F Marital therapy has not been shown to be as effective as cognitive therapy for people who have unipolar depression and marital discord. (p. 205)

15. T / F Children are at increased risk for suicide if they have lost a parent or have been abused. (p. 207)

16. T / F Genetic factors, as well as alterations in serotonin functioning can contribute to causal factors for suicide. (p. 209)

17. T / F ECT is often used for severely depressed patients who present with an immediate and serious suicidal risk, including those with psychotic or melancholic features. (p. 203)

18. T / F Those who threaten suicide seldom attempt suicide. (p. 210)

Essay Questions

1. Describe Aaron Beck's cognitive theory of depression. (pp. 188–189)

2. Discuss the controversy regarding a person's right to die. (p. 212)

3. Discuss the causal factors in bipolar disorder. (pp. 198–200)

4. Explain the sociocultural factors affecting unipolar and bipolar disorders. (pp. 200–202)

5. Explain what suicide prevention centers do. (pp. 210–211)

WHEN YOU HAVE FINISHED

WEB LINKS TO ITEMS OR CONCEPTS DISCUSSED IN CHAPTER 6

American Psychological Association Web Page on Depression
   http://www.apa.org/topics/topicdepress.html
The American Psychological Association hosts this Web page on depression with links to treatments, finding a therapist, books, videos, journals, press releases, and the *Monitor on Psychology,* which has cutting edge articles and information on various topics.

Medline Plus Web Site on Depression
   http://www.nlm.nih.gov/medlineplus/depression.html
The Medline Plus Web site on depression provides the latest news, treatments, information on research and clinical trials, links to the NIMH, statistics, and separate links for information on the disorder in men and women, children and adolescents, and the elderly.

The International Foundation for Research and Education on Depression
http://www.ifred.org/

The International Foundation for Research and Education on Depression strives to bring together various sources and organizations to educate and further the research of depression. This site offers not only those with depression the hope and information they are seeking but also family and friends the understanding and tools to help their loved ones.

Depression Inventory
http://psychcentral.com/depquiz.htm

While this inventory cannot take the place of a diagnostic assessment performed by a mental health professional, it does provide a gauge of one's level of depression.

Center for Epidemiologic Studies Depression Scale
http://intelihealth.com/IH/ihtIH/WSIHW000/8271/9025/197543.html?d=dmtMHSurvey&screen=2

This is the Center for Epidemiologic Studies Depression Scale, which provides a good overall assessment of one's answers to the scale and a printout to give to one's clinician.

The Depression and Bipolar Support Alliance
http://www.dbsalliance.org/

The Depression and Bipolar Support Alliance is one of the nation's largest organizations devoted to depression and bipolar disorder. The organization promotes awareness of these disorders by presenting timely, relevant, and empirically based resources, tools, and information in an understandable and useful format.

The Medline Plus Web Site on Bipolar Disorder
http://www.nlm.nih.gov/medlineplus/bipolardisorder.html

The Medline Plus Web site on Bipolar Disorder provides a wealth of information, a link to the Mood Disorder Questionnaire, treatments, and a variety of useful links.

The Psychiatric Times
http://www.psychiatrictimes.com/dis-bip.html

Psychiatric Times posts a wide variety of topics on bipolar disorder at this Web address.

FAQ's on Bipolar Disorder
http://www.mhsource.com/bipolar/bdfaq.html

The most-frequently asked questions on mood disorders are answered by Dr. Paul Keck.

Lithium Treatment
http://www.miminc.org/aboutlithinfoctr.html

This is a great Web site by the Madison Institute of Medicine that discusses lithium treatment as well as other mood stabilizers. Be sure to check out the other links as well.

Suicide Information from Medline Plus
> http://www.nlm.nih.gov/medlineplus/suicide.html

Terrific links and information from the Medline Plus Web site on suicide.

American Foundation for Suicide Prevention (AFSP)
> http://www.afsp.org/index.cfm?fuseaction=home.viewPage&page_id=1

This is the official Web site of the American Foundation for Suicide Prevention (AFSP). This organization funds research, develops prevention initiatives, and offers numerous educational programs for mental health professionals, survivors, and the public. There is a wealth of information on suicide and ways you can get involved in advocacy and volunteer programs.

American Association of Suicidology
> http://www.suicidology.org/

This is official site of the American Association of Suicidology where one can find prevention information, support groups, training, conferences, and crisis centers.

USE IT OR LOSE IT
Provide an answer to the thought question below, knowing that there is more than one way to respond. Possible answers are presented in the Answer Key.

Why do you think rates of depression and anxiety are increasing in Western societies despite increasing prosperity and material comfort?

CRISSCROSS
Now that you know all there is to know about this chapter, here's your opportunity to put that knowledge to work.

Across
1. A markedly elevated, euphoric, and expansive mood
4. Being persistently depressed for at least two years
7. Experiencing only depressive episodes
9. Experiencing depressive and manic episodes
10. Ending one's own life
11. Answers humans give to Why? (as in why does everything happen to me?)
12. Different patterns of symptoms or features

Down
2. Elevated or euphoric episode
3. Cyclical mood changes less severe than in bipolar disorder
5. Severe alterations in mood for a long period of time
6. Same as recurrence, except in a fairly short time
8. Depression recurs at some point after remission

Puzzle created with Puzzlemaker at DiscoverySchool.com

ANSWERS TO TEST QUESTIONS – CHAPTER 6

MATCHING
C. Martin Seligman
F. Emile Durkheim
A. Aaron Beck
B. Sigmund Freud
E. Emil Kraepelin
D. Abramson et al., 1989

SHORT ANSWERS
Your answer should contain the following points.

1. Normal response phases to the loss of a grandparent:
a. Numbing and disbelief; a few hours to a week
b. Yearning and searching; weeks or months
c. Disorganization and despair
d. Some level of reorganization

2. The women who experienced stressful life events but did not become depressed had in common:
a. Having an intimate relationship with spouse or lover
b. Having no more than three children
c. Having a part-time or full-time job
d. Having a serious religious commitment

3. Interpersonal problems can play a causal role in depression and how depression affects others by:
a. Lack of social support; more vulnerable to depression
b. Lack of social skills; speak more slowly or monotonously, maintain less eye contact, difficulty solving interpersonal problems
c. Behavior elicits negative feelings in others
d. Negative feelings make people less willing to interact with depressed person
e. Depression can lead to marital discord, and marital discord can lead to depression
f. Depression in one family member extends to infants, children, and adolescents

THE DOCTOR IS IN

1. Helen
<u>Diagnosis</u>: Dysthymia—persistent depressed mood for at least two years with symptoms of poor appetite, sleep disturbances, low energy, and low self-esteem, and fleeting periods of feeling normal.
<u>Additional information</u>: Family history of mood disorders, relationship with husband, last time she had a physical check-up, outside interests and how often the periods of feeling

normal appear and how long these last.

2. Expert
a. Conduct disorders and substance abuse common among completers
b. Mood disorders common among nonfatal attempts
c. Those with two or more disorders are at higher risk for completion
d. Availability of firearms in the home more common for completers
e. Adolescents more sensitive to lack of control and may have maladaptive family settings
f. Limited problem-solving abilities
g. Exposure to suicide in media

3. Miles
Diagnosis: Seasonal affective disorder—depressed for two winters in a row with symptoms disappearing in the spring
Additional information: Did Miles have any depressive episodes at other times of the year? Did he experience anything similar where he used to live?

4. Ed
Diagnosis: Bipolar. Manic behavior—excessive ideas, violent when wife wouldn't give him a credit card. Mania lasted a week. Depression preceded the manic episode.

PRACTICE TESTS

Q#	TEST 1	TEST 2	TEST 3
1	D	A	A
2	C	C	B
3	A	A	C
4	D	C	B
5	A	B	A
6	D	D	C
7	D	D	C
8	C	C	D
9	A	A	C
10	D	B	D

COMPREHENSIVE PRACTICE TEST

Q#	M/C	T/F
1	C	F
2	A	T
3	B	T
4	D	T
5	C	F
6	A	T
7	D	F

8	B	F
9	C	T
10	B	T
11	C	F
12	D	T
13	B	T
14	C	F
15	D	T
16	A	T
17	A	T
18	B	F

Essay Questions
Your answer should contain the following points.

1 Aaron Beck's cognitive theory of depression:
a. Depressogenic schemas or dysfunctional beliefs—rigid, extreme, and counterproductive thoughts
b. Negative automatic thoughts—thoughts just below the surface and are unpleasant pessimistic predictions
c. Negative cognitive triad—what negative automatic thoughts focus on. These are negative thoughts about self, negative thoughts about one's experience and surrounding world, and negative thoughts about one's future
d. The above is maintained by negative cognitive biases, which are dichotomous reasoning, selective abstraction, and arbitrary inference

2. The controversy regarding a person's right to die:
a. Has always been an issue with some cultures/societies supporting a person's right to commit suicide, e.g., classical Greece, the Netherlands, Hemlock Society, and the Oregon Death with Dignity Act
b. A terminally ill person has a right to die with dignity—legislative pressure to pass laws to allow physician assisted suicide, e.g., Dr. Kervorkian
c. Some people fear that people who are terminally ill will be pressured into taking their own lives
d. Another issue is someone who isn't terminally ill who wants to take his/her own life and the use of prevention tactics, such as involuntary hospitalization
e. Civil rights suits, if a person is restrained against his/her will, thus raising legal issues

3. Causal factors in bipolar disorder:
Biological
• Genetic component—80 percent of the variance in the tendency to develop bipolar depression
• Abnormalities in the hypothalamic, pituitary, thyroid axis
• Disturbance in biological rhythms
• Shifting patterns of brain activity

Biochemical
• Perhaps excesses of neurotransmitters norepinephrine, serotonin, and dopamine
Psychosocial
• Stressful life events
• Personality and cognitive variables interacting with stressful life events associated with relapse
• Extreme defense against or reaction to depression

4. Explain the sociocultural factors affecting unipolar and bipolar disorders.
a. Depression occurs in all cultures, but form and prevalence vary.
b. China and Japan: some time and vegetative manifestations. No Western concept of guilt, self-recrimination.
c. Australian aborigines: no guilt or self-recrimination and no suicide. Vent hostility on others.
d. Kaluli of New Guinea: relieve losses. Prevents hopelessness.
e. United States: unipolar depression higher in lower socioeconomic groups. Bipolar more common in higher socioeconomic classes.

5. When working with someone who is contemplating suicide, suicide prevention centers:
a. Maintain supportive and directive contact with person for short period of time
b. Help the person realize acute distress is impairing his/her ability to access the situation accurately
c. Help the person see that present distress and emotional turmoil will not be endless

USE IT OR LOSE IT

Rates of depression are thought to be on the rise because of changes in mobility, media exposure, personal expectations, and social structure, which have resulted in people in Western cultures expecting more out of life, while dealing with rapid change and diminished social support.

CRISSCROSS ANSWERS
Across
1. Hypomania
4. Dysthymic
7. Unipolar
9. Bipolar
10. Suicide
11. Attributions
12. Specifiers

Down
2. Manic
3. Cyclothymic
5. Mood disorders
6. Relapse
8. Reoccurrence

Chapter 7: Somatoform and Dissociative Disorders

BEFORE YOU READ

The somatoform disorders are characterized by physical complaints or disabilities in the absence of any physical pathology. Because of the absence of physical pathology, they presumably reflect underlying psychological difficulties. In the dissociative disorders, the central problem is a failure of certain aspects of memory due to an active process of dissociation. For example, in dissociative amnesia, individuals cannot remember their names, do not know how old they are, or where they live. According to the text, both types of disorders appear to be ways of avoiding psychological stress while denying personal responsibility for doing so. There are suggestions, as well, that both may be associated with traumatic childhood experiences. Because the dissociative disorders are unfamiliar territory, they are among the most difficult to grasp of the disorders that we discuss in this book. However, as you will see, these disorders may easily overlap and be difficult to differentiate from other disorders. For example, body dysmorphic disorder and obsessive-compulsive disorder have similar presenting features. Dissociative identity disorder (DID) is one of the more controversial disorders and debated among clinicians as to its existence. In addition, these disorders can be faked by individuals seeking compensation or to avoid legal consequences. Yet, in light of this, there are individuals who authentically suffer from these disorders, and that is where we present our focus.

- **SOMATOFORM DISORDERS**
    Hypochondriasis
    Somatization Disorder
    Pain Disorder
    Conversion Disorder
    Body Dysmorphic Disorder

- **DISSOCIATIVE DISORDERS**
    Depersonalization Disorder
    Dissociative Amnesia and Fugue
    Dissociative Identity Disorder (DID)
    General Sociocultural Causal Factors in Dissociative Disorders
    Treatment and Outcomes in Dissociative Disorders

- **UNRESOLVED ISSUES:**
    DID and the Reality of "Recovered Memories"

OBJECTIVES
After reading this chapter, you should be able to do the following:

1. Describe the major manifestations of somatoform disorders.

2. List the primary presenting symptoms of somatization disorder and hypochondriasis and note the similarities and differences between these closely related disorders.

3. Explain what is meant by a pain disorder. Discuss the difficulties of determining that pain is of psychological, rather than physical, origin and of reliably assessing an entirely subjective phenomenon.

4. Characterize the symptoms of conversion disorder, trace the history of the concept of "conversion," and describe the likely cause and chain of events in the development of a conversion disorder.

5. Discuss the etiological contributions of biological, psychosocial, and sociocultural factors to the somatoform disorders.

6. Compare and contrast the treatments for the somatoform disorders. What is known regarding their effectiveness, as compared to no treatment at all?

7. Compare the major features of dissociative amnesia and fugue, dissociative identity disorder, and depersonalization disorder.

8. Discuss the causal factors that contribute to the dissociative disorders, and note the critical difficulty caused by the fallibility of memory in determining the contribution of childhood abuse to these disorders.

9. Describe the most appropriate treatments for the dissociative disorders, as well as the limitations of biological and psychological treatments.

10. Describe the issues related to DID and recovered memories.

KEY WORDS
Each of the words below is important in understanding the concepts presented in this chapter. Write the definition next to each word.

Term	Page	Definition
Alter identities	231	
Body dysmorphic disorder (BDD)	224	
Conversion disorder	221	
Depersonalization	228	
Depersonalization disorder	228	
Derealization	228	
Dissociation	216	
Dissociative amnesia	229	
Dissociative disorders	216	
Dissociative fugue	230	
Dissociative identity	231	

disorder (DID)		
Factitious disorder	224	
Factitious disorder by proxy	225	
Host identity	231	
Hypochondriasis	216	
Malingering	224	
Pain disorder	220	
Primary gain	222	
Secondary gain	222	
Soma	216	
Somatization disorder	218	
Somatoform disorders	216	

AS YOU READ
Answers can be found in the Answer Key at the end of the book.

MATCHING
Who's Who and What's What?
Match the following psychological disorders with their descriptions.

Disorder
____D____ Somatoform disorder
____B____ Hypochondriasis
____E____ Somatization disorder
____A____ Pain disorder
____C____ Conversion disorder
____J____ Body dysmorphic disorder
____K____ Dissociative disorders
____H____ Depersonalization disorder
____I____ Dissociative fugue
____G____ Dissociative identity disorder
____F____ Dissociative amnesia

Description
A. Severe pain but no medical pathology to explain it
B. Anxious preoccupation with having a disease based on a misinterpretation of bodily signs or symptoms
C. Patterns of symptoms affecting sensory or voluntary motor functions, even though medical examination reveals no physical basis for these
D. Psychological problems are manifested in physical disorders that often mimic medical conditions, for which no medical evidence can be found

E. Many different complaints of physical ailments in four symptom categories spread over several years
F. Inability to recall previously sorted information that cannot be accounted for by ordinary forgetting; common initial reaction to severe stress
G. Person manifests two or more distinct identities or personality states that alternate in some way in taking control of behavior
H. Normal processes regulating awareness and multichannel capacities of the mind apparently become disorganized, leading to various anomalies
I. A person not only goes into an amnesic state, but also leaves home surroundings and becomes confused about his or her identity
J. An obsessive preoccupation with some perceived flaw in one's appearance
K. Persistent or recurrent experiences of feeling detached from their own bodies and mental processes

SHORT ANSWERS
Provide brief answers to the following questions.

1. Briefly explain the four criteria for somatization disorder. (p. 218)

2. List four categories of symptoms for donversion disorder. (p.222)

3. How can people with malingering/factitious disorders be distinguished from those with somatoform disorders? (p. 224)

4. Name and describe two types of psychogenic amnesia. (p. 229)

5. Describe the characteristics of dissociative identity disorder (pp. 231–232)

THE DOCTOR IS IN...PSYCHIATRIC HELP—5¢

Read the following scenarios and diagnose the client. Remember to look carefully at the criteria for the disorder before you make a decision as to the diagnosis. Make a list of other information you might need to help you understand the causal factors.

1. As the psychiatrist in a large hospital, you have been called in to evaluate a patient who had been admitted two days before. The patient, Cathy, had awakened in the morning and had been unable to see. She was blind. A complete medical and neurological exam were done, but found nothing that would account for the blindness. You were called in to see if there could be a psychological cause. After talking to her for a while, you find out that her husband had died unexpectedly about three months ago, leaving her with financial problems. She was going to have to get a job and she was worried about her employability. You ask if she has a picture of her husband. She says, "Yes," and walks to the shelf skirting a chair that is in her way.

How would you diagnose Cathy and why? How would you treat her?

2. Frank comes to see you because he has been urged to talk to somebody. He is wearing sunglasses, even though he is in your office, and it is dark outside. When you ask him about the glasses, he tells you that his eyelids are horrible and ugly. He doesn't want anyone to see them—ever. Frank tells you that he spends much of the day checking his eyelids and trying to make them look better. He is saving for another surgery, his third, because he just can't stand the way his eyes look. You ask if he dates, has friends, or has a job. Frank says that he doesn't date (Who would want to be with someone as ugly as he is?), so he has started to withdraw even from his few friends. He recently lost his job because he was unable to meet clients, looking the way he does.

How would you diagnose Frank and why? How would you treat him?

3. Jackie comes to see you because she has been feeling rather odd lately. She tells you that she is feeling "unreal"—like she is not a part of her body. Jackie says that she is beginning to see her life as a movie because she feels so isolated from herself. She explains that when this experience occurs, it is like looking at the world through someone else's eyes. These experiences are now happening two or three times per week and last for several hours.

What would be your diagnosis for Jackie and why? How would you treat her and what would you expect treatment outcomes to be?

AFTER YOU READ

PRACTICE TESTS
Take the following three multiple-choice tests to see how much you have comprehended from the chapter. Each represents roughly one third of the chapter. As you study the chapter, use these to check your progress.

Practice Test 1

1. Dissociative disorders are some of the most dramatic phenomena to be observed in the entire domain of psychopathology, for example, (p. 216)
    a. people who cannot recall who they are or where they may have come from.
    b. people who have two or more distinct identities or personality states that alternatively take control of the individual's behavior.
    c. people who have intense pain for which no medical symptoms can be found.
    d. a and b

2. People with _____ are preoccupied with fears of having a serious disease, based on misinterpretation of one or more bodily signs or symptoms, and are not reassured when medical examination can find no physical problem. (p. 216)
    a. depersonalization disorder
    b. dissociative fugue
    c. hypochondriasis
    d. halitosis

3. Somatization disorder very commonly occurs with (p. 218)
    a. major depression.
    b. panic disorder and phobic disorders.
    c. generalized anxiety disorder.
    d. All of the above

4. Evidence exists that somatization disorder (p. 220)
    a. runs in families.
    b. is racially based.
    c. seems concentrated in individual communities.
    d. occurs mostly near oceans.

5. Patients with somatization disorder tend to think of themselves as (p. 220)
    a. physically weak.
    b. unable to tolerate stress.
    c. unable to tolerate physical activity.
    d. All of the above

6. All of the following are part of a chain of events in the development of a conversion disorder EXCEPT (p. 221)
    a. a conscious plan to use illness as an escape.
    b. a desire to escape from an unpleasant situation.
    c. a fleeting wish to be sick in order to avoid the situation.
    d. the appearance of the symptoms of some physical ailment.

7. A typical example of symptoms of conversion disorder would be (p. 221)
    a. partial paralysis.
    b. blindness or deafness.
    c. pseudoseizures.
    d. All of the above

8. Freud used the term *conversion hysteria* because he believed the symptoms were an expression of (p. 221)
    a. widespread anger.
    b. built-up hostility.
    c. repressed sexual energy.
    d. being a parent.

9. Conversion disorder occurs _____ often in women than in men. (p. 222)
    a. much less
    b. two to ten times more
    c. three to five times more
    d. a little less

10. Although it can develop at any age, conversion disorder most commonly occurs (p. 222)
    a. between early adolescence and early adulthood.
    b. during middle age.
    c. during infancy or early childhood.
    d. about eight weeks before death.

Practice Test 2

1. The prevalence of conversion disorders has _____ in the past thirty years or so. (p. 222)
    a. risen
    b. remained about the same

      c. declined
      d. stagnated

2. People with _____ disorders are intentionally producing or grossly exaggerating psychological or physical symptoms for external reasons, such as avoiding work or military service. (p. 224)
      a. malingering and factitious
      b. conversion
      c. pain
      d. somatoform

3. A person with _____ disorder is obsessed with a perceived or imagined flaw or flaws in his or her appearance. It is so intense that it causes clinically significant distress and/or impairment in social or occupational functioning. (p. 224)
      a. conversion
      b. pain
      c. factitious
      d. body dysmorphic

4. People with body dysmorphic disorder (BDD) may think (p. 224)
      a. their skin has ugly blemishes.
      b. their breasts are too small.
      c. their face is too thin.
      d. All of the above

5. Dissociative disorders are thought to represent attempts to avoid stress by (p. 228)
      a. escaping from personal identities.
      b. projecting blame onto others.
      c. separating from significant others.
      d. facing stressful situations.

6. It is likely that some people may have certain _____ that make them more susceptible to developing dissociative symptoms than others. (p. 228)
      a. ineffective genes
      b. mystical properties
      c. lack of self-control
      d. personality traits

7. In _____, one's sense of one's self and one's reality is temporarily lost, usually occurring during or after periods of severe stress. (p. 228)
      a. psychogenic pain disorder
      b. retrograde measles
      c. depersonalization
      d. hypochondriasis

8. When episodes of depersonalization become persistent and recurrent and interfere with normal functioning, _____ may be diagnosed. (p. 228)
     a. psychogenic pain disorder
     b. depersonalization disorder
     c. dissociative amnesia
     d. hypochondriasis

9. Retrograde amnesia involves the failure to remember (p. 229)
     a. previously learned information.
     b. new information.
     c. emotional information.
     d. only names and dates.

10. _____ is a fairly common initial reaction to intolerably stressful circumstances. (p. 229)
     a. Dissociative amnesia
     b. Brain pathology
     c. Hypochondriasis
     d. Retrograde measles

Practice Test 3

1. In cases of _____, which is very rare, a person is not only amnesic for some or all aspects of his or her past, but also departs from home surroundings. (p. 229)
     a. retrograde measles
     b. dissociative fugue
     c. disappropriate stressful symnabulolism
     d. multiple personality disorder

2. Dissociative identity disorder (DID) was formerly known as (p. 231)
     a. Scarlett O'Hara fever.
     b. dissociative fugue.
     c. multiple personality disorder.
     d. depersonalization disorder.

3. The identity switches in DID typically occur (p. 231)
     a. very quickly (in a matter of seconds).
     b. over a period of several hours.
     c. during a full moon.
     d. just prior to taking a test.

4. DIDs alter identities may differ in (p. 231)
     a. gender, age, and sexual orientation.
     b. handedness, handwriting, and prescription for eyeglasses.
     c. foreign languages spoken and general knowledge.

        d. All of the above

5. _____ may or may not be aware of each other, or may attempt to take over control from the host identity. (p. 231)
        a. Escapists
        b. Malingerers
        c. Alter identities
        d. Localized amnesiacs

6. DID was rare until around _____, but now thousands of cases have been reported. (p. 232)
        a. 1800
        b. World War I
        c. 1979
        d. September 11, 2001

7. DID has now been identified throughout the world. It has been found (p. 238)
        a. in all racial groups.
        b. in all cultures.
        c. in countries ranging from Nigeria and Ethiopia, to Turkey, Australia, and the Caribbean.
        d. All of the above

8. A major cause of DID appears to be (p. 237)
        a. the rise of individual anger and inner rage.
        b. childhood sexual abuse.
        c. air and water pollution.
        d. broken families and the fast pace of modern society.

9. For _____ patients, most therapists set integration of the previously separate alters, together with their collective merging into the host personality, as the ultimate goal of treatment. (p. 238)
        a. conversion disorder
        b. BDD
        c. DID
        d. JPG

10. Typically, the treatment for DID is (p. 238)
        a. psychologic and insight-oriented.
        b. psychotropic and insight-oriented.
        c. psychosocial and insight-oriented.
        d. psychodynamic and insight-oriented.

COMPREHENSIVE PRACTICE TEST

The following tests are designed to give you an idea of how well you understood the entire chapter. There are three different types of tests: multiple-choice, true/false, and essay.

Multiple Choice

1. Body dysmorphic disorder (BDD) usually occurs in adolescence when many people start to become preoccupied with their appearance and appears to be (p. 224)
    a. more prevalent in men than women.
    b. approximately equal in men and women.
    c. more prevalent in women than men.
    d. unheard of in Canada.

2. Treatment approaches for BDD focus on (p. 227)
    a. getting patients to identify and change distorted perceptions of their body.
    b. exposure to anxiety-provoking situations (e.g., wearing something that highlights, rather than disguises, their defect).
    c. prevention of checking responses (e.g., mirror checking, reassurance seeking, and repeatedly examining their imaginary defect).
    d. All of the above

3. Dissociative disorders have been a major research area in the field of cognitive psychology for the past (p. 228)
    a. few months.
    b. few years.
    c. quarter-century.
    d. 150 years.

4. Which of the following disorders is thought to mainly be a way of avoiding anxiety and stress and of managing life problems that threaten to overwhelm the person's usual coping resources? (p. 228)
    a. dissociative
    b. generalized
    c. hypochondriasis
    d. low self-esteem

5. In which of the following disorders might a person feel drastically changed or unreal? (p. 228)
    a. depersonalization disorder
    b. psychogenic pain disorder
    c. hypochondriasis
    d. cognitive psychology

6. The loss of memory following a catastrophic event is called (p. 229)
   a. psychogenic pain disorder.
   b. dissociative amnesia.
   c. hypochondriasis.
   d. alter ego.

7. In DID, the primary or host identity is most frequently encountered, but alter identities may (p. 231)
   a. be more concerned with personal-identity issues.
   b. take control at different points in time.
   c. become moody and refuse to cooperate.
   d. become an alter ego.

8. People with DID often show (p. 231)
   a. moodiness and erratic behavior.
   b. headaches, hallucination, and substance abuse.
   c. post-traumatic symptoms, and other amnesic and fugue symptoms.
   d. All of the above

9. In _____ amnesia, the individual forgets his or her entire life history. (p. 229)
   a. localized
   b. selective
   c. generalized
   d. continuous

10. Approximately _____ more females than males are diagnosed as having DID, believed by some to be due to the greater proportion of abuse among females than males. (p. 233)
   a. 25 percent
   b. 75 percent
   c. 3–9 times
   d. The numbers for females and males are about the same.

11. One of the primary techniques used in most treatments of DID is (p. 238)
   a. esteem exercise.
   b. hypnosis.
   c. projection.
   d. withdrawing stress.

12. DID patients who recover memories of abuse (often in therapy) have sued _____ for inflicting abuse. (p. 239)
   a. each other
   b. their parents
   c. schools and teachers
   d. anyone who seems to have a lot of money

13. DID patients have also sued _____ for implanting memories or abuse they later came to believe had not actually occurred. (p. 239)
    a. their parents
    b. schools and teachers
    c. therapists and institutions
    d. everyone who seems to have any money at all

14. Some parents, asserting they had been falsely accused, formed an international support organization called _____ and have sued therapists for damages, alleging therapists induced false memories of parental abuse in their children. (p. 240)
    a. the False Memory Syndrome Foundation
    b. Parents Against False Memories
    c. the International Order of Falsely Accused Parents
    d. the International Support Organization

15. Alter personalities would be expected in cases of (p. 240)
    a. psychogenic pain disorder.
    b. conversion disorder.
    c. hypochondriasis.
    d. dissociative identity disorder.

16. Carole was sitting in the dining room with her family but appeared to be split off from everything around her. It was like she was in another world. Carole was having a (p. 216)
    a. dissociation.
    b. a migraine headache.
    c. a panic attack.
    d. a dysthymic moment.

17. Julie's doctor finally sent her to a psychiatrist, as he could find nothing physically wrong with her despite her belief that she had the Avian Flu. Julie may most likely be suffering from (p. 216)
    a. psychogenic pain disorder.
    b. conversion disorder.
    c. hypochondriasis.
    d. dissociative identity disorder.

18. Fran has been seeing four doctors lately, one for her "nervous" bladder, one for her "anxious" bowel, one for her neck and back pain, and one for her "small lung capacity." Her diagnosis would most likely be (p. 219)
    a. psychogenic pain disorder.
    b. conversion disorder.
    c. somatization disorder.
    d. dissociative identity disorder.

19. Greg's physician did not feel that the constant lower back pain had a psychological origin and attributed it to diabetic neuropathy rather than to (p. 220)
   a. depression.
   b. conversion disorder.
   c. somatization disorder.
   d. pain disorder.

20. Michael had been in trouble with the law since he was 12. Now 20, he finds himself facing a lengthy prison sentence. He has decided to pretend he has numerous health problems to avoid prosecution or at least postpone his court date. He has been fainting and says he cannot breathe. This condition is known as (p. 224)
   a. malingering.
   b. conversion disorder.
   c. somatization disorder.
   d. pain disorder.

21. Molly suffered a terrible case of the flu during the winter, and she enjoyed all of the attention she received from her normally busy husband. She seems to get an extreme cold at least once a month that requires her husband's attention for one to two days. Molly may meet the criteria for (p. 224)
   a. factitious disorder.
   b. conversion disorder.
   c. somatization disorder.
   d. pain disorder.

TRUE/FALSE

1. T / F Somatoform disorders are characterized by physical symptoms without a physical explanation. (p. 216)

2. T / F People with hypochondriasis are not malingering to achieve specific goals. (p. 216)

3. T / F Somatization disorder is not extremely difficult to treat because much systematic research has been conducted. (p. 220)

4. T / F According to the DSM-IV-TR, symptoms of somatization disorder are not intentionally produced or feigned. (p. 219)

5. T / F Pain disorder can be associated only with psychological factors. (p. 221)

6. T / F Indications exist that people with hypochondriasis often had an excessive amount of illness in their families while growing up. (p. 218)

7. T / F Contemporary views of conversion disorder see it as serving the function of providing a plausible excuse, enabling the individual to escape or avoid an intolerably stressful situation without having to take responsibility for doing so. (p. 221)

8. T / F Conversion disorder was not very common in the past and hardly ever occurred prior to World War II. (p. 222)

9. T / F Conversion disorder typically involves unstable men. (p. 221)

10. T / F Most of us have concerns about our appearance, but people with body dysmorphic disorder are unrealistically preoccupied with their bodies. (p. 224)

11. T / F We all dissociate to a degree occasionally. (p. 228)

12. T / F Dissociative disorders appear mainly to provide a way to avoid anxiety and stress and of managing life problems that threaten to overwhelm the person's usual coping resources. (p. 228)

13. T / F Many researchers believe that BDD is closely related to OCD and have proposed it as one of the obsessive-compulsive spectrum disorders. (p. 226)

14. T / F Body dysmorphic disorder is thought to be closely related to generalized anxiety disorder. (p. 227)

15. T / F There are no treatments available for dissociative identity disorder. (p. 238)

Essay Questions

1. Discuss pain disorder. (pp. 220–221)

2. Describe the criteria commonly used for distinguishing between conversion disorders and true organic disturbances. (p. 221)

3. Describe body dysmorphic disorder using the DSM-IV-TR criteria as well as treatment options. (pp. 224–226)

4. Explain whether you believe dissociative identity disorder is a real diagnosis. Please use examples. (pp. 234–236)

WHEN YOU HAVE FINISHED

WEB LINKS TO ITEMS OR CONCEPTS DISCUSSED IN CHAPTER 7

Body Dysmorphic Disorder, Mayo Clinic
http://www.mayoclinic.com/health/body-dysmorphic-disorder/DS00559
The well-respected Mayo Clinic has a Web page devoted entirely to body dysmorphic disorder.

Conversion Disorder
http://www.nlm.nih.gov/medlineplus/ency/article/000954.htm
A brief overview of conversion disorder is provided on the Medline Plus Web site.

Somatization Disorder
http://www.nlm.nih.gov/medlineplus/ency/article/000955.htm
Medline Plus provides a synoptic overview of somatization disorder.

Munchausen by Proxy
http://www.mbpexpert.com/definition.html
This is the Web site of one of the foremost experts in Munchausen by Proxy, Louisa Lasher.

Kids Health Munchausen by Proxy
http://www.kidshealth.org/parent/system/ill/munchausen.html
Kids Health provides basic and very digestible information on Munchausen by Proxy.

A Malpractice Case Involving Dissociative Identity Disorder
http://www.astraeasweb.net/politics/braun.html
This Web page chronicles one of the most well-known malpractice cases in the field of psychiatry involving dissociative identity disorder.

False Memory Syndrome Foundation
        http://www.fmsfonline.org
The False Memory Syndrome Foundation strives to raise awareness to prevent false memories, to help those affected by false memories, and to provide insight into this interesting and highly controversial area.

USE IT OR LOSE IT

Dissociative identity disorder is characterized by the expression of different behaviors, voices, and even handwriting by the same person at different times. How would you explain this disorder to someone unfamiliar with psychological issues?

CRISSCROSS
Now that you know all there is to know about this chapter, here's your opportunity to put that knowledge to work.

Across
9. may include partial paralysis, blindness, pseudoseizures, but without any known medical condition

Down
1. seemingly medical conditions without evidence of physical pathology to account for these
2. the human mind's capacity to engage in complex activity independent of conscious awareness
3. not only amnesic but leaves home and may assume a new identity
4. intentionally over-exaggerating physical symptoms to avoid work
5. when one's sense of the reality of the outside world is temporarily lost
6. failure to recall when that failure cannot be accounted for by ordinary forgetting
7. presence of persistent and severe pain without a purely medical cause
8. new term for multiple personality disorder

Puzzle created with Puzzlemaker at DiscoverySchool.com

ANSWERS TO TEST QUESTIONS – CHAPTER 7

MATCHING
D. Somatoform disorder
B. Hypochondriasis
E. Somatization disorder
A. Pain disorder
C. Conversion disorder
J. Body dysmorphic disorder
H. Dissociative disorders
K. Depersonalization disorder
I. Dissociative fugue
G. Dissociative identity disorder
F. Dissociative amnesia

SHORT ANSWERS
Your answer should contain the following points.

1. Four criteria must be met for somatization disorder to be present:
a. Four pain symptoms. The patient must report a history of pain experienced in at least four different sites or functions.
b. Two gastrointestinal symptoms. The patient must report a history of at least two symptoms, other than pain, pertaining to the gastrointestinal system.
c. One sexual symptom. The patient must report at least one reproductive system symptom other than pain.
d. One pseudoneurological symptom. The patient must report a history of at least one symptom, not limited to pain, suggestive of a neurological condition.

2. Conversion disorder's four categories of symptoms:
a. Sensory—most often visual, auditory, or sensitivity to feeling
b. Motor—paralysis of an arm or leg
c. Seizures—resemble epileptic seizures
d. Mixed presentation from a–c

3. One way of telling the difference between people with malingering/factitious disorders and other somatoform disorders is by the response given when asked to describe the symptoms. Fakers are inclined to be defensive, evasive, and suspicious, but individuals with conversion disorders are very willing to discuss them, often in excruciating detail.

4. Your books discusses two types of psychogenic amnesia recognized by the DSM-IV-TR:
a. localized—a person remembers nothing that happened during a specific period
b. selective—a person forgets some, but not all, of what happened during a given period present

5. In very rare cases, called dissociative fugue, a person is not only amnesic for some or all aspects of his or her past, but also departs from home surroundings. During the fugue these persons are unaware of memory loss for prior stages in their life, but their memory for what happens during the fugue state itself is intact, during which they may live a quite normal life. Days, weeks, or even years later, such persons may suddenly come out of the fugue state and find themselves in strange places working in a new occupation and not knowing how they got there.

THE DOCTOR IS IN

1. Cathy
Diagnosis: conversion disorder, blind with no medical or neurological cause, recent large stressors in life, doesn't seem to be faking it, walks around a chair but is blind
Treatment: behavioral approaches, possibly hypnosis combined with other problem-solving therapies

2. Frank
Diagnosis: body dysmorphic disorder, preoccupation with eyelids to the point of interfering with his life; two surgeries and saving for a third
Treatment: antidepressants and cognitive-behavioral therapy that focuses on having Frank identify and change distorted perceptions about his body.

3. Jackie
Diagnosis: depersonalization disorder—Jackie feels separate from her body and like she is in a movie. She feels unreal and sees herself and her friends as automatons.
Treatment: no real controlled research has been done on treatment for depersonalization disorder. This disorder is thought to be resistant to treatment, making outcome difficult to predict. Treatment has focused on other psychopathology that may be associated with the disorder. Hypnosis and teaching self-hypnosis techniques may be useful but, again, no controlled research has been done.

PRACTICE TESTS

Q#	TEST 1	TEST 2	TEST 3
1	D	C	B
2	C	A	C
3	D	D	A
4	A	D	D
5	D	A	C
6	A	D	C
7	D	C	D
8	C	B	B
9	B	A	C
10	A	A	D

COMPREHENSIVE PRACTICE TEST

Q#	M/C	T/F
1	B	T
2	D	T
3	C	F
4	A	T
5	A	F
6	B	T
7	B	T
8	D	F
9	C	F
10	C	T
11	B	T
12	B	T
13	C	T
14	A	F
15	D	F
16	A	
17	C	
18	C	
19	D	
20	A	
21	A	

Essay Questions

Your answer should contain the following points.

1. Pain disorder essay:
a. Two types:
• pain disorder associated with psychological factors. Psychological factors are judged to play a major role in the onset or maintenance of the pain.
• pain disorder associated with psychological factors and a general medical condition. The pain experienced is considered to result from psychological factors and some medical condition that could cause pain.
b. Pain may be acute (duration of less than six months) or chronic (duration of more than six months).
c. Unknown in the general population; fairly common among patients at pain clinics.
d. More frequently diagnosed in women.
e. Frequently comorbid with anxiety and/or mood disorders.
f. Can lead to a vicious cycle of patient not being able to work or exercise and resulting inactivity may lead to depression and loss of physical strength and endurance. The loss of strength and fatigue can, in turn, exacerbate the pain.
g. Cognitive-behavior treatment techniques have been widely used. They generally include relaxation training, support and validation that the pain is real, scheduling of

daily activities, cognitive restructuring, and reinforcement of "no-pain" behaviors.

2. Criteria commonly used for distinguishing between conversion disorders and true organic disturbances:
a. Patient must receive a thorough medical and neurological examination.
b. The frequent failure of dysfunction to conform clearly to the symptoms of the particular disease or disorder simulated—no wasting away or atrophy of a "paralyzed" limb.
c. The selective nature of the dysfunction—"paralyzed" muscles can be used for some activities but not others.
d. Under hypnosis or narcosis, the symptoms can be removed, shifted, or reinduced at the suggestion of the therapist.

3. Your answer should include the following:
a. Markedly excessive preoccupation with some aspect of the body, either real or imagined.
b. This preoccupation causes significant distress or impairment.
c. Treatments include both pharmacological (SSRIs) and cognitive-behavioral treatment.

4. Your answer should support your stance and include a discussion about the controversies surrounding DID, whether it is real or faked, and recovered memories of abuse. Believers usually take DID and the idea of abuse as its cause to be established beyond doubt. Disbelievers are sympathetic to people suffering from DID symptoms, but have tended to doubt that it is usually caused by childhood abuse, and have challenged the validity or accuracy of recovered memories of abuse.

USE IT OR LOSE IT
Dissociative issues are often thought to be the result of self-hypnosis as a means of coping with early adversity, and in particular sexual abuse. To avoid anxiety or distress such individuals involuntarily slip into altered states, for which they may have little memory. Normal individuals may experience a minor version of this when they realize that they have engaged in an automatic behavior such as driving, while thinking about something completely different.

CRISSCROSS ANSWERS

Across
9. Conversion disorder

Down
1. Somatoform disorders
2. Dissociation
3. Dissociative fugue
4. Malingering
5. Derealization
6. Dissociative amnesia
7. Pain disorder
8. Dissociative identity disorder

Chapter 8: Eating Disorders and Obesity

BEFORE YOU READ

We are fortunate to live in a country of numerous opportunities, freedom, and choices. One such choice is food. No other the country in the world has as many choices and varieties of food and is as obsessed with food and with looking good as is the United States. These mixed signals affect us every day when we go to the supermarket and buy the larger size bag of chips, order the "value meal" in the drive-thru, and then see models in magazines and actors and actresses in the movies with "perfect" bodies. It is no wonder that a majority of Americans are obsessed with losing weight. Yet, Americans are also fighting rising rates of obesity and diabetes that may achieve epidemic proportions in the upcoming years. There are numerous explanations for the eating disorders and obesity, and chapter 8 provides insight into this complex world. The clinical aspects of eating disorders such as anorexia nervosa, bulimia nervosa, and binge-eating disorder will be discussed. The causes of these disorders will be examined including biological factors such as set-point, and the roles of serotonin, leptin and ghrelin, as well as the impact of societal and cultural factors. The implementation and efficacy of eating disorder interventions will also be reviewed. Finally, the emergence of obesity as a worldwide health problem will be considered, with an emphasis on the causes and possible means of responding to this growing issue.

- **CLINICAL ASPECTS OF EATING DISORDERS**
  Anorexia Nervosa
  Bulimia Nervosa
  Age of Onset and Gender Differences
  Medical Complications of Anorexia Nervosa and Bulimia Nervosa
  Other Forms of Eating Disorders
  Distinguishing Among Diagnoses
  Prevalence of Eating Disorders
  Eating Disorders Across Cultures
  Course and Outcome

- **RISK AND CAUSAL FACTORS IN EATING DISORDERS**
  Biological Factors
  Sociocultural Factors
  Family Influences
  Individual Risk Factors

- **TREATMENT OF EATING DISORDERS**
  Treating Anorexia Nervosa
  Treating Bulimia Nervosa
  Treating Binge-Eating Disorder

- **OBESITY**

- **RISK AND CAUSAL FACTORS IN OBESITY**
  The Role of Genes
  Hormones Involved in Appetite and Weight Regulation
  Sociocultural Influences
  Family Influences
  Stress and "Comfort Food"
  Pathways to Obesity
  Treatment of Obesity
  The Importance of Prevention

OBJECTIVES

After reading this chapter, you should be able to do the following:

1. Discuss the clinical aspects of eating disorders, such as age of onset and gender differences.

2. Define anorexia nervosa and bulimia nervosa and their subtypes.

3. Describe the medical complications of the various eating disorders.

4. Identify other forms of eating disorders, such as EDNOS and BED.

5. Discuss prevalence rates of eating disorders in this culture and across cultures.

6. Describe the biological, sociocultural, individual, and family risk and causal factors associated with eating disorders.

7. Explain the various methods used for treating eating disorders and be able to evaluate each.

8. Define obesity and identify risk and causal factors.

9. Discuss prevention and treatment methods for obesity.

<u>AS YOU READ</u>
Answers can be found in the Answer Key at the end of the book.

KEY WORDS
Each of the words below is important in understanding the concepts presented in this chapter. Write the definition next to each word.

Term	Page	Definition
Anorexia Nervosa	243	
Binge-eating disorder	249	

(BED)		
Body mass index (BMI)	260	
Bulimia nervosa	245	
Cognitive behavioral therapy (CBT)	258	
Eating disorder	243	
Eating disorder not otherwise specified (EDNOS)	249	
Grehlin	261	
Leptin	261	
Negative affect	256	
Obesity	260	
Perfectionism	256	
Purge	244	
Serotonin	252	

MATCHING
Who's Who and What's What
Match the following terms with their definitions.

Name/Term
_____ Perfectionism
_____ Richard Morton
_____ Charles Lasegue and Sir William Gull
_____ Anorexia nervosa—restricting type
_____ Anorexia nervosa—binge-eating purging type
_____ Bulimia nervosa
_____ Russell, a British psychiatrist

Definition
   A. Published the first medical account of anorexia nervosa in 1689
   B. Comes from the Greek words meaning "ox" and "hunger"
   C. Instrumental in naming the eating disorder, anorexia nervosa, in 1873
   D. Long regarded as an important risk factor for eating disorders
   E. Low weight is maintained by tightly controlling how much food is eaten
   F. Proposed the term *bulimia nervosa* in 1979

G. Breakdown of eating restraint, resulting in periods of binge-eating and efforts to purge

SHORT ANSWERS
Provide brief answers to the following questions.

1. Describe the risk factors for eating disorders in males. (p. 248)

2. What is the DSM-IV-TR criteria for bulimia nervosa? (p. 246)

3. Mary was diagnosed with an eating disorder—anorexia nervosa. She sought treatment for the disorder. Based on the research done by Lowe in 2001, what can you say about her recovery possibilities? (p. 251)

4. Explain how the study done by Anne Becker of the women in Fiji illustrates the impact the media has on thinness. (pp. 253–254)

THE DOCTOR IS IN...PSYCHIATRIC HELP—5¢
Read the following scenarios and diagnose the client. Remember to look carefully at the criteria for the disorder before you make a decision as to the diagnosis. Make a list of other information you might need to help you understand the causal factors.

1. Mary is 5 feet 6 inches and 96 pounds. She tells you that whenever she looks in the mirror, all she sees is a fat person. Mary has restricted her eating to just a few pieces of celery and carrots each day. There is a ritual to her eating pattern. Mary's hair is thin and her nails are brittle. She is still having regular menstrual periods.

How would you diagnose Mary and why?

2. Glenn, a 45-year-old male, comes to your office after his wife insisted that he come in to see you. Glenn is 5 feet 8 inches and 350 pounds. Even though his health is in jeopardy, he finds himself binging on all kinds of food from cakes and cookies to pizzas, fried chicken, and hamburgers. He feels disgusted with his behavior. You ask if he purges and he tells you that he does not. He says that he does not exercise excessively after binging.

How would you diagnose Glenn and why?

3. Diane, a 14-year-old girl, is referred to you because she has anorexia nervosa. Her parents are very concerned, but a bit shocked, when you suggest that you would like to see the whole family in therapy, not just Diane. What would you expect to see as family characteristics when you talk to Diane's family? How would you proceed with treatment?

AFTER YOU READ

PRACTICE TESTS
Take the following three multiple-choice tests to see how much you have comprehended from the chapter. Each represents roughly one third of the chapter. As you study the chapter, use these to check your progress.

Practice Test 1

1. An eating disorder that is found almost exclusively in men is (p. 248)
    a. anorexia nervosa.
    b. bulimia nervosa.
    c. male pattern eating disorder.
    d. reverse anorexia.

2. In this type of anorexia nervosa, every effort is made to limit how much food is eaten and caloric intake is tightly controlled. (p. 244)
    a. binge-eating purging type
    b. binge-eating disorder type
    c. restricting type
    d. bulimia nervosa

3. This type of anorexia nervosa involves a breakdown of restraint that results in periods of binge eating. (p. 244)
>   a. binge-eating purging type
>   b. binge-eating disorder type
>   c. restricting type
>   d. bulimia nervosa

4. Karen has the eating disorder bulimia nervosa. During her average binge, she could consume as much as _____ calories. (p. 246)
>   a. 2,000
>   b. 10,000
>   c. 4,800
>   d. 1,200

5. The DSM-IV-TR distinguishes between two types of bulimia nervosa. These are (p. 246)
>   a. purging and nonpurging.
>   b. starving and nonstarving.
>   c. binging and nonbinging.
>   d. None of the above

6. The difference between a person with the purging type of bulimia nervosa and a person with the restricting type of anorexia nervosa is (p. 246)
>   a. the nonpurging methods of weight maintenance.
>   b. the fear of gaining weight
>   c. their actual weight.
>   d. negative self-evaluation.

7. An eating disorder diagnosis found in the appendix of the DSM-IV-TR that warrants further study is (p. 249)
>   a. BED.
>   b. EDNOS.
>   c. OCD.
>   d. TNT.

8. Nicole has anorexia nervosa, and her doctor noted that she has thinning hair on her scalp, brittle nails, and a downy hair on her face, neck, arms, back, and legs. This downy hair is (p. 247)
>   a. longo.
>   b. lenugo.
>   c. lanugo.
>   d. lunugo.

9. A common disorder found in relatives of patients with eating disorders is (p. 252)
>   a. schizophrenia.
>   b. mood disorders.

    c. anxiety disorders.
    d. None of the above

10. Which of the following neurotransmitters is linked with mood disorders and impulsivity and modulates appetite and feeding behavior? (p. 252)
    a. serotonin.
    b. dopamine.
    c. GABA.
    d. All of the above

Practice Test 2

1. The majority of girls and women who have anorexia come from a (p. 254)
    a. single-parent home.
    b. middle-class background.
    c. higher social class background.
    d. a and b

2. The first model to exemplify the current sociocultural ideal of extreme thinness was (p. 253)
    a. Marilyn.
    b. Brittany.
    c. Sandra.
    d. Twiggy.

3. Internalizing the _____ is considered a risk factor for eating disorders. (p. 254)
    a. over-weight ideal
    b. Sleeping Beauty ideal
    c. Monroe ideal
    d. thin ideal

4. There seems to be a perceptual discrepancy between how young girls and women regard their own bodies and the media representation of the (p. 255)
    a. "ideal" female form.
    b. natural-looking woman.
    c. older woman.
    d. None of the above

5. Which of the following factors has the most controversy surrounding whether or not it is a causal factor in developing an eating disorder? (p. 255)
    a. dieting
    b. internalizing the "ideal" female form
    c. perfectionism
    d. All of the above have been proven to be causal factors.

6. A causal risk factor for body dissatisfaction is (p. 256)
        a. negative affect.
        b. upbeat attitude.
        c. high self-esteem.
        d. social support.

7. Which of the following is true about bulimics after they have received intense CBT treatment? (p. 259)
        a. Most fully recover.
        b. Most revert to their bulimic behavior.
        c. Most stop binging and purging but continue to severely restrict their diets.
        d. Most continue to be very concerned with weight and body image.

8. Most studies show a _____ link between child sexual abuse and eating disorders. (p. 257)
        a. weak but positive association
        b. moderate but positive association
        c. strong and positive association
        d. moderate but negative association

9. For adolescents with anorexia nervosa, this is the treatment of choice. (p. 258)
        a. family therapy
        b. antidepressants
        c. individual therapy
        d. cognitive-behavioral therapy

10. This type of treatment has proven effective in treating anorexia and bulimia by helping to modify distorted beliefs about weight, food, and self. (p. 259)
        a. EDT
        b. CNT
        c. DDT
        d. CBT

Practice Test 3

1. The _____ component of CBT for bulimia focuses on normalizing eating patterns. (p. 259)
        a. behavioral
        b. cognitive
        c. cathartic
        d. All of the above

2. The _____ component of CBT for bulimia challenges the dysfunctional thought patterns that perpetuate a binge cycle. (p. 259)
        a. behavioral
        b. cognitive

      c. cathartic
      d. All of the above

3. When patients with bulimia stop trying so hard to restrain their eating, they seem to (p. 259)
      a. get worse by eating more.
      b. stay about the same.
      c. improve.
      d. get better, then get worse.

4. Significant depression is a comorbid condition for binge eaters, affecting around _____ percent during their lifetime. (p. 260)
      a. 25
      b. 37
      c. 76
      d. 60

5. Obesity is defined based on a statistic called the (p. 260)
      a. CBT.
      b. BMI.
      c. GABA.
      d. MMPI.

6. From a diagnostic perspective, obesity is not a(n) (p. 261)
      a. problem if the person recognizes it.
      b. treatable problem like other eating disorders.
      c. eating disorder.
      d. health risk.

7. Adult obesity is related to the number and size of the _____ in the body. (p. 262)
      a. hormones
      b. T-cells
      c. adipose cells
      d. lymphocytes

8. A key influence on excessive eating and obesity is (p. 262)
      a. television.
      b. family behavior patterns.
      c. magazines.
      d. peers.

9. Obesity can result in all of the following medical conditions EXCEPT (p. 261)
      a. diabetes.
      b. high blood pressure.
      c. asthma.

       d. joint disease.

10. Which of the following has NOT been implicated as a possible contributor to obesity? (p. 263)
       a. genetic mutation of cells
       b. a society that discourages activity
       c. family influences
       d. more free time as society becomes wealthier

COMPREHENSIVE PRACTICE TEST

The following tests are designed to give you an idea of how well you understood the entire chapter. There are three different types of tests: multiple-choice, true/false, and essay.

Multiple Choice

1. At the heart of anorexia nervosa and bulimia nervosa is an intense and pathological fear of becoming (p. 243)
       a. too thin.
       b. overweight and fat.
       c. undernourished.
       d. All of the above

2. People with anorexia and bulimia will compromise their health to achieve (p. 243)
       a. muscle.
       b. obesity.
       c. thinness.
       d. a career.

3. Although people of all different ages have been known to develop eating disorders, the period of greatest risk is in (p. 247)
       a. the teenage years.
       b. early adulthood.
       c. middle age.
       d. a and b

4. The clinical picture of the binge-eating/purging type of anorexia has much in common with (p. 245)
       a. EDNOS.
       b. BED.
       c. bulimia nervosa.
       d. None of the above

5. This accounts for more morbidity and mortality than all other eating disorders combined. (p. 260)

    a. EDNOS
    b. obesity
    c. bulimia nervosa
    d. anorexia nervosa

6. Eating disorders are no longer confined to industrialized Western countries but can be found in (p. 250)
    a. India.
    b. Africa.
    c. Asia.
    d. All of the above

7. The long-term mortality rate for bulimia nervosa is around ___ percent. (p. 251)
    a. 10
    b. 6
    c. 0.5
    d. 1

8. People with anorexia and bulimia often show a long-standing pattern of excessive (p. 257)
    a. upbeat attitude.
    b. high self-esteem.
    c. social support.
    d. perfectionism.

9. Currently there is not enough empirical evidence to show that _____ is a risk factor for eating disorders. (p. 257)
    a. an overly indulgent grandmother
    b. a single-parent family
    c. childhood sexual abuse
    d. being an only child

10. Which of the following groups responds well to family treatment? (p. 259)
    a. adolescents
    b. mid-twenties
    c. young adults
    d. None of the above

11. Because many patients with bulimia also suffer from mood disorders, they are often treated with (p. 259)
    a. psychotherapy.
    b. behavioral therapy.
    c. antidepressants.
    d. hospitalization.

12. Which treatment for patients with bulimia has shown the greatest promise? (p. 259)
    a. CBT
    b. antidepressants
    c. ECT
    d. a and b

13. Obesity can result in (p. 260)
    a. diabetes.
    b. high blood pressure.
    c. musculoskeletal problems.
    d. All of the above

14. The rates of obesity are rising too quickly to be only a result of genetics. This rise implies what has become a significant influence? (p. 262)
    a. old age
    b. increase in activity
    c. unhealthy lifestyles
    d. All of the above

15. Being obese is defined as having a body mass index of _____ or above. (p. 260)
    a. 30
    b. 10
    c. 25
    d. 35

16. An extreme method for treating obesity involves (p. 264)
    a. antidepressants.
    b. psychotherapy.
    c. psychosurgery.
    d. gastric bypass surgery.

TRUE/FALSE

1. T / F Eating disorders in the elderly are easily diagnosed because doctors are aware of the problem. (p. 247)

2. T / F Even if they are painfully thin or emaciated, patients with anorexia often deny having any problems. (p. 243)

3. T / F Thirty to fifty percent of patients transition from the restricting type to the binge-eating purging type of anorexia nervosa during the course of their disorder. (p. 244)

4. T / F Death is often a direct outcome of the eating disorder bulimia nervosa. (p. 251)

5. T / F Psychiatric conditions often coexist with eating disorders. (p. 249)

6. T / F Recent research suggests that the restrictive type of anorexia has a genetic base. (p. 252)

7. T / F Body dissatisfaction is an important risk factor for pathological eating. (p. 256)

8. T / F Dieting is not regarded as a risk factor for the development of eating disorders in young women. (p. 255)

9. T / F About 17 percent of patients with severe eating disorders have to be committed to a hospital for treatment against their will. (p. 257)

10. T / F The most immediate concern with patients with anorexia is to restore their weight to a level that is not life-threatening. (p. 257)

11. T / F Young men never develop eating disorders. (p. 248)

12. T / F Per the DSM-IV-TR, one of the criteria for anorexia is the absence of at least four consecutive menstrual periods. (p. 243)

13. T / F Anorexia nervosa literally means lack of appetite induced by nervousness. (p. 243)

14. T / F Jayne binges and purges, but she also meets the criteria for anorexia nervosa. Her diagnosis would be anorexia nervosa (binge-eating/purging type). (p. 245)

15. T / F It is quite common for patients with bulimia nervosa to be treated with antidepressants. (p. 259)

16. T / F Obesity is not related to social class. (p. 260)

Essay Questions

1. Discuss the medical complications of anorexia nervosa and bulimia nervosa. (pp. 247–248)

Anorexia

Bulimia

2. Describe Garner's set-point theory and its relation to eating disorders. (p. 252)

3. Discuss at least three of the risk and causal factors for eating disorders. (pp. 252–257)

4. Describe the treatments for anorexia nervosa and bulimia nervosa. (pp. 259–260)

5. Describe the sociocultural and family influences on obesity. (pp. 261–263)

WHEN YOU HAVE FINISHED

WEB LINKS TO ITEMS OR CONCEPTS FOUND IN CHAPTER 8

National Association of Anorexia Nervosa and Associated Disorders
http://www.anad.org/site/anadweb/
This is the National Association of Anorexia Nervosa and Associated Disorders Web site, which is dedicated to educating the public on the problems of eating disorders, providing research on the treatment, prevention, and causes of eating disorders as well as acting as a resource center for friends, families, and for those suffering from eating disorders.

Mirror-Mirror Web Site
http://www.mirror-mirror.org/eatdis.htm
This site is dedicated to the recovery and awareness of eating disorders and provides inspiration by dispelling myths and realities, describing how to get help for recovery, and

posting links to other Web sites.

About-Face Web Site
http://www.about-face.org/
This is a very positive Web page devoted to the promotion of women's self-image and self-esteem.

Web MD Article on Eating Disorders and Gender
http://www.webmd.com/content/article/83/97764.htm
Eating disorders are not only seen in females.

National Eating Disorders Association
http://www.edap.org/p.asp?WebPage_ID=337
This is the Web site of the National Eating Disorders Association, which provides a wealth of information on eating disorders.

Something Fishy
http://www.something-fishy.org/
This Web site is dedicated to raising awareness and providing support to people with eating disorders.

The Eating Disorders Association
http://www.edauk.com/
The Eating Disorders Association provides knowledge and support.

USE IT OR LOSE IT
Provide an answer to the thought question below, knowing that there is more than one way to respond. Possible answers are presented in the Answer Key.

What role do you think the media plays in triggering eating disorders in young women?

CRISSCROSS
Now that you know all there is to know about this chapter, here's your opportunity to put that knowledge to work.

Across

7. A statistic used to define obesity

8. A neurotransmitter that has been implicated in modulating appetite and feeding behavior

Down

1. Means lack of appetite induced by nervousness

2. Frequent occurrence of episodes of out-of-control binge eating, followed by recurrent inappropriate behavior that is intended to prevent weight gain.

3. Having a BMI above 30

4. Physiologically regulated weight the body tries to defend or maintain

5. A causal risk factor; focusing on one's limitations and short-comings

6. May cause people to be much more likely to subscribe to the thin ideal; may help maintain bulimic pathology

Puzzle created with Puzzlemaker at DiscoverySchool.com

ANSWERS TO TEST QUESTIONS – CHAPTER 8

MATCHING
D. Perfectionism
A. Richard Morton
C. Charles Lasegue and Sir William
E. Anorexia nervosa—restricting type
G. Anorexia nervosa—binge-eating purging type
B. Bulimia nervosa
F. Russell, a British psychiatrist

SHORT ANSWERS
Your answer should contain the following points.

1. Describe risk factors for eating disorders in males.
a. homosexuality
b. premorbid obesity
c. being teased as a child
d. subgroups who need to "make weight" in order to work

2. What are the DSM-IV-TR criteria for bulimia nervosa?
a. frequent occurrence of episodes of binge eating
b. lack of control over eating
c. recurrent inappropriate behavior that is intended to prevent weight gain
d. person's self-evaluation has to be excessively influenced by weight and body shape

3. Very difficult to treat—Lowe's study looked at outcomes twenty-one years after patients sought treatment. He found that 16 percent of women with anorexia nervosa had died from starvation or suicide, 10 percent were still suffering from anorexia, 21 percent were partially recovered, and 51 percent were fully recovered. Mary has a little better than 50 percent chance of recovery.

4. In the early 1990s when Becker was first conducting her research, fat was associated with being strong, capable of work, and being kind and generous. Being thin was considered negative, thought to be sickly, incompetent, or having received poor treatment. There was no such thing as an eating disorder. In 1998, when Becker returned to Fiji, television has been introduced to Fiji, and the people were able to see such shows as *Beverly Hills 90210* and *Melrose Place*. The young women were expressing concerns about their weight and dislike of their bodies and dieting in earnest. This research provides anecdotal information about how the introduction of Western values about thinness might insinuate themselves into different cultures.

THE DOCTOR IS IN

1. Mary
Diagnosis: anorexia nervosa, note the abnormality of height and weight.

2. Glenn
<u>Diagnosis</u>: binge-eating disorder, note the excessive weight for a man his size.

3. Diane: the family dynamic would clearly come out during family therapy. Notably, rigidity, parental overprotectedness, excessive control, and possibly marital discord between the parents. Note where the parents and the patient sit. If they sit apart from one another, this may indicate marital discord as well as relationship issues with one or both parents. One or both parents may have had an eating disorder or are fighting one now. They may have a preoccupation with thinness, dieting, and good physical health. In terms of therapy, you as the therapist will be viewed as an outsider and possibly an "enemy" as you will expose a substantial amount of negative relationships that have been festering within this family for a good number of years. You will have to maintain control of the therapy and avoid taking sides or having one parent present as the "good guy." Objectivity as well as individual therapy with Diane will serve to provide stability that she may not have had previously.

PRACTICE TESTS

Q#	TEST 1	TEST 2	TEST 3
1	D	C	A
2	C	D	B
3	A	D	C
4	C	A	D
5	A	D	B
6	C	A	C
7	A	D	C
8	C	A	B
9	B	A	C
10	A	D	D

COMPREHENSIVE PRACTICE TEST

Q#	M/C	T/F
1	B	F
2	C	T
3	D	T
4	C	F
5	B	T
6	D	T
7	C	T
8	D	F
9	C	T
10	A	T
11	C	F
12	D	F

13	D	T
14	C	T
15	A	T
16	D	F

Essay Questions
Your answer should contain the following points.

1. Discuss the medical complications of anorexia nervosa and bulimia nervosa.

Anorexia
a. hair thins; nails and hair become brittle
b. skin becomes dry; downy hair grows on face neck, arms, back, and legs (langugo)
c. skin develops a yellowish tinge
d. hands and feet feel cold
d. low blood pressure
e. vitamin B1 deficiency, which could lead to depression and cognitive changes
f. sudden death from heart arrhythmias
g. low levels of potassium can result in kidney damage and renal failure

Bulimia
a. purging can cause electrolyte imbalances and hypokalemia
b. risk for heart abnormalities
c. damage to heart muscle caused by ipecac used to induce vomiting
d. callouses on their hands from sticking their fingers down their throat
e. damage to teeth from stomach acid when throwing up
f. mouth ulcers and dental cavities
g. small red dots around eyes, caused by the pressure of throwing up
h. swollen parotid glands, caused by repeatedly vomiting

2. Describe Garner's set-point theory and its relation to eating disorders.
Weight is physiologically regulated around a weight that the body tries to defend, a set-point. If a person tries to radically deviate from this weight, there are "physiological compensations" that take place to restore the weight. Hunger drive is an example of compensation. The more weight a person loses, the greater the hunger levels. This is an attempt to encourage eating, gain weight, and return to a state of equilibrium. People with anorexia think about food all the time and try very hard to suppress their hunger. Chronic dieting increases likelihood of person having periods of binging impulses—eating very high–caloric foods.

3. Biological factors, sociocultural factors, family influences, and individual risk factors.

4. For anorexia nervosa, family therapy is the treatment of choice, as medications do not elicit a significant response. CBT may be used, but is limited in obtaining full recovery from the disorder. For bulimia nervosa, medications such as the antidepressants are quite effective along with CBT.

5. Time pressures as well as less exercise are contributing to obesity. In families where high-fat, high-calorie diets or an overemphasis on food is encouraged, obesity may be produced in many or all family members.

USE IT OR LOSE IT

Many researchers believe that constant exposure to media images of extremely thin models may cause some young women to develop eating disorders in the pursuit of unrealistic body weights.

CRISSCROSS ANSWERS

Across
7. Body mass index
8. Serotonin

Down
1. Anorexia nervosa
2. Bulimia nervosa
3. Obesity
4. Set-point theory
5. Negative affect
6. Perfectionism

Chapter 9: Personality Disorders

BEFORE YOU READ

Personality disorders differ from other mental health diagnoses because they are ingrained "lifestyles" or characteristic patterns that are maladaptive and persist throughout the individual's lifetime. These Axis-II disorders are grouped into three clusters on the basis of similarities of features among the disorders. Cluster A includes paranoid, schizoid, and schizotypal personality disorders, which are all characterized by odd or eccentric behaviors. Cluster B is comprised of the disorders that tend to be dramatic and emotional, and includes histrionic, narcissistic, antisocial, and borderline personality disorder. Cluster C is made up of disorders that involve anxiety and fearfulness such as avoidant, dependent, and obsessive-compulsive personality disorders. Unfortunately, there is still disagreement about how best to define these disorders, and they can co-occur with Axis-I disorders as well as with each other, further complicating diagnosis. Nevertheless, new treatment approaches continue to emerge, and have shown some success with specific personality disorders. However, one of the most difficult and complicated of the personality disorders is antisocial personality disorder. This disorder is specifically focused on in chapter 9, as it is the most socially disruptive of the personality disorders.

- **CLINICAL FEATURES OF PERSONALITY DISORDERS**

- **DIFFICULTIES DOING RESEARCH ON PERSONALITY DISORDERS**
    Difficulties in Diagnosing Personality Disorders
    Difficulties in Studying the Causes of Personality Disorders

- **CATEGORIES OF PERSONALITY DISORDERS**
    Paranoid Personality Disorder
    Schizoid Personality Disorder
    Schizotypal Personality Disorder
    Histrionic Personality Disorder
    Narcissistic Personality Disorder
    Antisocial Personality Disorder
    Borderline Personality Disorder
    Avoidant Personality Disorder
    Dependent Personality Disorder
    Obsessive-Compulsive Personality Disorder
    General Sociocultural Causal Factors for Personality Disorders

- **TREATMENTS AND OUTCOMES**
    Adapting Therapeutic Techniques to Specific Personality Disorders
    Treating Borderline Personality Disorder
    Treating Other Personality Disorders

• **ANTISOCIAL PERSONALITY AND PSYCHOPATHY**
    Psychopathy and ASPD
    The Clinical Picture in Psychopathy and Antisocial Personality Disorder
    Causal Factors in Psychopathy and Antisocial Personality
    A Developmental Perspective on Psychopathy and Antisocial Personality
    Treatments and Outcomes in Psychopathic and Antisocial Personality

• **UNRESOLVED ISSUES:**
    Axis II of DSM-IV-TR

OBJECTIVES
After reading this chapter, you should be able to do the following:

1. List the clinical features of the personality disorders and the problems associated with diagnosis.

2. Compare and contrast the different types of personality disorders and identify the three clusters into which most personality disorders are grouped.

3. Summarize what is known about the biological, psychological, and sociocultural causal factors of personality disorders.

4. Discuss the difficulties of treating individuals with personality disorders and describe the approaches to treatment that have been tried.

5. Compare and contrast the DSM-IV-TR concept of antisocial personality and Cleckley's concept of psychopathy.

6. List the clinical features of psychopathy and antisocial personality.

7. Summarize the biological, psychosocial, and sociocultural causal factors in psychopathy and antisocial personality and the integrated developmental perspective.

8. Explain why it is difficult to treat psychopathy and antisocial personality and describe the most promising of the as yet unproven approaches to treatment.

AS YOU READ
Answers can be found in the Answer Key at the end of the book.

KEY WORDS
Each of the words below is important in understanding the concepts presented in this chapter. Write the definition next to each word.

Term	Page	Definition
Antisocial personality disorder (ASPD)	278	

Avoidant personality disorder	281	
Borderline personality disorder (BPD)	278	
Dependent personality disorder	282	
Histrionic personality disorder	275	
Narcissistic personality disorder	277	
Obsessive-compulsive personality disorder (OCPD)	283	
Paranoid personality disorder	272	
Personality disorder	269	
Psychopathy	287	
Schizoid personality disorder	274	
Schizotypal personality disorder	274	

MATCHING
Who's Who and What's What
Match the following personality disorders with the appropriate description.

Personality Disorder

_____ Paranoid
_____ Schizoid
_____ Schizotypal
_____ Histrionic
_____ Narcissistic
_____ Antisocial
_____ Borderline
_____ Avoidant
_____ Dependent
_____ Obsessive-compulsive

Description

A. Hypersensitivity to rejection, shyness, insecurity
B. Over concern with attractiveness; self-dramatization
C. Impulsive, drastic mood shifts, self-mutilation
D. Suspicious and mistrustful; blames others
E. Lacks desire to form attachments; poor relationships

    F. Grand preoccupation with self; lack of empathy
    G. Excessive concern with order, rules; perfectionistic
    H. Peculiar thought patterns; odd perception and speech
    I.   Lacking morals or ethics; deceitful, manipulative
    J. Discomfort being alone, indecisive, difficulty ending relationships

SHORT ANSWERS
Provide brief answers to the following questions.

1. List the five criteria used in DSM-IV-TR to define personality disorders. (p. 269)

2. Discuss the genetic influences and developmental perspectives for antisocial personality disorders. (pp. 291–294)

3. Many studies have found that people with borderline personality disorder report a large number of negative, even traumatic, events in childhood including abuse and neglect, separation and loss, and parental psychopathology. However, it is difficult to say childhood trauma plays a causal role. Why? (p. 279)

4. Discuss the difference between a loner with schizoid personality disorder and the loner who is avoidant. (p. 274)

PERSONALITY DISORDER
Personality disorders discussed in the text cover a lot of ground and can leave you confused. As you discover items while studying, jot down the facts and descriptive words for later reference.

Cluster A
Characteristics of Cluster A Disorders:

Paranoid personality disorder
Characteristics:
Causal factors:
Treatment or hope for treatment:
Miscellaneous points or terms:

Schizoid personality disorder
Characteristics:
Causal factors:
Treatment or hope for treatment:
Miscellaneous points or terms:

Schizotypal personality disorder
Characteristics:
Causal factors:
Treatment or hope for treatment:
Miscellaneous points or terms

Cluster B
Characteristics of Cluster B Disorders:

Histrionic personality disorder
Characteristics:
Causal factors:
Treatment or hope for treatment:
Miscellaneous points or terms:

Narcissistic personality disorder
Characteristics:
Causal factors:
Treatment or hope for treatment:
Miscellaneous points or terms:

<u>Antisocial personality disorder</u>
Characteristics:
Causal factors:
Treatment or hope for treatment:
Miscellaneous points or terms:

<u>Borderline personality disorder</u>
Characteristics:
Causal factors:
Treatment or hope for treatment:
Miscellaneous points or terms:

Cluster C
Characteristics of Cluster C Disorders:

<u>Avoidant personality disorder</u>
Characteristics:
Causal factors:
Treatment or hope for treatment:
Miscellaneous points or terms:

<u>Dependent personality disorder</u>
Characteristics:
Causal factors:
Treatment or hope for treatment:
Miscellaneous points or terms:

<u>Obsessive-compulsive personality disorder</u>
Characteristics:
Causal factors:
Treatment or hope for treatment:
Miscellaneous points or terms:

Antisocial Personality and Psychopathy
Characteristics of Antisocial Personality and Psychopathy:

<u>Antisocial personality</u>
Characteristics:
Causal factors:
Treatment or hope for treatment:
Miscellaneous points or terms:

Psychopathy
Characteristics:
Causal factors:
Treatment or hope for treatment:
Miscellaneous points or terms:

THE DOCTOR IS IN...PSYCHIATRIC HELP—5¢
Read the following scenarios and diagnose the client. Remember to look carefully at the criteria for the disorder before you make a decision as to the diagnosis. Make a list of other information you might need to help you understand the causal factors.

1. Helen, a 31-year-old waitress, comes to the office of a male therapist, seeking help trying to understand why she doesn't have a relationship. She is dressed rather provocatively in a tight red dress that, while flattering to her figure, is questionable attire for a doctor's appointment in the midafternoon. Notably, her hair is done up in a complicated manner and seems more appropriate for an evening out or a date. She tells the therapist about her life in a very dramatic and lively manner and makes flirtatious comments like, "I can't understand why no one likes me—what I wouldn't do to have some cute guy like you just sweep me off my feet." How would Helen be diagnosed and why?

2. Jack, a computer software engineer, comes to your office because he is having problems at work and may lose his job if things don't change. When you ask him what has happened, he looks at you suspiciously, and asks you who else you have been talking to. You assure him you haven't talked to anyone. He tells you that others at work are talking about him behind his back, and he knows they are responsible for his having to see a therapist. Jack tells you he has no friends at work or any place else. How would you diagnose Jack and why?

3. Pam sits in your office not saying much and is having some difficulty talking about herself. She manages to tell you that she is alone much of the time—something she doesn't like—and would like to feel comfortable meeting people. She is extremely self-conscious and avoids situations in which she might be criticized or rejected.
How would you diagnose Pam and why?

4. As a therapist, what issues will you face in treating the three patients above?

AFTER YOU READ

PRACTICE TESTS
Take the following three multiple-choice tests to see how much you have comprehended from the chapter. Each represents roughly one third of the chapter. As you study the chapter, use these to check your progress.

Practice Test 1

1. Personality disorders were formerly known as (p. 269)
    a. fatal flaws.
    b. character disorders.
    c. personality patterns.
    d. None of the above

2. Studies estimate that _____ people meet criteria for at least one personality disorder at some point in their lifetime. (p. 270)
    a. about 9 out of 10
    b. less than 1 percent of
    c. about 13 percent of
    d. 42 percent

3. Diagnostic criteria for personality disorders are (p. 270)
    a. not as sharply defined as for most Axis II diagnoses.
    b. not as sharply defined as for most Axis I diagnoses.
    c. not as sharply defined as for most Axis III diagnoses.
    d. not as sharply defined as for most Axis IV diagnoses.

4. This cluster includes the paranoid, schizoid, and schizotypal personality disorders. (p. 272)
	a. cluster C
	b. cluster B
	c. cluster A
	d. All of the above

5. People with _____ personality disorder often bear grudges, are unwilling to forgive perceived insults and slights, and are quick to react with anger. (p. 272)
	a. schizoid
	b. paranoid
	c. narcissistic
	d. antisocial

6. People with _____ personality disorder rarely experience strong positive or negative emotions, are unable to express their feelings, appear cold and distant, and can be classified as loners or introverts. (p. 274)
	a. schizoid
	b. paranoid
	c. narcissistic
	d. antisocial

7. People with _____ personality disorder are excessively introverted and show cognitive and perceptual distortions and eccentricities in their communication and behavior. (p. 274)
	a. schizoid
	b. schizotypal
	c. borderline
	d. antisocial

8. People with _____ personality disorder exhibit excessive attention-seeking behavior, are dramatic and extraverted, and tend to feel unappreciated if they are not the center of attention. (p. 275)
	a. histrionic
	b. narcissistic
	c. borderline
	d. antisocial

9. People with _____ personality disorder show an exaggerated sense of self-importance, a preoccupation with being admired, and a lack of empathy for the feelings of others. (p. 277)
	a. histrionic
	b. narcissistic
	c. borderline
	d. schizoid

10. Narcissistic personality disorder may be more frequently observed in (p. 278)
   a. older persons.
   b. men than in women.
   c. women than in men.
   d. television news anchors.

Practice Test 2

1. People with _____ personality disorder continually violate the rights of others through deceitful, aggressive, or antisocial behavior, without remorse. (p. 278)
   a. schizoid
   b. schizotypal
   c. borderline
   d. antisocial

2. _____ personality disorder is characterized by impulsivity and instability in interpersonal relationships, self-image, and moods. (p. 278)
   a. Schizoid
   b. Schizotypal
   c. Borderline
   d. Histrionic

3. People with _____ personality disorder display extreme affective instability and self-destructive behaviors such as gambling, sexual promiscuity, and suicide attempts. (p. 278)
   a. schizoid
   b. schizotypal
   c. borderline
   d. histrionic

4. Overall, about _____ of patients with borderline personality disorder reported some type of childhood abuse or neglect. (p. 279)
   a. 1.732 percent
   b. 20 percent
   c. half
   d. 90 percent

5. A study (Paris, 1999) suggests that borderline personality disorder may be more prevalent in our society today than in the past and in many other cultures, because of (p. 280)
   a. marital discord.
   b. the weakening of the family structure in our society.
   c. the increase of violence in entertainment and the media.
   d. All of the above

6. People with _____ personality disorder have a pattern of extreme social inhibition and introversion, leading to lifelong patterns of limited social relationships. (p. 281)
        a. avoidant
        b. schizotypal
        c. borderline
        d. antisocial

7. People with _____ personality disorder show an extreme need to be taken care of, which leads to clinging and submissive behavior. (p. 282)
        a. avoidant
        b. dependent
        c. borderline
        d. obsessive-compulsive

8. Dependent personality disorder occurs in about 2 to 4 percent of the population and is (p. 282)
        a. usually found east of the Mississippi.
        b. found mostly in older men.
        c. more common in women than men.
        d. a product of domineering grandparents.

9. People with _____ personality disorder are characterized by the need for perfectionism and an excessive concern with maintaining order and control. (p. 283)
        a. schizoid
        b. schizotypal
        c. obsessive-compulsive
        d. histrionic

10. People with an obsessive-compulsive personality (p. 284)
        a. believe they are helpless.
        b. are quite rigid and stubborn.
        c. have difficulty delegating tasks to others.
        d. b and c

Practice Test 3

1. Some features of this personality disorder may overlap with some features of the narcissistic, antisocial, and schizoid personality disorders, yet these individuals are characterized by their unwillingness to be generous with themselves. (p. 284)
        a. borderline
        b. obsessive-compulsive
        c. dependent
        d. histrionic

2. The most clinical and research attention has been paid to this personality disorder. (p. 285)
    a. avoidant
    b. depressive
    c. obsessive-compulsive
    d. borderline

3. The treatment of borderline personality disorder using drugs is controversial because (p. 286)
    a. victims become addicted rapidly.
    b. it is so frequently associated with suicidal behavior.
    c. drugs tend to cause them to "cross the border" and not return.
    d. drugs tend to cause them to develop other disorders.

4. People diagnosed with _____ personality disorder persistently disregard and violate the rights of others through a combination of deceitful, aggressive, or antisocial behavior. (p. 287)
    a. psychopathy
    b. antisocial
    c. obsessive-compulsive
    d. borderline

5. The prevalence of antisocial personality disorder in the general population is estimated to be about _____ percent for males and _____ percent for females. (p. 288)
    a. 3, 1
    b. 33, 3
    c. 3, 10
    d. 50, 0

6. People diagnosed with _____ personality disorder are characterized by callousness, selfishness, and an exploitative use of others, as well as being antisocial and impulsive and having socially deviant lifestyle. (p. 287)
    a. psychopathy
    b. dependent
    c. obsessive-compulsive
    d. borderline

7. Released prison inmates who were diagnosed as psychopaths were estimated to be _____ than those without a psychopathy diagnosis. (p. 288)
    a. three times more likely to reoffend.
    b. four times more likely to reoffend violently.
    c. less likely to reoffend.
    d. a and b

8. The probability that a child with a genetic or constitutional liability will develop conduct disorder, and later adult psychopathy, is increased if their own parents (p. 294)
  a. had poor and ineffective parenting skills.
  b. exhibited antisocial behavior.
  c. got divorced.
  d. All of the above

9. A "burned-out psychopath" is one who (p. 296)
  a. died.
  b. had a bad reaction to electroshock therapy.
  c. is an older, wiser person whose criminal activities have lessened after age 40.
  d. had a bad reaction to drugs.

10. The best multifaceted cognitive-behaviorally oriented treatment programs (p. 296)
  a. can cure 77 percnet of antisocial personalities and 34 percent of psychopaths.
  b. generally produce changes of only modest magnitude.
  c. greatly help at least half of the patients.
  d. have proven to only make things worse in the long run.

COMPREHENSIVE PRACTICE TEST
The following tests are designed to give you an idea of how well you understood the entire chapter. There are three different types of tests: multiple-choice, true/false, and essay.

Multiple Choice

1. Lucas is highly suspicious of everyone and never trusts anyone. He does not get along with his coworkers and prefers to "eat alone—that way they can talk about me." Just this past week, he accused his wife of cheating on him despite the fact that she normally works long hours at her job and has the pay stubs to prove it. He is convinced that she is out to embarrass him. Lucas may have this personality disorder. (p. 272)
  a. schizotypal personality disorder
  b. paranoid personality disorder
  c. avoidant personality disorder
  d. schizoid personality disorder

2. Morton was extremely introverted and kept to himself. The only pleasure he had seemed to be when he was organizing his paper clip and metal objects collection. He has never dated, and has no friends. He lives alone in a small one-bedroom apartment. At work, he handles the servers on the mainframe, which is solitary work. Morton would meet the criteria for this personality disorder. (p. 274)
  a. schizotypal personality disorder
  b. paranoid personality disorder
  c. avoidant personality disorder
  d. schizoid personality disorder

3. Marlene lacks any close friends. She wears the same clothes for days on end, and her clothes have "symbols" on them, designed by Marlene with rhinestones. She speaks of the paternal region quite often although no one seems to understand why or what she is talking about. When you speak to her she claims to know what you are thinking and that you think she is dirty. In fact, she says most people, especially those in groups, discuss her hygiene. Marlene would meet the criteria for this personality disorder. (p. 274)

      a. schizotypal personality disorder
      b. paranoid personality disorder
      c. avoidant personality disorder
      d. schizoid personality disorder

4. Brandy is very popular with all of the guys on the campus. She is always the life of the party, and the one girl you could always bet on to be dancing on the tables by the end of the evening. She is highly seductive with men, which has been a problem in the past although she continues to do it anyway. Even during midterms and finals week her hair is done up perfectly and she is dressed as if she is going to a party. Brandy would meet the criteria for this personality disorder. (p. 275)

      a. schizotypal personality disorder
      b. histrionic personality disorder
      c. avoidant personality disorder
      d. borderline personality disorder

5. While Tony had achieved reasonable success in his chosen profession, most who first met him thought he was an opinion leader. It was only after repeated meetings that they found him to be highly arrogant, self-serving, and highly critical of those around him. He would tell everyone how important he was, that the place could not run without him, and that he should be running things. He would always sit at the head of the table regardless of whether he was the chair of the meetings. On one occasion, when the vice president of the company asked him to move out of his VP chair during a conference, Tony replied, "Fine, I need you to keep my seat warm anyway." Tony would meet the criteria for this personality disorder. (p. 277)

      a. narcissistic personality disorder
      b. histrionic personality disorder
      c. avoidant personality disorder
      d. borderline personality disorder

6. Julie was admitted to the unit with numerous cuts on her arms, some deep others superficial. Her mother said Julie's boyfriend had just broken up with her a week ago, and she tried to get him back by attempting to hurt herself. He had become tired of her needy behaviors (calling him at two or three in the morning to ask if he still loved her, her constant questions about why he needed to go places without her, and her jealousy if he even said hello to another woman). She would easily get enraged and then start crying about how lonely she was. Julie would meet the criteria for this personality disorder. (p. 278)

      a. narcissistic personality disorder

    b. histrionic personality disorder
    c. avoidant personality disorder
    d. borderline personality disorder

7. Kelly is an attractive 25-year-old woman who is extremely shy, does not feel she is "good enough" although she excels in her studies and is very well regarded. She is hypersensitive to criticism even when it is positive. Kelly would meet the criteria for this personality disorder. (p. 281)
    a. narcissistic personality disorder
    b. histrionic personality disorder
    c. avoidant personality disorder
    d. borderline personality disorder

8. Denise worked part-time as a receptionist. Her husband, Ralph, while not physically, verbally abused her on regular basis. When she and her family were invited to parties, she would say she needed to ask Ralph if it was okay. She does not handle the financial matters nor any of the day-to-day activities of the home. She refused to decorate the home without Ralph's approval. Even at work, she constantly is asking others if she did things right. Denise would meet the criteria for this personality disorder. (p. 282)
    a. dependent personality disorder
    b. histrionic personality disorder
    c. avoidant personality disorder
    d. borderline personality disorder

9. While quite possibly one of the best accountants the firm has ever had, it was at a cost. David was extremely particular about everything. It was not uncommon for him to restart a project if he lost his place. He maintained the rule of three, meaning he had to triple check all calculations before it left his desk. David's boss appreciated the extra time he put in on evenings and weekends; however, David was very territorial and would not let anyone even help him make copies. David would meet the criteria for this personality disorder. (p. 283)
    a. dependent personality disorder
    b. obsessive-compulsive personality disorder
    c. avoidant personality disorder
    d. borderline personality disorder

10. Rico is a very charming individual; however, beneath that charm is a ruthless con artist. He has feigned illness twice to avoid prosecution, has been in trouble with the law since age 12, does not care about anyone and feels no remorse. He has lit fires, robbed elderly women, and broken into numerous homes. Rico would meet criteria for this personality disorder. (p. 287)
    a. dependent personality disorder
    b. obsessive-compulsive personality disorder
    c. antisocial personality disorder
    d. borderline personality disorder

11. The most comprehensive, systematic early description of psychopathy was made by this person in the 1940s. (p. 287)
    a. Cleckley
    b. Bleurler
    c. Morrison
    d. Buckley

12. Cluster A personality disorders are described as (p. 272)
    a. odd/eccentric.
    b. anxious/fearful.
    c. erratic/dramatic.
    d. All of the above

13. To be considered an antisocial personality disorder, the pattern of behavior must have been occurring since the age of 15, and before age 15, the person must have shown (p. 287)
    a. destruction of property, or deceitfulness or theft.
    b. persistent patterns of aggression toward people or animals.
    c. serious violation of rules at home or in school.
    d. All of the above

14. Approximately 75 percent of borderline personalities have cognitive symptoms that include (p. 279)
    a. relatively short or transient episodes in which they appear to be out of contact with reality.
    b. experiencing delusions or other psychotic-like symptoms such as hallucinations, paranoid ideas, body image distortions, or dissociative symptoms.
    c. complaints about personal misfortunes or of being misunderstood and unappreciated.
    d. a and b

15. People with avoidant personality disorder (p. 281)
    a. do not seek out other people but do not enjoy their aloneness.
    b. have great anxiety due to their inability to relate comfortably to other people.
    c. tend to be hypersensitive and may see ridicule or disparagement where none was intended.
    d. All of the above

16. A person with dependent personality disorder (p. 282)
    a. may remain in an abusive relationship due to a fear that defending herself might cause her to lose her partner.
    b. may not function well on his own.
    c. has great difficulty making even simple everyday decisions due to a lack of self-confidence.
    d. All of the above

17. Although not well studied, treatment of this cluster of personality disorders seems more promising. (p. 287)
    a. cluster A
    b. cluster C
    c. cluster B
    d. cluster D

18. Personality disorders are generally very difficult to treat, in part, because (p. 285)
    a. people suffering from these disorders view themselves as nearly perfect and in no need of change.
    b. these are, by definition, enduring, pervasive, and inflexible patterns of behavior.
    c. it is very difficult to get and keep the attention of persons suffering these disorders.
    d. All of the above

19. People who suffer from _____ personality disorder may experience transient psychotic symptoms, believe that they have magical powers, and engage in magical rituals. (p. 274)
    a. schizoid
    b. paranoid
    c. schizotypal
    d. antisocial

20. Psychopaths are (p. 289)
    a. often charming, spontaneous, and likeable on first acquaintance.
    b. deceitful and manipulative, callously using others to achieve their own ends.
    c. prone to acting out impulses in remorseless and often senseless violence.
    d. All of the above

21. Psychopaths (p. 289)
    a. seem to have good insight into other people's needs and weaknesses and are adept at exploiting them.
    b. are irresponsible and unfaithful mates, being manipulative and exploitative in sexual relationships.
    c. have learned to take, rather than earn, what they want and seldom forgo immediate pleasure for future gains and long-range goals.
    d. All of the above

22. _____ in childhood is the single best predictor of who develops an adult diagnosis of psychopathy or antisocial personality. (p. 294)
    a. An absorption in computer games
    b. Excess access to television, particularly violent television
    c. The number of antisocial behaviors exhibited
    d. Heavy metal and other violent and antisocial forms of music

23. The criminal activities of many people with ASPD declines after the age of _____, but the egocentric, callous, and exploitative dimension does not. (p. 296)
    a. 25
    b. 40
    c. 60
    d. 92

TRUE/FALSE

1 T / F Personality disorder seems to stem from the development of inflexible and distorted personality and behavioral patterns. (p. 269)

2. T / F People with mild personality disorders generally function adequately, but may be seen by others as troublesome or eccentric. (p. 269)

3. T / F Personality disorders are easily changed. (p. 285)

4 T / F Personality disorders rarely overlap. (p. 298)

5. T / F Histrionic personality disorder is estimated at 20 to 30 percent and never occurs in women. (p. 276)

6. T / F In a sense, all children begin life as narcissists and only gradually acquire a perspective-taking ability. (p. 277)

7. T / F Self-mutilation is one of the most characteristic features of borderline personality. (p. 279)

8. T / F Approximately 75 percent of individuals diagnosed as borderline personalities are women. (p. 279)

9. T / F There are cases of generalized social phobia without avoidant personality disorder, but very few cases of avoidant personality disorder without generalized social phobia. (p. 281)

10. T / F A person with dependent personality disorder may fail to get appropriately angry with others because of a fear of losing their support. (p. 282)

11. T / F People with obsessive-compulsive personality disorder have lifestyles characterized by over-conscientiousness, inflexibility, and perfectionism. (p. 283)

12. T / F No systematic studies of treating people yet exist for paranoid, schizoid, narcissistic, or histrionic disorders. (p. 285)

13. T / F The psychopath's conscience seems to be severely retarded or nonexistent. (p. 289)

14. T / F There are three clusters of personality disorders in the DSM-IV-TR. (p. 272)

15. T / F Individuals with paranoid personality disorder have a pervasive suspiciousness and distrust of others, leading to numerous interpersonal difficulties. (p. 272)

16. T / F Persons with borderline personality disorder tend to feel unappreciated if they are not the center of attention, and their lively, dramatic, and excessively extraverted styles often ensure that they can charm others into attending to them. (p. 278)

17. T / F Narcissistic personalities are willing and able to take the perspective of others. (p. 277)

18. T / F Eight to ten percent of those with borderline personality disorder may ultimately complete suicide. (p. 279)

19. T / F The person with schizoid personality disorder is cold, aloof, and indifferent to criticism as opposed to the avoidant personality, who is shy, insecure, and hypersensitive to criticism. (p. 274)

20. T / F Some studies suggest that histrionic personality disorder occurs more often in women than in men. (p. 276)

Essay Questions

1. Why do more misdiagnoses occur in diagnosing personality disorders than any other category? Explain. (pp. 270–271)

2. Antisocial personality disorder can be an extremely serious affliction, and persons suffering from it can be a danger to society. Name and explain the criteria that need to be met before a diagnosis can be made. (pp. 287–288)

3. People with psychopathic and antisocial personalities are extremely difficult to treat. Why is this so? (pp. 296–297)

WHEN YOU HAVE FINISHED

WEB LINKS TO ITEMS OR CONCEPTS DISCUSSED IN CHAPTER 9

American Psychological Association Web Site on Personality Disorders
http://www.apa.org/topics/topicperson.html
This is the American Psychological Association's official Web site on personality disorders.

All Clusters of Personality Disorders
http://mentalhelp.net/poc/center_index.php?id=8
Here you will find descriptions and treatment information on all of the personality disorders.

Histrionic Personality Disorder
http://www.clevelandclinic.org/health/health-nfo/docs/3700/3795.asp?index=9743
The Cleveland Clinic provides a terrific overview of histrionic personality disorder.

Antisocial Personality Disorder
http://www.intelihealth.com/IH/ihtIH/WSIHW000/9339/10529.html
This is a good starting point for gathering research on antisocial personality disorder.

Dr. Robert Hare's Web Site
http://www.hare.org/
This is the official Web site of Dr. Robert Hare, a well-known clinician, researcher, and author on antisocial personality disorder.

Avoidant Personality Disorder
http://www.nlm.nih.gov/medlineplus/ency/article/000940.htm
A brief description of avoidant personality disorder is provided on this Web page.

Obsessive Compulsive Personality Disorder
http://psyweb.com/Mdisord/jsp/ocpd.jsp
Treatments as well as a complete explanation are provided for obsessive-compulsive personality disorder on the PsyWeb site.

Dependent Personality Disorder
http://www.clevelandclinic.org/health/health-nfo/docs/3700/3794.asp?index=9783
The Cleveland Clinic provides a thorough overview of dependent personality disorder.

USE IT OR LOSE IT

Provide an answer to the thought question below, knowing that there is more than one way to respond. Possible answers are presented in the Answer Key.

You suspect that your boss has narcissistic personality disorder. What characteristics would you need to observe to confirm this diagnosis?

CRISSCROSS
Now that you know all there is to know about this chapter, here's your opportunity to put that knowledge to work.

Across
3. Mistrust of others, sees self as blameless
10. Perfectionist, excessive concern with order, rules

Down
1. Peculiar; oddities of perception and speech
2. Self-dramatization, over-concern with attractiveness
4. Grandiosity, self-promoting
5. Disregards and violates the rights of others
6. Impulsiveness, mood shifts
7. Hypersensitivity to rejection
8. Antisocial, impulsive, socially deviant lifestyle
9. Subordination of needs to keep others involved in relationships
11. Impaired social relationships, no desire for relationships

Puzzle created with Puzzlemaker at DiscoverySchool.com

ANSWERS TO TEST QUESTIONS – CHAPTER 9

MATCHING
Personality Disorder
D. Paranoid
E. Schizoid
H. Schizotypal
B. Histrionic
F. Narcissistic
I. Antisocial
C. Borderline
A. Avoidant
J. Dependent
G. Obsessive-compulsive

SHORT ANSWERS
Your answer should contain the following points.

1. The five criteria used in DSM-IV-TR to define personality disorders are that the pattern
a. must be manifested in at least two areas.
b. must be inflexible and pervasive.
c. leads to clinically significant distress or impairment in functioning.
d. is stable and of long duration.
e. is not better accounted for as another mental disorder.

2. a. Genetic Influences
• Twin studies have shown highly heritable emotional traits
• Increasing evidence for genetic contributions to certain disorders
b. Developmental Perspectives
• Learning-based habit patterns and maladaptive cognitive styles
• May originate in disturbed parent-child attachment relationships
• Role of parental psychopathology and ineffective parenting practices
• Early emotional and physical abuse as well as ADHD and ODD

3. It difficult to say childhood trauma plays a causal role in developing borderline personality disorder because
a. most children who experienced early abuse and neglect do not end up with any serious personality disorders.
b. the studies that suggested this have serious shortcomings.
c. childhood abuse is not a specific risk factor, because it also is reported at relatively high rates with other personality disorders.
d. childhood abuse nearly always occurs in families with other pathological dynamics that actually may be more important than the abuse per se.

4. The difference between a loner with schizoid personality disorder and the loner who is avoidant is
a. a schizoid's primary focus is on avoiding humiliation and rejection.
b. an avoidant's primary focus is avoiding people in general.

THE DOCTOR IS IN...PSYCHIATRIC HELP—5¢

1. Histrionic personality disorder—very dramatic, is flirtatious, wants approval, moves to be closer to therapist than would be considered healthy.

2. Paranoid personality disorder—pervasive suspiciousness and distrust, interpersonal difficulties, others are to blame for his problems, is not psychotic.

3. Avoidant personality disorder—extreme social inhibition and introversion. Hypersensitivity to criticism. She is aware of a problem but is afraid of rejection if she were to get involved socially, and is self-conscious.

4. As a therapist, what issues will you face in treating the three patients above?
a. Personality disorders are difficult to treat because these are enduring, pervasive, and inflexible patterns of behavior.
b. There are many different goals of treatment such as reducing subjective distress and enhancing well-being, changing specific dysfunctional behaviors, changing whole patterns of behavior, and changing the entire structure of the personality.
c. Therapeutic techniques must be modified and boundaries maintained.
d. Possible hospitalization or partial hospitalization.
e. Use of a new cognitive approach, which assumes that the dysfunctional feelings and behavior associated with the personality disorder are the result of schema that produce biased judgments and the tendency to make cognitive errors in many situations.

PRACTICE TESTS

Q#	TEST 1	TEST 2	TEST 3
1	B	D	B
2	C	C	D
3	B	C	B
4	C	D	B
5	B	B	A
6	A	A	A
7	B	B	D
8	A	C	D
9	B	C	C
10	B	D	B

COMPREHENSIVE PRACTICE TEST

Q#	M/C	T/F
1	B	T
2	D	T
3	A	F
4	B	F
5	A	F
6	D	T
7	C	T
8	A	T
9	B	T
10	C	T
11	A	T
12	A	T
13	D	T
14	D	T
15	D	T
16	D	F
17	B	F
18	B	T
19	C	T
20	D	T
21	D	
22	C	
23	B	

Essay Questions
Your answer should contain the following points.

1. More misdiagnoses occur in diagnosing personality disorders than any other category because
a. the criteria are not as sharply defined.
b. the categories are not mutually exclusive.
c. personality characteristics are dimensional in nature—that is, these can range from normal to severe, which can lead to unreliable diagnoses.

2. Antisocial personality disorder can be an extremely serious affliction, and persons suffering from it can be a danger to society. The criteria that need to be met before a diagnosis can be made are
a. at least three behavioral problems occurring after age 15.
b. at least three instances of deviant behavior before age 15.
c. the antisocial behavior is not a symptom of another mental disorder.

3. People with psychopathic and antisocial personalities are extremely difficult to treat because
a. biological treatments (drugs) do not seem to have any substantial impact on the disorder as a whole.
b. individuals have little motivation to take their medications.
c. of inherent factors in the psychopath's personality—the inability to trust, to learn from experience, to accept responsibility for one's actions.
d. information given by psychopaths is not reliable.

USE IT OR LOSE IT

Narcissists tend to be grandiose and self-absorbed. They may demand that employees constantly agree with them, but will also blame the people around them when things go wrong. To deal with a narcissistic boss you would need to understand why they behave as they do, and learn to stand up for yourself, ignore unreasonable behavior, and document your own actions in order to make sure that you get credit for the things you do, and avoid blame for things that are not your fault.

CRISSCROSS ANSWERS

Across
3. Paranoid
10. Obsessive-compulsive

Down
1. Schizotypal
2. Histrionic
4. Narcissistic
5. Antisocial
6. Borderline
7. Avoidant
8. Psychopathy
9. Dependent
11. Schizoid

Chapter 10: Substance-Related Disorders

BEFORE YOU READ

Throughout history, human beings have experimented and used various drugs for medicinal and for recreational purposes. Most commonly, alcohol, tobacco, and marijuana have historically been used, abused, and the subject of various debates. There are other drugs that date back thousands of years, yet our understanding of their negative impact on health and behavior has grown only in the past fifty years. When individuals have difficulty controlling their use of such substances, or of other behaviors, the term *addiction* is used. This chapter explores alcohol abuse and dependence, and explains the differences between these two conditions. The effects of drugs such as narcotics, stimulants, sedatives, and hallucinogens are also explored. Possible causes for addictions are discussed, along with differences in substance use as a function of cultural factors. An evaluation of treatment options for specific types of addictive disorders is also provided.

• ALCOHOL ABUSE AND DEPENDENCE

The Prevalence, Comorbidity, and Demographics of Alcohol Abuse and
    Dependence
The Clinical Picture of Alcohol Abuse and Dependence
Biological Factors in the Abuse of and Dependence on Alcohol and Other
    Substances
Psychosocial Causal Factors in Alcohol Abuse and Dependence
Sociocultural Factors
Treatment of Alcohol Abuse Disorders

• DRUG ABUSE AND DEPENDENCE

Opium and Its Derivatives (Narcotics)
Cocaine and Amphetamines (Stimulants)
Barbiturates (Sedatives)
LSD and Related Drugs (Hallucinogens)
Ecstasy
Marijuana

• UNRESOLVED ISSUES

Exchanging Addictions: Is This an Effective Approach?

OBJECTIVES

After reading this chapter, you should be able to do the following:

1. Outline the major divisions of psychoactive substance-related disorders, define alcohol abuse and alcohol dependence, summarize the many negative consequences of alcohol use for both the individual and society, and indicate the prevalence and gender ratio of excessive drinking.
2. Describe the clinical picture of alcohol abuse including the biological and psychological effects of chronic consumption of alcohol.

3. Review the biological, psychosocial, and sociocultural contributors to alcohol abuse and dependence.

4. Summarize the research findings on the results of treatment and relapse prevention for alcohol-dependent persons.

5. List the specific drugs and their effects, summarize theories of causal factors, and review treatments for the following drugs of abuse: opium and its derivatives, cocaine and amphetamines, barbiturates, LSD and other hallucinogens, marijuana, and caffeine and nicotine.

6. Discuss the controversy surrounding controlled drinking versus abstinence.

AS YOU READ
Answers can be found in the Answer Key at the end of the book.

KEY WORDS
Each of the words below is important in understanding the concepts presented in this chapter. Write the definition next to each word.

Term	Page	Definition
Addictive behavior	301	
Alcoholism	301	
Amphetamine	324	
Barbiturates	325	
Caffeine	317	
Cocaine	323	
Ecstasy	326	
Endorphins	322	
Flashback	326	
Hallucinogens	326	
Hashish	327	
Heroin	319	
LSD	326	
Marijuana	327	
Mescaline	326	
Mesocorticolimbic dopamine pathway (MCLP)	308	
Methadone	322	
Morphine	319	
Nicotine	317	
Opium	319	

Psilocybin	326	
Psychoactive drugs	301	
Substance abuse	301	
Substance dependence	301	
Tolerance	301	
Toxicity	301	
Withdrawal symptoms	301	

MATCHING
Who's Who and What's What
Match the following drugs with their effects.

Drug

_____ Alcohol
_____ Caffeine
_____ Nicotine
_____ Ecstasy
_____ Opium
_____ Morphine
_____ Heroin
_____ Methadone
_____ Cocaine
_____ Amphetamine
_____ Barbiturates
_____ LSD
_____ Mescaline
_____ Marijuana

Effects

A. Intoxicant found in coffee and chocolate
B. Mild hallucinogen from a plant; can produce mild euphoria or unpleasant experiences depending upon the mood of the user
C. Synthesized drug first used in inhalant for stuffy noses; recalled when discovered that customers were chewing the wicks for "kicks"; newer, more powerful preparation is methedrine, also known as speed
D. A hallucinogen and a stimulant; popular among young adults
E. Poisonous alkaloid associated with 14 percent of all deaths in the United States
F. Hallucinogen distorts sensory images, causing users to see or hear things differently and unusually
G. The major problem drug in the United States; associated with more than half of highway deaths, 50 percent of all rapes, 40–50percent of murders, 40 perecent of all assaults

H. Drug from a plant, costly, a "high" for the affluent
I. A mixture of about 18 alkaloids; morphine and heroin made from this
J. Derived from peyote cactus; hallucinogen used for centuries
K. Derived from opium; was used during Civil War as pain killer; legal as prescription only
L. Derived from opium; first used in cough syrup around 1900; highly addictive; illegal in the United States
M. Addictive drug used as substitute for heroin during treatment
N. Sedatives, depressants that slow down the nervous system; large doses produce immediate sleep or death

SHORT ANSWERS
Provide brief answers to the following questions.

1. Discuss the relationship between being pregnant and drinking alcohol. (p. 306)

2. Discuss the two factors apparently involved in the overpowering addiction to drugs such as opium, cocaine, and alcohol. (pp. 319–321)

3. Discuss the neurochemical process underlying addiction and the role the drug plays in activating the "pleasure pathway." (p. 308)

4. Discuss how environmental factors promote substance abuse. (pp. 309–313)

5. Is there an "alcoholic personality"—a type of character organization that predisposes a person to use alcohol, rather than some other defensive pattern of coping with stress? Explain. (p. 310)

6. Discuss the immediate effects of mainlined or snorted heroin. (p. 319)

7. The view that cocaine users did not develop physiological dependence has changed over the past twenty years. Explore this change of view. (p. 323)

THE DOCTOR IS IN...PSYCHIATRIC HELP—5¢

Read the following scenarios and diagnose the client. Remember to look carefully at the criteria for the disorder before you make a decision as to the diagnosis. Make a list of other information you might need to help you understand the causal factors.

1. You have been working with Tony, who is dependent on alcohol. He has had several problems with the law and has lost his job as a result of his drinking. His wife has told him that if he doesn't get help, she is going to leave. As Tony's therapist, how would you treat him? Be sure to look at relapse prevention.

2. Lupe brings her father, Martin, into to see you. Recently, she found him asleep on the kitchen table, a bottle of pills and an alcoholic drink sitting near by. He is an older gentleman who lost his wife to cancer about a year ago. As you are talking, he tells you that he had been having difficulty sleeping until his doctor had given him something. These helped, but he found that having a drink made these work faster, and, since he was on a fixed income, the pills lasted longer even though the label said not to drink. Lupe tells you that her father has become very sluggish and is having sudden mood shifts. Lately, it seems that she is finding him in this state more often.

AFTER YOU READ

PRACTICE TESTS
Take the following three multiple-choice tests to see how much you have comprehended from the chapter. Each represents roughly one third of the chapter. As you study the chapter, use these to check your progress.

Practice Test 1

1. As a problem facing our society today, addictive behavior is (p. 301)
    a. just beginning to be understood and controlled.
    b. one of the most pervasive and intransigent mental health problems.
    c. overrated and overblown.
    d. a severe problem only in lower income neighborhoods.

2. Substance abuse generally involves (p. 301)
    a. use of a substance, resulting in potentially hazardous behavior.
    b. a continued use, despite persistent social, psychological, occupational, or health problems.
    c. a marked psychological need for increasing amounts of a substance to achieve the desired effects.
    d. a and b

3. Substance dependence involves (p. 301)
    a. use of a substance, resulting in potentially hazardous behavior.
    b. a continued use, despite persistent social, psychological, occupational, or health problems.
    c. a marked psychological need for increasing amounts of a substance to achieve the desired effects.
    d. b and c

4. The need for increased amounts of a substance to achieve the desired effects is called (p. 301)
    a. abuse.
    b. dependence.
    c. tolerance.
    d. withdrawal.

5. Depression and alcoholism frequently occur together since alcohol (p. 302)
    a. is excitatory.
    b. activates the dancing gene.
    c. is a depressant.
    d. causes many problems, which is depressing.

6. When the blood-alcohol level reaches approximately 0.5 percent, the individual passes out, which is a good thing, because (p. 304)
   a. any more drinking would just be a waste of money.
   b. both dancing and driving at that level are pretty much out of the question.
   c. concentrations above 0.55 percent are usually lethal.
   d. All of the above

7. The effects of alcohol vary for different drinkers, depending on (p. 305)
   a. their physical condition.
   b. the amount of food in their stomach.
   c. the duration of their drinking.
   d. All of the above

8. A physiological effect of alcohol is (p. 304)
   a. a tendency toward decreased sexual inhibition, but lowered sexual performance.
   b. a lapse of memory—a blackout.
   c. headache, nausea, and fatigue of a hangover.
   d. All of the above

9. Researchers believe that genetics contribute to one's susceptibility to alcoholism because (p. 308)
   a. almost one third of alcoholics in a study had at least one parent with an alcohol problem.
   b. females in a study were five times more likely to be alcoholic if both of their parents were alcoholic.
   c. children of alcoholic parents who had been adopted by nonalcoholic foster parents had nearly twice the number of alcohol problems by their late 20s as did a control group.
   d. All of the above

10. Certain ethnic groups, particularly Asians and Native Americans, have abnormal physiological reactions to alcohol, known as "_____," including flushing of the skin, a drop in blood pressure, heart palpitations, and nausea. (p. 309)
   a. the fatal flaw
   b. alcohol flush reaction
   c. hypnotic effect
   d. pressure-and-palpitation flush reaction

Practice Test 2

1. Stable family relationships and parental guidance are often _____ in families of substance abusers. (pp. 309–310)
   a. lacking
   b. very strong
   c. inconsistent

d. not discussed

2. About _____ percent of persons with schizophrenia abuse either alcohol or drugs. (p. 310)
>   a. 10
>   b. 25
>   c. 50
>   d. 99.44

3. According to a recent survey, what percentage of college students identified themselves as binge drinkers? (p. 312)
>   a. 21
>   b. 30
>   c. 44
>   d. 85

4. In cultures whose religious values restrict or prohibit the use of alcohol, the incidence of alcoholism is (p. 313)
>   a. about the same as other groups.
>   b. minimal.
>   c. actually higher.
>   d. unknown, as they refuse to discuss it.

5. In the Alcoholics Anonymous (AA) view, (p. 315)
>   a. one's alcoholism can be cured through group meetings and the understanding of peers.
>   b. one is never cured but an alcoholic for life, whether or not one is drinking.
>   c. the alcoholic is weak-willed and lacking in moral strength.
>   d. having a drink or occasionally "falling off the wagon" is nothing to worry about.

6. Drug abuse and dependence are most common during (p. 317)
>   a. adolescence and young adulthood.
>   b. childhood.
>   c. retirement age individuals.
>   d. All of the above

7. Their religious values prohibit the use of alcohol. (p. 312)
>   a. Muslims
>   b. Mormons
>   c. New Zealand
>   d. a and b

8. Because morphine is so addictive, a chemical called acetic anhydride was added to it around the turn of the 20th century in hopes of converting it into a more controllable substance. This new mix was called (p. 319)
    a. aspirin.
    b. heroin.
    c. acetydride.
    d. the Whopper.

9. Opium and its derivatives, morphine, codeine, and heroin, were outlawed in 1914 by (p. 319)
    a. President Woodrow Wilson.
    b. World War I.
    c. the Harrison Act.
    d. the Mann Act.

10. Withdrawl from nicotine is characterized by (p. 318)
    a. craving for nicotine.
    b. irritability and frustration.
    c. anger.
    d. All of the above

Practice Test 3

1. The desire to obtain narcotics can (p. 321)
    a. lead to socially maladaptive behavior.
    b. force the addict to lie, steal, and associate with undesirable contacts.
    c. cause females to turn to prostitution as a means to finance their addiction.
    d. All of the above

2. The most frequently cited reason for beginning to use heroin was (p. 321)
    a. pleasure.
    b. curiosity.
    c. peer pressure.
    d. All of the above

3. Cocaine _____ the action of the central nervous system. (p. 323)
    a. increases
    b. decreases
    c. equalizes
    d. negates

4. In 2000 about _____ percent of emergency room visits were cocaine related. (p. 323)

       a. 1.732

       b. 4

       c. 13

       d. 29

5. Many life problems experienced by cocaine abusers result, in part, from (p. 323)

       a. the low quality of people they are forced to deal with.

       b. the considerable amounts of money required to support their habits.

       c. dysfunction and disinterest in sexual performance.

       d. fetal crack syndrome.

6. The earliest amphetamine—Benzedrine—was first synthesized as an inhalant to relieve stuffy noses. However, it was soon withdrawn because (p. 324)

       a. it was so powerful that stuffy noses ceased to be a problem.

       b. some customers were chewing the wicks in the inhalers for "kicks."

       c. it didn't work.

       d. it was discovered that nutmeg worked just as well.

7. Curiously, amphetamines have _____ effect on many youngsters. (p. 324)

       a. a stimulating

       b. a calming

       c. an invigorating

       d. no

8. Methedrine, used in large amounts, can raise blood pressure (p. 324)

       a. enough to cause immediate death.

       b. slightly.

       c. over a period of time.

       d. it does not raise blood pressure in any amount.

9. A common effect of barbiturates is (p. 325)

       a. slow speech.

       b. impaired decision making and problem solving.

       c. sudden mood shifts.

       d. All of the above

10. Psychedelic drugs do not, in fact, "create" sensory images, but (p. 326)

       a. increase the effects.

       b. distort them, so that a person sees or hears things in different and unusual ways.

       c. categorizes odd events.

       d. None of the above

COMPREHENSIVE PRACTICE TEST

The following tests are designed to give you an idea of how well you understood the entire chapter. There are three different types of tests: multiple-choice, true/false, and essay.

Multiple Choice

1. Alcohol abuse and dependency are _____ in the United States. (p. 302)
    a. not a serious problem
    b. a major problem
    c. required at some fraternities
    d. easily cured

2. The life expectancy with alcohol dependency is about _____ than that of the average citizen. (p. 302)
    a. 12 years shorter
    b. 12 years longer
    c. a couple of years shorter
    d. the same, but it seems longer

3. Excessive drinkers often suffer from (pp. 303–304)
    a. chronic fatigue, oversensitivity, and depression.
    b. lowered feelings of adequacy and worth, impaired reasoning and judgment, and gradual personality deterioration.
    c. coarse and inappropriate behavior, lowered pride and personal appearance, and generally touchiness and irritability.
    d. All of the above

4. A number of investigators have pointed out that the typical alcohol abuser is (p. 311)
    a. unable or unwilling to tolerate tension and stress.
    b. discontented with his or her life.
    c. misunderstood and just looking for a good time.
    d. a and b

5. Many young people begin to use alcohol because they expect that it will (p. 311)
    a. lower tension and anxiety.
    b. increase their popularity.
    c. increase sexual desire and pleasure in life.
    d. All of the above

6. Alcohol abuse and dependence are difficult to treat because (p. 313)
    a. many alcoholics refuse to admit they have a problem.
    b. they refuse to seek assistance before they "hit bottom."
    c. many leave treatment before therapy is completed.
    d. All of the above

7. A multidisciplinary approach to the treatment of drinking problems appears to be most effective because (p. 313)
  a. the problems are often complex.
  b. researchers really aren't sure what works yet.
  c. a substance abuser's needs change as treatment progresses.
  d. a and b

8. Caffeine and nicotine are (p. 317)
  a. drugs of dependence.
  b. mild hallucinogens.
  c. mild depressants.
  d. harmless pastimes.

9. Factors that predispose an individual to substance abuse probably include (p. 312)
  a. the presence of an alcoholic father.
  b. marital accord.
  c. feelings of inadequacy.
  d. a and c

10. The use of opium derivatives over a period of time usually results in a physiological craving for the drug. The time required varies, but it has been estimated that continual use over a period of _____ is sufficient. (p. 321)
  a. three days
  b. two weeks
  c. thirty days
  d. one year

11. Strong doses of barbiturates cause sleep almost immediately. Excessive doses (p. 325)
  a. are lethal.
  b. are extremely enlightening.
  c. cause the dance gene to take control, and the user will not be able to sit still.
  d. None of the above

12. When people quit using cocaine they (p. 323)
  a. do not develop any physiological signs of dependence.
  b. develop transient depressive symptoms.
  c. feel better within a few weeks of therapy.
  d. b and c

13. Ecstasy users have been found to be more likely to (p. 327)
  a. use marijuana.
  b. engage in binge drinking.
  c. have multiple sexual partners.
  d. All of the above

14. Until the late 1960s, marijuana use in the United States was confined largely to (p. 327)
    a. members of lower socioeconomic minority groups.
    b. people in the entertainment and related fields.
    c. British rock groups.
    d. a and b

15. Continued use of high dosages of marijuana over time tends to produce (p. 328)
    a. increased energy.
    b. clear and concise thinking.
    c. lethargy and passivity.
    d. None of the above

16. Alcohol inhibits _____ in the brain, which impairs the organism's ability to learn and affects the higher brain centers, impairing judgment and other rational processes and lowering self-control. (p. 304)
    a. glutamate
    b. acetylcholine
    c. serotonin
    d. dopamine

17. Dennis had abused Vicodin for the past eleven months. He experienced extremely painful withdrawal as his body needed time to produce its own opium-like substance called (p. 322)
    a. acetylcholine.
    b. endorphins.
    c. catecholamines.
    d. dopamine.

18. Terence exceeded his dosage of this type of drug, which resulted in elevated blood pressure, enlarged pupils, rapid speech, tremors, sweating, confusion, and extreme excitability. (p. 324)
    a. amphetamine
    b. barbiturates
    c. anxiolytics
    d. antidepressants

19. Jimmy noticed that this new medication his doctor prescribed made him relaxed, sluggish, and drowsy. He was given which type of drug? (p. 325)
    a. amphetamine
    b. barbiturates
    c. anxiolytics
    d. antidepressants

20. As Sam and Sarah were partying in the club, they decided to try this new pill, and in twenty minutes they felt a rush sensation, then a feeling of calmness, energy, and well-being. They started to sweat profusely, and Sarah began clenching her teeth. They most likely ingested (p. 326)

        a. amphetamine.
        b. heroin.
        c. MDMA.
        d. MNDA.

TRUE/FALSE

1. T / F Tolerance for a substance is the need for less and less to achieve the desired effect. (p. 301)

2. T / F Substance dependence means that an individual will show tolerance for a drug and/or withdrawal symptoms when the drug is unavailable. (p. 301)

3. T / F One in seven deaths are associated with cigarette consumption. (p. 318)

4. T / F Men are about five times more likely to have an alcohol problem then women. (p. 302)

5. T / F In a study, college freshmen from families with alcohol-abusing parents viewed their families as less healthy and had more problematic family relationships than those with nonalcohol-abusing parents. (p. 310)

6. T / F There is a strong association between antisocial personality disorder and alcohol, aggression, and high rates of substance abuse. (p. 310)

7. T / F Excessive use of alcohol is one of the most frequent causes of divorce in the United States. (p. 311)

8. T / F Users of opium derivatives gradually build up a tolerance to the drug, so that increasingly larger amounts are needed to achieve the desired effects. (p. 321)

9. T / F The efficacy of Alcoholics Anonymous has been carefully tested clinically. (p. 315)

10. T / F Planning for relapse actually helps people to cope with a substance abuse problem. (p. 317)

11. T / F Addicts often dread the discomfort of withdrawal, but in a hospital setting, it is less abrupt and usually involves the administration of medications that eases the distress. (p. 322)

12. T / F Amphetamines were initially considered to be "wonder pills" that helped people stay alert, and were used by both the Allied and German soldiers to ward off fatigue during World War II. (p. 324)

13. T / F Chronic alcohol use may result in cirrhosis of the liver as well as malnutrition. (p. 305)

14. T / F Antidepressants such as diazepam reduce the severity of alcohol withdrawal symptoms. (p. 313)

15. T / F Caffeine and nicotine are widely available and are NOT considered drugs of dependence by the DSM-IV-TR. (p. 318)

16. T / F Cocaine precipitates a euphoric state of two to four hours' duration, during which a user experiences feelings of confidence and contentment. (p. 323)

17. T / F LSD can produce intoxication with an amount smaller than a grain of salt. (p. 326)

18. T / F There is a strong relationship between daily marijuana use and the occurrence of psychotic symptoms. (p. 327)

19. T / F Marijuana does NOT induce memory dysfunction and a slowing of information processing. (p. 328)

20. T / F An interesting and unusual phenomenon that may occur some time following the use of LSD is the flashback. (p. 326)

Essay Questions

1. Alcohol has complex and seemingly contradictory effects on the brain from the activation of the brain's "pleasure areas" to the health risks and degradation that can result from heavy and long-term use. Discuss this, particularly in relation to the items below. (pp. 303–312)

a. physiological effects

b. abilities

c. pregnancy

d. chronic use

e. dependence

f. organic damage

g. physical and mental decline

2. Discuss the controversy about whether alcoholics need to give up drinking altogether or can learn to drink moderately. (pp. 313–315)

3. Discuss heroin withdrawal. (pp. 321–323)

WHEN YOU HAVE FINISHED

WEB LINKS TO ITEMS OR CONCEPTS DISCUSSED IN CHAPTER 10

Web Site of the Substance Abuse and Mental Health Services Administration (SAMHSA)
http://www.samhsa.gov/

This is the official Web site of the Substance Abuse and Mental Health Services Administration (SAMHSA), which focuses on programs and funding to improve the lives of people with or who are at risk for mental and substance abuse disorders. There are many trusted links and a wealth of information on substance abuse and dependence.

Addiction Treatment Forum
http://www.atforum.com/

The homepage of the Addiction Treatment Forum provides up-to-date information on substance abuse and addiction therapies, current research, and the latest news in the field.

National Institute on Alcohol Abuse and Alcoholism (NIAAA)
http://www.niaaa.nih.gov/

The home page of the National Institute on Alcohol Abuse and Alcoholism (NIAAA) provides current information on the research that it conducts and supports, information on alcoholism, useful links, and a copy of its newsletter.

SAMHSA's National Clearinghouse for Alcohol and Drug Information
http://ncadi.samhsa.gov/links/
This is SAMHSA's National Clearinghouse for Alcohol and Drug Information, which covers nearly every topic on substance, and substance-related disorders as well as links to recovery, support, and self-help.

Marijuana Use Presented by the National Institute on Drug Abuse
http://www.nida.nih.gov/DrugPages/Marijuana.html
The National Institute on Drug Abuse presents a Web page devoted entirely to marijuana use and dependence.

Cocaine Use Presented by the National Institute on Drug Abuse
http://www.nida.nih.gov/DrugPages/Cocaine.html
The National Institute on Drug Abuse presents a Web page devoted entirely to cocaine use and dependence.

LSD Use Presented by the National Institute on Drug Abuse
http://www.nida.nih.gov/Infofacts/LSD.html
The National Institute on Drug Abuse has a Web page devoted entirely to facts and information on LSD.

The University of Indiana Web Page on Frequently Used Substances
http://www.drugs.indiana.edu
The University of Indiana developed this Web site to make available information about frequently abused substance. This page will link you to cocaine, ecstasy, ketamine, and benzodiazepines.

USE IT OR LOSE IT
Provide an answer to the thought question below, knowing that there is more than one way to respond. Possible answers are presented in the Answer Key.

Do you think that people can be addicted to positive behaviors such as exercise in much the same way they can become addicted to various substances?

CRISSCROSS

Now that you know all there is to know about this chapter, here's your opportunity to put that knowledge to work.

Across

1. Hallucinogen and stimulant currently popular as a party drug
5. The poisonous nature of a substance
6. A person with a serious drinking problem
7. Involves marked physiological need for a substance and produces withdrawal symptoms, if unavailable
8. The need for increasing amounts of a substance
9. Widely used poisonous alkaloid; very addictive; difficult withdrawal; causes many deaths annually
10. Grows as a plant, highly addictive; morphine and heroin are derived from it
11. Opium derivative; removed from medical practice
12. Thought to be a mild pick-me-up, has intoxicating and/or withdrawal potential

Down

2. Pathological use resulting in potentially hazardous behavior, or persistent social or health problems
3. Behavior based on the pathological need for a substance
4. Drug used as replacement for heroin during treatment

Puzzle created with Puzzlemaker at DiscoverySchool.com

ANSWERS TO TEST QUESTIONS – CHAPTER 10

MATCHING
G. Alcohol
A. Caffeine
E. Nicotine
D. Ecstasy
I. Opium
K. Morphine
L. Heroin
M. Methadone
H. Cocaine
C. Amphetamine
N. Barbiturates
F. LSD
J. Mescaline
B. Marijuana

SHORT ANSWERS
Your answer should contain the following points.

1. With reference to drinking any alcohol during pregnancy:
   a. even moderate amounts of alcohol believed to be dangerous.
   b. fetal alcohol syndrome (FAS) may occur.
   c. birth defects, such as mental retardation, may also occur.

2. The two factors apparently involved in the overpowering hold that occurs in some people after only a few uses of a drug, such as opium, cocaine, or alcohol, are
   a. some drugs activate areas of the brain that produce pleasure;
   b. a person's genetic and biological make-up.

3. The neurochemical process underlying addiction and the role the drug plays in activating the "pleasure pathway" includes a discussion of
   a. the mesocorticolimbic dopamine pathway (MCLP).
   b. alcohol and other drugs that produce euphoria by stimulating this area in the brain.

4. Alcohol-related problems that may result from living in an environment that promotes use of the substance:
   a. lack of stability in family relationships and parental guidance.
   b. children witness parents using alcohol or drugs.
   c. negative parental models have long-range negative consequences.
   d. role models and media promote alcohol as stress reducer.
   e. alcohol promoted to increase popularity and acceptance in younger persons.

5. An "alcoholic personality"
   a. self-medicates with alcohol to reduce discomfort.
   b. is emotionally immature, expects a great deal of the world, requires praise, feels inferior, has low frustration for tolerance, is unsure of abilities to fulfill expected male or female roles.
   c. tends to be impulsive and aggressive.

6. The immediate effects of mainlined or snorted heroin are
   a. euphoric spasm (60 seconds or so);
   b. followed by a high (lethargic, withdrawn—typically four to six hours);
   c. negative phase that produces a desire for more.

7. The view that cocaine users did not develop physiological dependence has changed over the past twenty years because
   a. acute tolerance has now been demonstrated.
   b. of a significant increase in knowledge of cocaine's addictive properties
   c. a new disorder is described—cocaine withdrawal.
   d. the psychological and life problems experienced by cocaine users are often great—often related to the considerable amount of money required to support their habits.

THE DOCTOR IS IN...PSYCHIATRIC HELP—5¢
Your answer should include the following points.

1. a. Possible use of medications to reduce cravings and ease detoxification process
b. Group therapy—peers who will provide a confrontational give-and-take atmosphere; possibly have Tony's wife take part in a group for spouses of alcohol abusers
c. Family therapy/treatment—to work out the family dynamics
d. Behavioral therapy—aversive conditioning, behavioral couples therapy
e. Cognitive-behavioral approach recommended by Marlatt—combines cognitive-behavioral strategies of intervention with social-learning and modeling of behavior
f. Possibly look at controlled drinking or AA meetings
g. Be sure to look at relapse prevention

2. Martin is taking barbiturates. His behavior; not sleeping, then being able to do so with the pill; sluggishness; impaired cognition and mood swings all indicate the use of sedatives. Potential danger is death, since he is taking the barbiturates and drinking.

PRACTICE TESTS

Q#	TEST 1	TEST 2	TEST 3
1	B	A	D
2	D	C	D
3	D	C	A
4	C	B	D
5	C	B	B

6	C	A	B
7	D	D	B
8	D	B	A
9	D	C	D
10	B	D	B

COMPREHENSIVE PRACTICE TEST

Q#	M/C	T/F
1	B	F
2	A	T
3	D	T
4	D	T
5	D	T
6	D	T
7	D	T
8	A	T
9	D	F
10	C	F
11	A	T
12	B	T
13	D	T
14	D	F
15	C	F
16	A	F
17	B	T
18	A	T
19	B	F
20	C	T

Essay Questions
Your answers should contain the following points.

1. a. physiological effects—depresses brain functioning, inhibiting glutamate, affects higher brain center, impairing judgment and other rational processes and lowering self control.
b. abilities—decreased sexual performance, blackouts (lapses of memory), hangover
c. pregnancy—possible fetal alcohol syndrome, producing birth defects, such as mental retardation
d. chronic use—suffers chronic fatigue, oversensitivity, and depression
e. dependence—can produce lowered feelings of adequacy and worth
f. organic damage—alcohol must be assimilated by the liver, which may suffer irreversible damage; 26,000 annual cirrhosis deaths from alcohol

g. physical and mental decline—impaired reasoning and judgment, and gradual personality deterioration

2. a. controlled drinking, the ability to start drinking after drying out, is possible, it seems, in some cases of less severe situations
b. AA view is that once a person is an alcoholic that person is always at risk and always in recovery, one day at a time.

3. a. addicted users find they feel physically ill when they do not take it
b. after approximately eight hours withdrawal symptoms begin
• severity depends on many factors: amount used, duration of addiction, addict's health and personality
c. can be agonizing with symptoms including runny nose, tearing eyes, perspiration, restlessness
• symptoms get worse as time rolls on: chilliness alternates with flushing and excessive sweating, vomiting, diarrhea, abdominal cramps, pains, dehydration
• occasionally symptoms include delirium, hallucinations, manic activity
• cardiovascular collapse and death is a possibility
d. symptoms are usually on the decline by the third or fourth day, gone by seventh or eighth

USE IT OR LOSE IT

The correct answer to this question is a matter of opinion. Some people believe that the term *addiction* should only be used to refer to negative behaviors. However, others argue that people can be addicted to things like exercise, if they are unable to discontinue the behavior even when it is causing problems in their health or personal life.

CRISSCROSS ANSWERS

Across
1. Ecstasy
5. Toxicity
6. Alcoholic
7. Dependence
8. Tolerance
9. Nicotine
10. Opium
11. Heroin
12. Caffeine

Down
2. Substance abuse
3. Addictive behavior
4. Methadone

Chapter 11: Sexual Variants, Abuse, and Dysfunctions

BEFORE YOU READ

Paradoxically, sex is a common topic in the movies, on television, and in music, yet we rarely talk about it openly in our own lives, and often wonder about other people's sexuality, whether we are normal, and how to manage sexual problems. This chapter emphasizes the variability in sexual attitudes and behaviors across cultures. It also focuses on a particularly timely topic, homosexuality, which is not considered a sexual deviation in the current version of the DSM-IV-TR. Sexual issues that do cause psychological difficulty for individuals can be classified as sexual variants, sexual abuse, or sexual dysfunctions. Sexual variants include paraphilias in which individuals seek sexual arousal via nonhuman subjects, hurting others or being hurt, or interacting with nonconsenting partners. For example touching or fondling shoes excites people with a shoe fetish, masochists and sadists are people who are sexually aroused by suffering humiliation or hurting others respectively, and pedophiles respond sexually to minors. Gender identity disorders, characterized by strong discomfort with one's own sex, are also classified as sexual variants. Sexual abuse or sexual behavior, characterized by coercion and lack of consent, is discussed in terms of its negative psychological impact on the victim and its adverse impact on society. The third section concerns sexual dysfunctions—problems that may interfere with an individual's full enjoyment of sexual relations, but fortunately are the most treatable disorders discussed.

- **SOCIOCULTURAL INFLUENCES ON SEXUAL PRACTICES AND STANDARDS**
  Homosexuality and American Psychiatry

- **SEXUAL AND GENDER VARIANTS**
  The Paraphilias
  Causal Factors and Treatments for Paraphilias
  Gender Identity Disorders

- **SEXUAL ABUSE**
  Childhood Sexual Abuse
  Pedophilia
  Incest
  Rape
  Treatment and Recidivism of Sex Offenders

- **SEXUAL DYSFUNCTIONS**
  Dysfunctions of Sexual Desire
  Dysfunctions of Sexual Arousal
  Orgasmic Disorders
  Dysfunctions Involving Sexual Pain

- **UNRESOLVED ISSUES**
  How Harmful Is Childhood Sexual Abuse?

CHAPTER 11: CORE CONCEPTS

OBJECTIVES
After reading this chapter, you should be able to do the following:

1. Provide a number of examples of sociocultural influences on sexual practices.

2. Describe the clinical features of the following paraphilias: fetishism, transvestic fetishism, voyeurism, exhibitionism, sadism, masochism, and pedophilias.

3. Discuss the most effective treatments for paraphilias, and summarize causal factors implicated in their etiology.

4. Define and describe the clinical features and treatment of the gender identity disorders (gender identity disorder of childhood, transsexualism).

5. Review what is known about the frequency and nature of childhood sexual abuse. Discuss the controversies surrounding childhood testimony regarding sexual abuse and adult "recovered memories" of childhood sexual abuse.

6. Define pedophilia and summarize what is known about pedophiles.

7. Review what is known about the frequency and nature of incest.

8. Summarize what is known about rape and rapists, and discuss the issues regarding the frequency of rape and the motivation of rapists.

9. Describe attempts to treat sex offenders.

10. Define the sexual dysfunctions, describe their general features, review etiological theories, and summarize the major approaches to treatment.

11. Knowledgeably discuss the difficulty of deciding the extent of the harm caused by childhood sexual abuse.

AS YOU READ
Answers can be found in the Answer Key at the end of the book.

KEY WORDS
Each of the words below is important in understanding the concepts presented in this chapter. Write the definition next to each word.

Term	Page	Definition
Autogynephilia	343	
Cross-gender identification	341	
Desire phase	353	
Dyspareunia	358	

Excitement phase	353	
Exhibitionism	339	
Female orgasmic disorder	357	
Female sexual arousal disorder	356	
Fetishism	336	
Gender dysphoria	341	
Gender identity disorder	341	
Hypoactive sexual desire disorder	353	
Incest	347	
Male erectile disorder	355	
Male orgasmic disorder	357	
Masochism	340	
Orgasm	353	
Paraphilias	335	
Pedophilia	346	
Premature ejaculation	356	
Rape	347	
Resolution	353	
Sadism	339	
Sexual abuse	344	
Sexual aversion disorder	353	
Sexual dysfunction	352	
Transsexualism	342	
Transvestic fetishism	336	
Vaginismus	358	
Voyeurism	338	

MATCHING
Who's Who and What's What
Match the following dysfunction with the appropriate answer.

Dysfunction

       of Sexual Desire
_____ Hypoactive sexual desire disorder
_____ Sexual aversion disorder

       of Sexual Arousal
_____ Male erectile disorder
_____ Female sexual arousal disorder

       of Orgasm
_____ Premature ejaculation
_____ Male orgasmic disorder
_____ Female orgasmic disorder

       Sexual Pain Disorders
_____ Vaginismus
_____ Dyspareunia

Characteristics
    A. A. Inability to achieve or maintain an erection
    B. Difficulty in achieving orgasm, either manually or during sexual intercourse
    C. Painful coitus; may have either organic or psychological basis
    D. Little or no sexual drive or interest
    E. Nonresponsiveness to erotic stimulation, physically and emotionally
    F. Inability to ejaculate during intercourse
    G. Involuntary muscle spasm at the entrance to the vagina preventing penetration
    H. Total lack of interest in sex and avoidance of sexual contact
    I. Unsatisfactorily brief period between the beginning of sexual stimulation and ejaculation

SHORT ANSWERS
Provide brief answers to the following questions.

1. Why has research on childhood sexual abuse increased in the past decade?
(p. 344)

2. What are the controversies concerning childhood sexual abuse? (p. 344)

3. Discuss the difference between incest and rape. (pp. 347–348)

4. Describe the four phases of human sexual response. (p. 353)

5. Per the DSM-IV-TR, during which phases can disorders occur? (p. 353)

THE DOCTOR IS IN...PSYCHIATRIC HELP—5¢
Read the following scenarios and diagnose the client. Remember to look carefully at the criteria for the disorder before you make a decision as to the diagnosis. Make a list of other information you might need to help you understand the causal factors.

1. Jim was referred to you by the courts. He was caught after breaking into a woman's house to steal her underwear. Jim says that he is almost relieved at being caught, as his problem was getting worse. He uses the underwear to fantasize while he masturbates. You ask him how long this behavior has been going on and he tells you that he has had these feelings since he was an adolescent; he found one of his sister's girlfriend's underwear in the bathroom (he had a crush on her).

How would you diagnose Jim and why?

2. Darla comes to your office. She is an attractive female in her late 40s. She begins by telling you that she was born a boy but always felt like a girl. She never wanted to play boy games, preferred to be with girls, and often wished she would wake up in the morning and find that she had become a girl. She began cross-dressing almost twenty years ago and has lived full-time as a female for the past ten years. Darla has been on hormones for several years and is planning to have surgery. She is employed as a secretary and has passed as a woman for many years.

How would you diagnose Darla? Why and what would you recommend as treatment?

3. Susan and Ben come to your office seeking couple's counseling. They are both frustrated with their sexual relations. Susan experiences involuntary spasms around her vagina when they attempt to have intercourse. It is very painful, and she can't go on. This has begun to affect Ben, and he has started to have erectile dysfunctions. They love each other very much and want to work this out.

How would you diagnose the problem and what else would you want to know about the couple?

AFTER YOU READ

PRACTICE TESTS
Take the following three multiple-choice tests to see how much you have comprehended from the chapter. Each represents roughly one third of the chapter. As you study the chapter, use these to check your progress.

Practice Test 1

1. Several prominent sexologists suggested that homosexuality is (p. 333)
   a. wrong.
   b. questionable.
   c. natural and consistent with psychological normality.
   d. natural and consistent with psychological abnormality.

2. Homosexuality was removed as a sexual deviation from the DSM in (p. 334)
   a. 1966.
   b. 1974.
   c. 1981.
   d. 1977.

3. Glenn is a 35-year-old married man who cross-dresses. He becomes sexually aroused while looking at himself dressed as a woman. His wife is aware of his cross-dressing and doesn't have a problem with it. Glenn is considered to have a (p. 337)
   a. transvestic fetish.
   a. exhibitionistic fetish.
   c. voyeuristic fetish.
   d. fetish fetish.

4. A Peeping Tom is another name for someone who is a(n) (p. 338)
    a. exhibitionist.
    b. transvestite.
    c. erotophilia.
    d. voyeur.

5. The legal term for _____ is *indecent exposure*. (p. 339)
    a. exhibitionism
    b. transvestism
    c. erotophilism
    d. voyeurism

6. Steve finds great sexual pleasure in being bound by his lover and humiliated—and sometimes whipped. He has participated in this behavior for more than two years now. Steve would be considered a(n) (p. 340)
    a. sadist.
    b. transvestite.
    c. exhibitionist.
    d. masochist.

7. Voyeurs tend to be (p. 339)
    a. violent.
    b. otherwise noncriminal in their behavior.
    c. egocentric.
    d. rapists.

8. _____ appears in genetic males and is a paraphilia characterized by sexual arousal at the thought or fantasy of being a woman. (p. 343)
    a. Autoeroticism
    b. Autogynephilia
    c. Gynoplasticism
    d. None of the above

9. The accuracy of children's testimony is an issue because children (p. 344)
    a. are susceptible to the influence of others.
    b. can't always distinguish fact from fantasy.
    c. are not called on to testify all that often.
    d. a and b

10. Recovered memories are considered (p. 346)
    a. controversial.
    b. absolutely true.
    c. totally false.
    d. b and c

Practice Test 2

1. _____ is diagnosed when an adult has recurrent, intense sexual urges or fantasies about sexual activity with a prepubescent child. (p. 346)
    a. Paraphilia
    b. Pedophilia
    c. Erotophilia
    d. Fetishism

2. The typical victim of a pedophile is a girl between the ages of (p. 346)
    a. 5 and 8.
    b. 15 and 18.
    c. 12 and 15.
    d. 8 and 11.

3. _____ is sexual activity that occurs under actual or threatened forcible coercion of one person by another. (p. 347)
    a. Incest
    b. Rape
    c. Sadism
    d. Masochism

4. In most societies incest is (p. 347)
    a. promoted.
    b. forbidden.
    c. tolerated.
    d. forgiven.

5. What percentage of rapes is committed in the rapist's neighborhood? (p. 348)
    a. 50
    b. 80
    c. 45
    d. 38

6. About how many rapes are single-offender rapes in which the victim may know the offender? (p. 349)
    a. One third
    b. One half
    c. Two thirds
    d. One quarter

7. The psychological impact of rape is called (p. 348)
    a. rape trauma disorder.
    b. rape stress disorder.
    c. acute trauma syndrome.

    d. post-traumatic stress disorder.

8. Rape is motivated by the need to (p. 348)
    a. dominate, assert power, and humiliate the victim.
    b. dominate, assert power, and anger the victim.
    c. share, assert power, and humiliate the victim.
    d. excite, assert power, and humiliate the victim.

9. _____ rape is a favorite tactic of defense attorneys, which some police and court jurisdictions still believe, even though it is a myth. (p. 349)
    a. Victim-credibility
    b. Victim-consent
    c. Victim-precipitated
    d. None of the above

10. Rapists show some deficits in their cognitive appraisals of women's (p. 350)
    a. feelings.
    b. intentions.
    c. boundaries.
    d. a and b

Practice Test 3

1. Recently, both explanations and treatments of sexual dysfunction have become increasingly (pp. 352–353)
    a. psychological.
    b. behavioral.
    c. biological.
    d. less obvious.

2. The DSM-IV-TR says that sexual dysfunction can occur in which phase? (p. 353)
    a. desire
    b. excitement
    c. orgasm
    d. All of the above

3. Hypoactive sexual desire disorder seems to have a very strong _____ component, especially for women. (p. 353)
    a. psychological
    b. physiological
    c. behavioral
    d. None of the above

4. In this type of sexual desire dysfunction, the person shows extreme avoidance of all genital sexual contact with a partner. (p. 353)
    a. hypoactive sexual desire disorder
    b. sexual aversion disorder
    c. erectile insufficiency
    d. sexual repulsion disorder

5. Sexual interest in men and women depends on (p. 353)
    a. estrogen.
    b. dopamine.
    c. serotonin.
    d. testosterone.

6. The general neglect of research and treatment of female sexual dysfunction is an implicit attitude that women don't care about (p. 355)
    a. their bodies.
    b. their relationships.
    c. sex.
    d. the NFL.

7. _____ was formerly called impotence. (p. 355)
    a. Erectile contraction disorder
    b. Male erectile disorder
    c. Priapism
    d. All of the above

8. Masters, Johnson, and Kaplan believed that erectile dysfunction was primarily a function of _____ about sexual performance. (p. 355)
    a. excitement
    b. interest
    c. anxiety
    e. fantasizing

9. Viagra will promote an erection only if _____ is present. (p. 356)
    a. a partner
    b. sexual desire
    c. an opportunity
    d. All of the above

10. Premature ejaculation is most likely to occur in (p. 356)
    a. young men
    b. after abstinence
    c. men over 60
    d. a and b

COMPREHENSIVE PRACTICE TEST
The following tests are designed to give you an idea of how well you understood the entire chapter. There are three different types of tests: multiple-choice, true/false, and essay.

Multiple Choice

1. The major reason that there are fewer sex researchers than other researchers is (p. 352)
      a. sexual taboos.
      b. sexual issues are controversial.
      c. nobody is interested in sexual issues.
      d. a and b

2. This person is distinguished by the recurrent, intense sexually arousing fantasies, urges, and behaviors involving the use of some inanimate object to obtain gratification. (p. 335)
      a. fetishist
      b. voyeur
      c. pedophile
      d. sexual sadist

3. Terry is a 40-year-old married man, but he likes to dress up in his wife's clothing. He also buys women's clothing for himself under the illusion he is buying it for his wife. Terry would have (p. 336)
      a. fetishism.
      b. voyeurism.
      c. pedophilia.
      d. transvestic fetishism.

4. The DSM-IV-TR criteria for this group of disorders is a persistent pattern, lasting at least six months, that causes significant distress or impairment, in which unusual objects, rituals, or situations are required for full sexual satisfaction. (p. 336)
      a. pedophilias
      b. paraphilias
      c. erotophilias
      d. All of the above

5. Ted Bundy and Jeffrey Dahmer were cited in your textbook as extreme examples of this paraphilia. (p. 340)
      a. masochism
      b. sadism
      c. voyeurism
      d. frotteurism

6. Sexual abuse includes (p. 344)
     a. pedophilia.
     b. rape.
     c. incest.
     d. All of the above

7. Although short-term consequences of childhood sexual abuse include fears, PTSD, sexual inappropriateness, and poor self-esteem, approximately _____ of sexually abused children show no symptoms. (p. 344)
     a. one half
     b. a quarter
     c. two thirds
     d. one third

8. Long-term consequences of childhood sexual abuse may include (p. 344)
     a. dissociative symptoms.
     b. somatization disorder.
     c. borderline personality disorder.
     d. All of the above

9. Culturally prohibited relations between family members, such as brother and sister or parent and child, are known as (p. 347)
     a. rape.
     b. acquaintance rape.
     c. incest.
     d. paraphilia.

10. This is the most common form of incest but it is rarely reported. (p. 347)
     a. father-daughter
     b. mother-son
     c. uncle-niece
     d. brother-sister

11. According to the FBI Uniform Crime Reports, the greatest concentration of rapists arrested is between _____ years old. (p. 349)
     a. 18 and 24
     b. 25 and 35
     c. 15 and 20
     d. 16 and 23

12. It is difficult to establish the prevalence rates for rape, because studies may (p. 349)
     a. vary in the definitions used.
     b. vary in the way information is gathered.
     c. not have enough subjects.
     d. a and b

13. The age distribution of rape victims is not at all random but includes a very high proportion of women in their (p. 348)
    a. teens and early forties.
    b. teens and early thirties.
    c. teens and late twenties.
    d. teens and early twenties.

14. _____ is most likely to occur after a lengthy abstinence and is the most common male sexual dysfunction. (p. 356)
    a. Impotence
    b. Male erectile disorder
    c. Male orgasmic disorder
    d. Premature ejaculation

15. When treating female orgasmic disorder, it is important to distinguish between a(n)_____ and a(n) _____ dysfunction. (p. 357)
    a. past, present
    b. subjective, objective
    c. lifelong, situational
    d. interest, disinterest

16. _____ in women is more likely to have an obvious organic basis. (p. 358)
    a. Female orgasmic disorder
    b. Female sexual arousal disorder
    c. Vaginismus
    d. Dyspareunia

17. Lou keeps getting caught in the women's locker room at the gym. At first, the managers thought he was just lost; however, this is now the fifth time. Lou also likes to watch his neighbor across the street at various times of the day. This is an example of (p. 338)
    a. masochism.
    b. sadism.
    c. voyeurism.
    d. frotteurism.

18. Peter was finally arrested after a three-month spree of exposing himself to women and children in the park. This is an example of (p. 339)
    a. masochism.
    b. exhibitionism.
    c. voyeurism.
    d. frotteurism.

19. After being arrested, Paul confessed to the police psychologist that his date did not consent to the twenty lashes he gave her with a riding crop. He said that while she did not like it, he enjoyed every minute of it and had an orgasm. This case is an example of (p. 339)
>   a. masochism.
>   b. exhibitionism.
>   c. voyeurism.
>   d. sadism.

20. George enjoyed when his wife took the dominant role and he became her slave. She would dress up in leather, tie him to the bed face down, and whip him repeatedly with a stick. George said it kept his relationship fresh. This is an example of (p. 340)
>   a. masochism.
>   b. exhibitionism.
>   c. voyeurism.
>   d. sadism.

TRUE/FALSE

1. T / F Homosexuality is still considered a mental disorder by the American Psychiatric Association. (p. 334)

2 T / F The belief that homosexuality is a mental illness has been associated with people's discomfort concerning the sexual behaviors of homosexual people. (p. 334)

3. T / F Nearly all the people with paraphilias are female. (p. 335)

4. T / F Fetishes cause overt harm to others only when accompanied by illegal acts like theft or destruction of property. (p. 336)

5. T / F Voyeurism is the most common sexual offense reported to the police in the United States, Canada, and Europe. (p. 338)

6. T / F The DSM-IV-TR recognizes eight specific paraphilias. (p. 335)

7 T / F Sexual abuse is sexual contact that involves physical or psychological coercion or at least one individual who cannot reasonably consent to the contact. (p. 344)

8. T / F Research has shown that the use of anatomically correct dolls greatly increases the accuracy of 3- or 4-year-olds' reports of what happened to them. (p. 346)

9. T / F The incest taboo is virtually universal among human societies. (p. 347)

10. T / F If the partner is under 18, but consents, it can't be considered statutory rape. (p. 347)

11. T / F Most rapes involve more than one rapist. (p. 347)

12. T / F Conviction rates for rape are low. (p. 349)

13. T / F Megan's Law, intended to protect potential victims, has also encouraged harassment of sex offenders. (p. 351)

14. T / F A high percentage of people will never experience a sexual dysfunction in their lifetime. (p. 353)

15. T / F Autogynephilia is paraphilic sexual arousal by the thought or fantasy of being a woman. (p. 343)

16. T / F Exhibitionism is the most common sexual offense reported to the police in the United States, Canada, and Europe. (p. 339)

17. T / F The most common short-term consequences of childhood sexual abuse are PTSD, sexual inappropriateness, and poor self-esteem. (p. 344)

18. T / F Nearly all are pedophiles are female, and about two thirds of their victims are boys. (p. 346)

19. T / F The most frequent cause of erectile disorder in older men is due to vascular disease. (p. 355)

20. T / F Female sexual arousal disorder can be diagnosed in women who are readily sexually excitable and who otherwise enjoy sexual activity but who show persistent or recurrent delay in or absence of orgasm following a normal sexual excitement phase. (p. 356)

Essay Questions

1. Discuss the types of treatment that are used with sex offenders (psychological, biological, surgical), the goals, and effectiveness. (pp. 350–352)

2. What were some of the conclusions of Bruce Rind's research on the association between early sexual experiences and mental health in young adulthood? (p. 359)

3. Please explain three of the eight specific paraphilias. (pp. 335–346)

4. Please describe the difference between sadism and masochism. (pp. 339–340)

5. Please describe the motivation behind rape. (p. 348)

WHEN YOU HAVE FINISHED

WEB LINKS TO ITEMS OR CONCEPTS DISCUSSED IN CHAPTER 11

Female Sexual Dysfunction and Treatments
http://www.aafp.org/afp/20000701/127.html
Dr. Nancy Philips provides an excellent and detailed explanation of female sexual dysfunction and associated treatments.

Female Sexual Dysfunction and Treatments
http://www.nlm.nih.gov/medlineplus/femalesexualdysfunction.html
There are numerous links and information on female sexual dysfunction on the Medline Plus Web site.

The Male Health Center
http://www.malehealthcenter.com/
The Male Health Center Web site provides numerous links and up-to-date information on all aspects of male health including sexual dysfunction.

Paraphilias and Fetishes
http://health.discovery.com/centers/sex/sexpedia/paraphilia.html
The Discovery Health Channel provides complete and detailed explanations of the paraphilias and fetishes.

Frotteurism
http://www.behavenet.com/capsules/disorders/frotteurismTR.htm
Information and diagnostic criteria of this little known disorder is presented here.

Forensic Psychiatry and the Paraphilias
>   http://www.forensicpsychiatry.ca/paraphilia/overview.htm
This Web site puts a forensic spin on paraphilias and was developed by a forensic psychiatrist.

Autoerotic Asphyxiation
>   http://www.aarrgghh.com/no_way/autoErot.htm
This is an interesting article on autoerotic asphyxiation and includes statistics and examples of cases.

Autoerotic Asphyxiation
>   http://www.autoerotic-asphyxiation.com/
This is probably one of the most informative Web sites on this curious and very dangerous form of sexual gratification.

Gender Identity Disorder
>   http://www.leaderu.com/jhs/rekers.html
Dr. George Rekers presents a well-written article on gender identity disorder.

Southern Arizona Gender Alliance
>   http://sagatucson.org/saga/
Southern Arizona Gender Alliance offers information on a wide variety of gender identity disorders, as well as pages on treatments, including gender reassignment, and links to other resources.

USE IT OR LOSE IT

Provide an answer to the thought question below, knowing that there is more than one way to respond. Possible answers are presented in the Answer Key.

Do you believe that people should be allowed to surgically change gender if they feel that their body is the wrong sex?

CRISSCROSS

Now that you know all there is to know about this chapter, here's your opportunity to put that knowledge to work.

Across

1. When an adult has sexual urges, fantasies, or activity with a prepubescent child
4. Sexual arousal by the thought of being a woman (males only)
5. Receiving sexual fantasies and behavior while observing unsuspecting females undressing or couples having sex
7. Behaviors involving exposure of genitals to others in inappropriate circumstances
8. Third sexual phase, resulting in the release of sexual tension and peak of sexual pleasure
9. Obtaining sexual gratification involving the use of some inanimate object (shoes, for instance)
10. Persons with gender identity disorder wishing to change their sex
11. Sexual contact that involves physical or psychological coercion

Down

2. Culturally prohibited sexual relations between family members
3. Experiencing sexual gratification by inflicting pain and cruelty
5. Involuntary spasm of the muscles at the entrance to the vagina, preventing penetration
6. Experiencing sexual stimulation from pain and degradation

Puzzle created with Puzzlemaker at Discoveryschool.com

ANSWERS TO TEST QUESTIONS – CHAPTER 11

MATCHING
Dysfunction

of Sexual Desire
D. Hypoactive sexual desire disorder
H. Sexual aversion disorder
of Sexual Arousal
A. Male erectile disorder
E. Female sexual arousal disorder
of Orgasm
I. Premature ejaculation
F. Male orgasmic disorder
B. Female orgasmic disorder
Sexual Pain Disorders
G. Vaginismus
C. Dyspareunia

SHORT ANSWERS
Your answer should contain the following points.

1. a. much more common than once was assumed
b. possible links between childhood sexual abuse and some mental disorders
c. some dramatic and well-publicized cases involving allegations of childhood sexual abuse have raised issues concerning validity of children's testimony and accuracy of recovered memories

2. There are questions as to the degree of validity of children's testimony, well-meaning therapists may coax recovered memories, and recovered memories are also questionable.

3. Incest is prohibited sexual relations between family members and more than likely involves forced or coerced sexual acts. Rape is sexual activity that occurs under actual or threatened conditions.

4. The desire phase, the excitement phase, orgasm, and resolution.

5. Disorders can occur in any of these phases: desire phase, the excitement phase, and orgasm.

THE DOCTOR IS IN...PSYCHIATRIC HELP—5¢
1. Jim has a fetish. He uses an inanimate (women's underwear) to obtain sexual gratification and has had the problem for more than six months. Also, it is causing him distress, and he seems to be concerned that it is getting worse.

2. a. Diagnosis: gender identity disorder/transsexualism. Darla meets the criteria for gender identity disorder. She has had a strong cross-gender identification (desire and insistence on being the opposite sex) and gender dysphoria (discomfort about her biological sex). She is now an adult and considered a transsexual.
b. Treatment: Psychotherapy is not effective in resolving gender dysphoria, so the best treatment would be to help Darla obtain sexual reassignment surgery.

3. a. Diagnosis: Vaginismus for Susan and situational erectile dysfunction for Ben
b. What else to know: Any past traumatic sexual experience for Susan, when did the problem start, and how have they handled the problem so far.

PRACTICE TESTS

Q#	TEST 1	TEST 2	TEST 3
1	C	B	C
2	B	D	D
3	A	B	A
4	D	B	B
5	A	B	D
6	D	C	C
7	B	D	B
8	B	A	C
9	D	C	B
10	A	D	B

COMPREHENSIVE PRACTICE TEST

Q#	M/C	T/F
1	D	T
2	A	T
3	D	F
4	B	T
5	B	F
6	D	F
7	D	T
8	D	F
9	C	T
10	D	F
11	A	T
12	D	T
13	D	T
14	D	F
15	C	T
16	D	T
17	C	T

18	B	F
19	D	T
20	A	F

Essay Questions
Your answer should contain the following points.

1. Goals:
-modify patterns of sexual arousal
-modify cognitions and social skills
-change habits or behaviors that increase the chance of reoffending
-reduce sexual drive

Therapies:
-Aversion therapy—growing skepticism about its efficacy as sole form of treatment aversion. *Therapy can involve these methods:* covert sensitization assisted covert sensitization satiation.
-Cognitive restructuring—attempts to eliminate cognitive distortions. *Often involves* social-skills training—learning to process information from women more effectively; relapse prevention—helps offender to understand the antecedents of his decision to offend. Cognitive-behavioral techniques appear more effective than aversion therapy.
-Surgical and chemical castration—lower the testosterone level, which lowers the sex drive, allowing the offender to resist any inappropriate impulses; relapse rates when the drugs/chemicals are discontinued are very high; recidivism rates of castrated offenders are typically less than three percent.

2. a. Correlations between childhood sexual abuse and later problems were of surprisingly small magnitude, suggesting that such experiences are not typically very harmful.
b. After statistically controlling for general family problems, the small association between CSA and adult problems was reduced to essentially zero—suggesting family problems might play a greater problem.
c. Incest and forced sex both associated with more problems than sex between nominally consenting nonrelated individuals.
d. Age at which CSA was experienced was unrelated to adult outcome.

3. Your answer should be specific and include three of the following: fetishism, transvestic fetishism, voyeurism, exhibitionism, sexual sadism, sexual masochism, pedophilia, and frotteurism.

4. In sadism, a person has recurrent, intense sexually arousing fantasies, urges, or behaviors that involve inflicting psychological or physical pain on another individual to gain sexual excitement.

In masochism, the person experiences recurrent, intense, sexually arousing fantasies, urges, or behaviors involving the act of being humiliated, beaten, or bound, often in a ritualistic pattern of behavior.

5. Rape is motivated by the need to dominate, to assert power, and to humiliate a victim rather than sexual desire for her. Rape is always an act of violence and is certainly not a sexually pleasurable experience, whatever the rapist's motivation.

USE IT OR LOSE IT

This is a complex question that depends on your personal beliefs about gender, sexual behaviors, and values. As more people speak out about transgender issues, and medical treatments advance, individual and societal approaches to changing ones gender may change as well.

CRISSCROSS ANSWERS

Across
1. Pedophilia
4. Autogynephilia
5. Voyeurism
7. Exhibitionism
8. Orgasm
9. Fetishism
10. Transsexualism
11. Sexual abuse

Down
2. Incest
3. Masochism
5. Vaginismus
6. Sadism

Chapter 12: Schizophrenia and Other Psychotic Disorders

BEFORE YOU READ

Schizophrenia is one of—if not the—most difficult of the mental disorders to treat and manage. By definition, schizophrenia impacts reasoning, thoughts, emotion, language, and motor behaviors. Additionally, it affects one's perception and social interactions, and has direct and indirect impacts on the person's health. This debilitating disorder affects one out of every hundred people. However, its distribution varies as a function of ethnicity, father's age and mother's condition during pregnancy, and even where in the world and what time of the year a person is born.

Schizophrenic behavior patterns can be classified into different subtypes including paranoid, catatonic, and disorganized patterns. Additionally, abnormal behaviors such as delusions and hallucinations are called positive symptoms, while those characterized by the absence of normal behaviors are called negative symptoms. Given this complex pattern of behaviors, it is not surprising that there are a variety of possible causes of schizophrenia, most of which are thought to interact. These include genetic and organic factors, variations in transmitter activity, family and social interactions, and even developmental experiences. The treatment of schizophrenia was revolutionized by the advent of psychotropic medications that alter transmitters, such as dopamine and GABA, and can dramatically improve symptoms in some individuals. Despite the amount of research devoted to understanding schizophrenia, many questions still remain about the causes, prevention, and treatment of the disorder, and whether it is really a collection of disorders rather than a single disease.

- **SCHIZOPHRENIA**
  The Epidemiology of Schizophrenia
  Origins of the Schizophrenia Construct

- **THE CLINICAL PICTURE IN SCHIZOPHRENIA**
  Delusions
  Hallucinations
  Disorganized Speech
  Disorganized and Catatonic Behavior
  Negative Symptoms

- **SUBTYPES OF SCHIZOPHRENIA**
  Paranoid Type
  Disorganized Type
  Catatonic Type
  Undifferentiated Type
  Residual Type
  Other Psychotic Disorders

- **WHAT CAUSES SCHIZOPHRENIA?**
  Genetic Aspects
  Prenatal Exposures

Genes and Environment in Schizophrenia: A Synthesis
A Neurodevelopmental Perspective
Biological Aspects
Neurocognition
Psychosocial and Cultural Aspects

• TREATMENT AND CLINICAL OUTCOME
Pharmacological Approaches
Psychosocial Approaches

• UNSOLVED ISSUES:
Can Schizophrenia Be Prevented?

OBJECTIVES
After reading this chapter, you should be able to do the following:

1. Explain the epidemiology of schizophrenia, as well as the origins of its construct.

2. Describe the clinical picture of schizophrenia including the diagnostic signs of the positive and negative symptoms.

3. Compare and contrast the subtypes of schizophrenia.

4. Describe the clinical features of other psychotic disorders.

5. Summarize the biological, psychosocial, and sociocultural causal influences in schizophrenia.

6. Evaluate the various biological and psychosocial treatments for schizophrenia.

7. Discuss current issues in treating schizophrenia including limitations of antipsychotics and the need for expanded psychosocial intervention.

8. Explain the difficulties associated with trying to prevent schizophrenia.

AS YOU READ
Answers and page numbers can be found in the Answer Key at the end of the book.

KEY WORDS
Each of the words below is important in understanding the concepts presented in this chapter. Write the definition next to each word.

Term	Page	Definition
Antipsychotics (neuroleptics)	388	

Brief psychotic disorder	371	
Candidate genes	377	
Catatonic schizophrenia	369	
Cognitive remediation	390	
Delusion	365	
Delusional disorder	370	
Disorganized schizophrenia	369	
Dopamine	382	
Endophenotypes	380	
Expressed emotion (EE)	386	
Glutamate	384	
Hallucination	365	
Linkage analysis	377	
Negative symptoms	367	
Paranoid schizophrenia	368	
Positive symptoms	367	
Residual schizophrenia	370	
Schizoaffective disorder	370	
Schizophreniform disorder	370	
Shared psychotic disorder (folie à deux)	371	
Undifferentiated schizophrenia	370	

MATCHING
Who's Who and What's What
Match the following names and terms with their correct definitions or descriptions.

Name/Term

_____ Genain quadruplets
_____ Emil Kraepelin
_____ Eugen Bleuler
_____ Neologisms
_____ Echopraxia
_____ Echolalia
_____ Communication deviance

_____ Sociogenic hypothesis
_____ Social drift hypothesis

Description/Definition

A. Imitation of the act of others
B. Swiss psychiatrist who in 1911 used the term *schizophrenia* to characterize a split within the intellect and between the intellect and emotion and external reality
C. Completely new made-up words by a patient with schizophrenia
D. Studied by David Rosenthal at NIMH in the mid-1950s, because all developed schizophrenia but were discordant with severity
E. Theory that schizophrenic individuals find themselves unable to maintain a job or relationships; thus, they are likely to end up at the lower end of the socioeconomic ladder
F. Mimicking of another's phases
G. Theory that the lower the SES, the higher the prevalence of schizophrenia, because the conditions of lower-class existence are stressful, increasing the risk for schizophrenia
H. German psychiatrist who used the term *dementia praecox* to refer to a group of conditions that feature mental deterioration beginning early in life
I. Measure of how understandable and "easy to follow" the speech of a family member is

Match the following types of schizophrenia with their definitions.

Schizophrenia

_____ Undifferentiated
_____ Paranoid type
_____ Catatonic type
_____ Disorganized type
_____ Residual type
_____ Schizoaffective disorder
_____ Schizophreniform disorder

Definition

A. Those persons who are in remission following a schizophrenic episode and show only mild signs of schizophrenia
B. A form of schizophrenia that occurs at an early age and includes blunting, inappropriate mannerisms, and bizarre behavior
C. A person in whom symptoms of schizophrenia have existed for six months or less
D. A person who shows absurd, illogical, changeable delusions and frequent hallucinations
E. A form of schizophrenia in which all the primary indications of schizophrenia are seen but does not meet one of the other subtypes
F. A person who shows some schizophrenic signs, as well as obvious depression or elation

G. A type of schizophrenia characterized by alternating periods of extreme excitement and extreme withdrawal

SHORT ANSWERS
Provide brief answers to the following questions.

1. Describe the types of delusions common in schizophrenia. (p. 365)

2. Provide examples of prenatal factors that could trigger or cause schizophrenia. (pp. 377–378)

3. List examples of the positive and negative symptoms of schizophrenia. (pp. 367–368)

4. List the five subtypes of schizophrenia. (p. 368)

5. Describe the three types of prevention programs with relation to schizophrenia. (p. 393)

THE DOCTOR IS IN...PSYCHIATRIC HELP—5¢
Read the following scenarios and diagnose the client. Remember to look carefully at the criteria for the disorder before you make a decision as to the diagnosis. Make a list of other information you might need to help you understand the causal factors.

1. Sharon is a 22-year-old single female that comes to visit you. Her sister has referred her to you after the police arrested her outside of Tom Hanks' house. She told the police

that she and Tom were getting married and that she was the love of his life. Sharon said that his latest movie was dedicated to her, and that he conveyed it through a secret message on the screen that only she could pick up. With Sharon's permission, you talk to her sister and discover that other than this behavior, Sharon seems normal. How would you diagnosis Sharon and why?

2. You are a family therapist. A family comes to see you, bringing their 23-year-old son who suffers from schizophrenia. They are exhausted as each family member has been taking turns staying up and "watching" over him at night as he has broken things, left the house unexpectedly, and repeatedly accuses them of trying to "keep him beneath the realm of Vulcar". He is confrontational at times, never physically, only verbally. How would you treat this patient, his family, and, based on studies, what would you expect the son's outcome to be?

AFTER YOU READ

PRACTICE TESTS
Take the following three multiple-choice tests to see how much you have comprehended from the chapter. Each represents roughly one third of the chapter. As you study the chapter, use these to check your progress.

Practice Test 1

1. The hallmark of schizophrenia is a significant loss of contact with reality, referred to as (p. 363)

      a. hallucinations.
      b. delusions.
      c. psychosis.
      d. manic reaction.

2. Symptoms of schizophrenia include oddities in (p. 363)
      a. perception.
      b. thinking.
      c. sense of self.
      d. All of the above

3. Schizophrenia is about as prevalent as (p. 363)
      a. epilepsy.
      b. heart disease.
      c. stroke.
      d. None of the above

4. Schizophrenia tends to develop earlier in _____ than in _____. (p. 364)
      a. women, men
      b. men, women
      c. old age, adulthood
      d. preschoolers, elementary-age children

5. He is best known for his careful description of what we now regard as schizophrenia. (p. 364)
      a. John Bonds
      b. Sigmund Freud
      c. Eugen Bleuler
      d. Emil Kraepelin

6. Delusions of grandeur are common in _____ schizophrenia. (p. 368)
      a. disorganized
      b. catatonic
      c. residual
      d. paranoid

7. In the past, _____ schizophrenia was called hebephrenic. One of its characteristics is flat or inappropriate affect. (p. 369)
      a. disorganized
      b. catatonic
      c. residual
      d. paranoid

8. _____ schizophrenia was once common in Europe and North America but has become less prevalent in recent years. It is still found in less industrialized regions of the world. (p. 369)

    a. Disorganized
    b. Catatonic
    c. Residual
    d. Paranoid

9. _____ schizophrenia is considered by the authors as something of a wastebasket category, because a patient may meet the criteria for schizophrenia but not fit into one of the other types. (p. 370)
    a. Undifferentiated
    b. Residual
    c. Disorganized
    d. Paranoid

10. The category used for people who have suffered at least one episode of schizophrenia, and now don't have positive symptoms but clinically show negative symptoms, is (p. 370)
    a. undifferentiated.
    b. residual.
    c. disorganized.
    d. paranoid.

Practice Test 2

1. Most instances of an acute, schizophrenic breakdown appear to show symptoms of the _____ type, which may later lead to a change in diagnosis to a specific subtype. (p. 370)
    a. undifferentiated
    b. paranoid
    c. catatonic
    d. disorganized

2. This diagnosis is something of a hybrid in that it is used to describe people who have features of schizophrenia and severe mood disorder. (p. 370)
    a. undifferentiated schizophrenia
    b. schizoaffective
    c. schizoeffective
    d. schizotypal

3. A _____ is an erroneous belief that is fixed and firmly held despite clear and contradictory evidence. (p. 365)
    a. hallucination
    b. delusion
    c. differentiation
    d. dementia

4. A _____ is a sensory experience that occurs in the absence of any external perceptual stimulus. (p. 365)
     a. hallucination
     b. delusion
     c. differentiation
     d. dementia

5. Disorganized speech is the external manifestation of a disorder in thought (p. 366)
     a. form.
     b. content.
     c. interpretation.
     d. All of the above

6. _____ symptoms reflect behavioral excesses or distortions in schizophrenic patients. (p. 367)
     a. Catatonic
     b. Negative
     c. Positive
     d. Alogia

7. _____ symptoms reflect behavioral deficits in schizophrenic patients. (p. 367)
     a. Catatonic
     b. Negative
     c. Positive
     d. Alogia

8. Schizoaffective disorder is characterized by the presence of (p. 370)
     a. schizophrenia and a mood disorder.
     b. schizophrenia and a substance addiction.
     c. schizophrenia and paranoia.
     d. OCD and a mood disorder.

9. Studies by Elaine Walker and her colleagues found what differences between preschizophrenic children and their healthy siblings? (pp. 378–379)
     a. motor abnormalities
     b. less positive facial emotions
     c. more negative facial emotions
     d. All of the above

10. Because the brain normally occupies the skull fully, the enlarged ventricles of some schizophrenics imply a(n) (p. 380)
     a. decreased pressure on the brain.
     b. loss of brain tissue mass.
     c. increased amount of spinal fluid.
     d. predisposition to hydrocephaly.

Practice Test 3

1. _____ is an excitatory neurotransmitter that researchers suspect might be involved in schizophrenia. (p. 382)
    a. GABA
    b. Dopamine
    c. Glutamate
    d. None of the above

2. A significant percentage of patients with schizophrenia are deficient in their ability to track a moving target. The skill required to do this task is called (p. 384)
    a. rapid eye movement.
    b. smooth-pursuit eye movement.
    c. tracking eye movement.
    d. following ability eye movement.

3. Researchers are also looking at this excitatory neurotransmitter that is widespread in the brain. (p. 384)
    a. GABA
    b. glutamate
    c. serotonin
    d. ACTH

4. As a genetic researcher, you have decided to move away from the family, twin, and adoption schizophrenia studies you had been focusing on and become involved in a new paradigm. This paradigm shift would probably be a study of (p. 377)
    a. behaviors.
    b. the unconscious thoughts of schizophrenic.
    c. treatment methods.
    d. molecular genetics.

5. In addition to prenatal viral infections, researchers are looking at _____ as a factor that could cause or trigger schizophrenia. (p. 377)
    a. Rhesus incompatibility
    b. early nutritional deficiency
    c. perinatal birth complications
    d. All of the above

6. In MRI studies of patients with schizophrenia, there is a ___ percent reduction in whole brain volume relative to controls. (p. 380)
    a. 8
    b. 7
    c. 5
    d. 3

7. These are discrete, measurable traits that are thought to be linked to specific genes that might be important in schizophrenia. (p. 380)
>   a. endophenotypes
>   b. ectophenotypes
>   c. eldophenotypes
>   d. emdophenotypes

8. Somewhere between ___ and ___ percent of people with schizophrenia also show eye-tracking dysfunction and are deficient in their ability to track a moving target such as a pendulum. (p. 384)
>   a. 84, 86
>   b. 74, 86
>   c. 64, 86
>   d. 54, 86

9. Dopamine and glutamate are affected by this hormone that is released when we are stressed. (p. 386)
>   a. GABA
>   b. ABBA
>   c. insulin
>   d. cortisol

10. All of the following are examples of second-generation antipsychotics EXCEPT: (p. 388)
>   a. Risperdal
>   b. Zyprexa
>   c. Geodon
>   d. Thorazine

COMPREHENSIVE PRACTICE TEST
The following tests are designed to give you an idea of how well you understood the entire chapter. There are three different types of tests: multiple-choice, true/false, and essay.

Multiple Choice

1. The most common form of hallucination is (p. 365)
>   a. tactile.
>   b. visual.
>   c. auditory.
>   d. olfactory.

2. Modern research has found support for the idea that auditory hallucinations are really misperceived (p. 366)
>   a. external stimuli.
>   b. radio signals.
>   c. thought insertions.
>   d. subvocal speech.

3. Which of the following choices is NOT a subtype of schizophrenia? (p. 368)
>   a. paranoid
>   b. disorganized
>   c. depressed
>   d. catatonic

4. This disorder is characterized by duration of days, not weeks or months, and usually presents both positive and negative schizophrenic symptoms; it often goes untreated and/or unrepeated. (p. 371)
>   a. acute onset schizophrenia
>   b. subchronic schizophrenia
>   c. acquired schizophrenia
>   d. brief psychotic disorder

5. The prevalence of schizophrenia in the first-degree relatives of a proband with schizophrenia is about what percent? (p. 372)
>   a. 25
>   b. 10
>   c. 3
>   d. 2

6. Wahlberg and colleagues found that children who were at genetic risk and lived with families that had high _____ showed high levels of thought disorder. (p. 376)
>   a. levels of affection
>   b. communication deviance
>   c. number of siblings
>   d. a and c

7. Donald's father was 55 years old when Donald was born. Donald's risk of developing schizophrenia is (p. 363)
>   a. two to five times the normal risk.
>   b. two to four times the normal risk.
>   c. two to three times the normal risk.
>   d. three to four times the normal risk.

8. During his psychiatric evaluation with Dr. Morton, Tom was convinced that Dr. Morton was a CIA operative sent by the government to "tap into his mind" and implant a sonar chip for further study and classification. Tom refused to eat anything that was not

sealed; as he feared this was also a way "they" would get the chip inside him. Tom would have this type of schizophrenia. (p. 368)

      a. paranoid schizophrenia
      b. undifferentiated schizophrenia
      c. catatonic schizophrenia
      d. disorganized schizophrenia

9. Schizophreniform disorder is characterized by schizophrenic-like psychosis that (p. 370)

      a. lasts at least a month, but not more than six months.
      b. lasts less than a year, but not more than six years.
      c. are exclusively visual in nature.
      d. are undetectable.

10. Negative symptoms of schizophrenia seem to be linked to which part of the brain? (p. 381)

      a. frontal lobe
      b. temporal lobe
      c. medial
      d. amygdala

11. Positive symptoms of schizophrenia seem to be linked to which part of the brain, especially on the left side? (p. 381)

      a. temporal lobe
      b. hippocampus
      c. amygdala
      d. All of the above

12. Tony was a 20-year-old single white male who presented to the Emergency Room of a local hospital wearing tattered clothing and appeared highly confused. When Dr. Miles introduced himself, Tony began laughing uncontrollably. As the interview progressed, Tony said there were "slov lovs all around, a bound, into the ground." In response to Dr. Miles's question of what year it was, Tony said it was "the year of the tear on the deer which is here, did you hear what I say, today, today, today?" Tony is displaying this type of schizophrenia. (p. 369)

      a. paranoid schizophrenia
      b. undifferentiated schizophrenia
      c. disorganized schizophrenia
      d. catatonic schizophrenia

13. Some evidence points to patients with schizophrenia as missing particular types of neurons known as (p. 381)

      a. inhibitory interneurons.
      b. micro neurons.
      c. macro neurons.

    d. excitatory neurons.

14. The first antipsychotics, developed more than fifty years ago to treat schizophrenia, are called (pp. 388–389)
    a. conventional antipsychotics.
    b. neuroleptics.
    c. unconventional antipsychotics.
    d. a and b

15. Which of the following symptoms/side effects are less likely to be encountered when taking second-generation antipsychotics? (p. 389)
    a. weight gain
    b. rehospitalization
    c. agitation
    d. diabetes

16. Betty, who is schizophrenic, goes to a group every day where she learns employment skills, relationship skills, and skills in managing medication. This type of training is referred to as (p. 390)
    a. real life.
    b. case management.
    c. social skills.
    d. family.

17. The goal of cognitive-behavioral therapy when treating schizophrenia is to (p. 390)
    a. decrease the intensity of positive symptoms.
    b. reduce relapse.
    c. decrease social disability.
    d. All of the above

18. _____ therapy is staged, which means that it comprises different components that are administered at different points in the patient's recovery. (p. 390)
    a. Personal
    b. Cognitive
    c. Psychodynamic
    d. Behavioral

19. Jane presented with little to no movements. During her psychiatric evaluation, she repeated the same questions asked of her and began imitating the movements of the psychiatrist. She could not be moved and sat in rather awkward and uncomfortable positions. Jane is presenting with this type of schizophrenia. (p. 369)
    a. paranoid schizophrenia
    b. undifferentiated schizophrenia
    c. disorganized schizophrenia
    d. catatonic schizophrenia

20. William's clinical presentation was somewhat complicated as he had had a manic episode, but was now experiencing delusions and hallucinations in the absence of any mood symptoms for the past two weeks. William may have this disorder. (p. 370)
    a. paranoid schizophrenia
    b. undifferentiated schizophrenia
    c. schizoaffective disorder
    d. catatonic schizophrenia

TRUE/FALSE

1. T / F The overall average age of onset of schizophrenia is around 25 years for men and around 29 years for women. (p. 363)

2. T / F People who have a parent with schizophrenia have a statistically higher risk of developing the disorder than those who do not. (p. 378)

3. T / F Delusions reflect a disorder of thought content. (p. 365)

4. T / F A preponderance of negative symptoms in the clinical picture is considered a good sign for the patient's future outcome. (p. 367)

5. T / F The prognosis for someone diagnosed with schizophreniform disorder is better than for established forms of schizophrenia. (p. 370)

6. T / F The terms *familial* and *genetic* are synonymous. (p. 372)

7. T / F Schizophrenia probably involves several, or perhaps many, genes working together to make a person susceptible. (p. 378)

8. T / F The first signs of schizophrenia may be found in the way that children move. (p. 379)

9. T / F The prognosis is very good for individuals who develop a disorganized schizophrenia. (p. 369)

10. T / F Schizophrenia manifests itself more in defective cognition than in defective biology. (p. 384)

11. T / F Patients living in more industrialized countries do better than patients living in less industrialized countries. (p. 389)

12. T / F Dopamine is the only neurotransmitter involved in schizophrenia. (p. 382)

13. T / F A large number of studies have shown that, compared with controls, patients with schizophrenia have enlarged brain ventricles, with males possibly more affected than females. (p. 380)

14. T / F Patients with schizophrenia show abnormally low frontal lobe activation when they engage in mentally challenging tasks. (p. 381)

15. T / F Extrapyramidal side effects are involuntary movement abnormalities such as muscle spasms, rigidity, and shaking, which resemble Parkinson's disease. (p. 389)

Essay Questions

1. Discuss how dopamine became implicated in schizophrenia. (pp. 382–383)

2. Define and explain expressed emotion (EE) and its connection to patient relapse. (p. 386)

3. Compare the conventional antipsychotics with the newer, novel ones in terms of effectiveness and side effects. (pp. 388–389)

WHEN YOU HAVE FINISHED

WEB LINKS TO ITEMS OR CONCEPTS DISCUSSED IN CHAPTER 12
The National Institute on Mental Health
   http://www.nimh.nih.gov/HealthInformation/schizophreniamenu.cfm
The National Institute on Mental Health provides facts and information on schizophrenia as well as current clinical trials and links to other areas of relevance.

One Man's Personal Struggle with Schizophrenia
   http://www.chovil.com/
Ian Chovil is a 52-year-old man who has suffered with schizophrenia for the past thirty-six years. He shares his story and his heart on his Web page.

Schizoaffective Disorder
   http://www.nlm.nih.gov/medlineplus/schizophrenia.html

A solid collection of information is located on the Medline Plus Web site on schizophrenia with links to schizoaffective disorder.

Psychotropic Medications for Schizophrenia
http://www.schizophrenia.com/meds.html
This Web site provides a general overview of the various psychotropic medications for schizophrenia.

Antipsychotic Use
http://www.nimh.nih.gov/publicat/medicate.cfm#antipsychotics
The NIMH provides a good primer into understanding the use of antipsychotics as well as useful advise for those taking them.

WED MD Discussion on First- and Second-Generation Antipsychotics
http://www.webmd.com/hw/schizophrenia/aa47186.asp
WebMD provides a terrific discussion on the differences between first- and second-generation antipsychotics.

American Psychiatric Association's Practice Guidelines for the Treatment of Schizophrenia
http://www.psych.org/psych_pract/treatg/pg/Practice%20Guidelines8904/Schizophrenia_2e.pdf
This is the American Psychiatric Association's Practice Guidelines for the Treatment of Schizophrenia as a PDF file, which you can print and save. It is a near-definitive collection of the currently available treatments for schizophrenia.

USE IT OR LOSE IT
Provide an answer to the thought question below, knowing that there is more than one way to respond. Possible answers are presented in the Answer Key.

Do you think people with schizophrenia should be institutionalized against their will to ensure they take their medications correctly, and receive treatment for their illness?

CRISSCROSS
Now that you know all there is to know about this chapter, here's your opportunity to put that knowledge to work.

Across

3. The most important neurotransmitter implicated in schizophrenia
6. An excitatory neurotransmitter that is widespread in the brain
7. Pronounced motor signs, either of an excited or stuporous type of schizophrenia
8. An erroneous belief that is fixed and firmly held
9. The hallmark of schizophrenia, a significant loss of contact with reality
10. A wide variety of disordered processes of varied etiology, developmental pattern, and outcome

Down

1. A measure of the family environment
2. An absence or deficit of behaviors normally present in schizophrenia
4. A sensory experience occurring without any external perceptual stimulus
5. A class of drugs introduced in the mid-1950s that transformed the environment in mental hospitals

Puzzle created with Puzzlemaker at DiscoverySchool.com

ANSWERS TO TEST QUESTIONS – CHAPTER 12

MATCHING
Name/Term
D. Genain quadruplets
H. Emil Kraepelin
B. Eugen Bleuler
C. Neologisms
A. echopraxia
F. echolalia
I. communication deviance
G. sociogenic hypothesis
E. social drift hypothesis

Schizophrenia
E. Undifferentiated
D. Paranoid type
G. Catatonic type
B. Disorganized type
A. Residual type
F. Schizoaffective disorder
C. Schizophreniform disorder

SHORT ANSWERS
Your answer should contain the following points.

1. Delusions common in schizophrenia.
a. mad feelings or impulses: thoughts, feelings, or actions are being controlled by external agents
b. thought insertion: thoughts are being inserted into one's brain by some external agency
c. thought withdrawal: some external agency has robbed one of one's thoughts
d. delusions of reference: neutral environmental event (television program or song) is believed to have special and personal meaning intended only for the patient
e. delusions of bodily changes: (e.g., bowels don't work) or removal of organs

2. Examples of prenatal factors that could trigger or cause schizophrenia.
a. prenatal viral infection: more people with schizophrenia are born between January and March, in a study done in Finland after a flu epidemic. It was found that there was a higher rate of schizophrenia in children born to mothers who had the flu in the second trimester of pregnancy
b. Rhesus incompatibility: a study done by Hollister, Laing, and Mednick showed that the rate of schizophrenia is about 2.1 percent in males who are Rh-incompatible with their mothers, as opposed to 0.8 percent of males who were compatible
c. birth complications: research has shown that mothers of patients with schizophrenia were more likely to have had some sort of problems with pregnancy or delivery. One

possibility is the problem might have caused oxygen deprivation
d. nutritional deficiency: the results of Dutch Hunger Winter's study, in which people suffered severe famine as a result of a Nazi blockade, found that children who were conceived at the height of the famine had a two-fold increase in their risk of later developing schizophrenia

3. The positive and negative symptoms of schizophrenia.
Positive:
a. delusions
b. hallucinations
c. disorganized speech
d. grossly disorganized behavior
e. sudden onset
f. derailment of associations

Negative:
a. flat or blunted emotional expressiveness
b. alogia
c. avolition
d. asociality
e. significant cognitive impairment

4. Paranoid, catatonic, disorganized, residual, and undifferentiated.

5. Three types of prevention programs with relation to schizophrenia.
a. primary prevention: to prevent new cases; improve obstetric care for women with schizophrenia and first-degree relatives of schizophrenic patients
b. secondary prevention: early intervention with people at risk; possible screening of at-risk people; problem with how to identify people and how harmful to tell someone they might develop schizophrenia
c. tertiary prevention: early treatment for those who already have the illness; vocational rehabilitation, family support and cognitive therapy

THE DOCTOR IS IN...PSYCHIATRIC HELP—5¢
1. Delusional disorder with erotomania subtype. Sharon's actions and beliefs are completely false and absurd. She seems normal outside of the belief that she and Tom Hanks are getting married. Sharon also seems to be stalking him. Given her young age, this may be the first sign of a more severe disorder that is just beginning to develop. However, for the time being, the working diagnosis is delusional disorder with erotomania subtype.

2. Treatment:
a. may need to have a physician hospitalize the patient to stabilize him
b. work to encourage a patient-relative relationship
b. educate the patient and family about schizophrenia during and after hospitalization

c. help to improve coping and problem-solving skills
d. enhance communication skills, especially the clarity of family communications
Outcome: better than average expectation for the patient to do better clinically and
have a low relapse rate

PRACTICE TESTS

Q#	TEST 1	TEST 2	TEST 3
1	B	A	B
2	D	B	B
3	A	B	B
4	B	A	D
5	D	B	D
6	D	C	D
7	A	B	A
8	B	A	D
9	A	D	D
10	B	B	D

Q#	M/C	T/F
1	C	T
2	D	T
3	C	T
4	D	F
5	B	T
6	B	F
7	C	T
8	A	T
9	A	F
10	A	T
11	D	F
12	C	F
13	A	T
14	D	T
15	B	T
16	C	
17	D	
18	A	
19	D	
20	C	

Essay Questions
Your answer should contain the following points.

1. Dopamine became implicated in schizophrenia because
a. mental changes associated with LSD had scientists interested in schizophrenia consider a possible biochemical basis for the disorder
b. the observation that chlorpromazine's therapeutic benefits were linked to its ability to block dopamine receptors
c. the abuse of amphetamines in the '50s and '60s led to the discovery that, if too much dopamine is produced, a form of psychosis that includes paranoia and auditory hallucinations occurs that looks a lot like schizophrenia
d. actual clinical studies that treated patients by giving them drugs, which increased the availability of dopamine

2. Expressed emotion (EE) and its connection to patient relapse.
a. EE is a measure of the family environment, which is based on how the family member speaks about the patient during a private interview with a researcher; there are three main elements: criticism, hostility, and emotional over involvement (EOI)
b. criticism, the most important, reflects dislike or disapproval; hostility, dislike, or rejection of patient as a person; EOI dramatic or over-concerned attitude with illness
c. it predicts relapse in patients
d. when EE levels in families are lowered, rates of patient relapse rates decrease
e. high EE behaviors exhibited by family members are perceived as stressful by patients and possibly triggering the release of cortisol, which triggers dopamine activity
f. studies show that an increase in patients' unusual thinking occurred immediately after the patient was criticized by a family member

3. Conventional: Haldol and Thorazine
a. work because these are dopamine antagonists
b. benefits appear within one to three weeks, with maximum results in six to eight weeks
c. work best for positive symptoms
d. side effects: drowsiness, dry mouth, weight gain, extrapyramidal side effects, tardive dyskinesia, and neuroleptic malignant syndrome

Novel: Clozaril, Risperdal, Zyprexa, Seroquel, Geodon
a. cause fewer extrapyramidal symptoms
b. don't block D2 receptors well, but block a much broader range of receptors including D4 dopamine receptor
c. relieve positive and negative symptoms
d. patients less likely to be rehospitalized
e. side effects: drowsiness and weight gain, diabetes, and, rarely, agranulocytosis

USE IT OR LOSE IT
When people are psychotic, they frequently make choices that are dangerous to themselves and others. Therefore, most mental health professionals believe that there are instances when people should be involuntarily committed for mental health

treatment in order to stabilize their behavior. Such commitments are typically time-sensitive, and subject to legal controls that vary by state.

CRISSCROSS ANSWERS

Across
3. Dopamine
6. Glutamate
7. Catatonic
8. Delusion
9. Psychosis
10. Schizophrenia

Down
1. Expressed emotion
2. Negative symptoms
4. Hallucination
5. Antipsychotics

Chapter 13: Cognitive Disorders

BEFORE YOU READ

The brain is essential for all things organisms do, including the most basic of functions such as breathing and temperature regulation and the most complex interactions of thought and feeling. However, many things can go wrong. Chapter 13 covers several types of brain impairments. The first part of the chapter discusses clinical signs of brain damage and neuropsychological brain disorders. This is followed by a more in-depth look at delirium, dementia (with particular attention paid to Alzheimer's disease), dementia from HIV infection, vascular dementia, and amnestic syndrome. Cognitive disorders can also stem from traumatic head injuries following car accidents, falls, sports accidents, and violence. Notably, temporary loss of consciousness and post-impact confusion are common following mild head injuries, while more severe injuries can cause long lasting impairment. Innovations in the treatment of head injuries including the use of medication, dietary supplements, and therapy offer hope for patients, but much remains to be learned about the process of rehabilitation and recovery. The brain truly is one of our last frontiers.

- **BRAIN IMPAIRMENT IN ADULTS**
  Clinical Signs of Brain Damage
  Diffuse Versus Focal Damage
  The Neuropsychology/Psychopathology Interaction

- **DELIRIUM**
  Clinical Presentation
  Treatment and Outcome

- **DEMENTIA**
  Alzheimer's Disease
  Dementia from HIV-1 Infection
  Vascular Dementia

- **AMNESTIC SYNDROME**

- **DISORDERS INVOLVING HEAD INJURY**
  The Clinical Picture
  Treatments and Outcomes

- **UNRESOLVED ISSUES:**
  Can Dietary Supplements Enhance Brain Functioning?

CHAPTER 13: CORE CONCEPTS

OBJECTIVES
After reading this chapter, you should be able to do the following:

1. Explain why the DSM-IV-TR dropped the terms *functional mental disorders* and *organic mental disorders*.

2. Discuss the clinical signs of brain damage.

3. Explain the diffuse versus focal damage as it relates to brain impairment.

4. Describe how neuropsychology and psychopathology interact with each other.

5. Define delirium in terms of clinical presentation and discuss clinical treatments and outcomes.

6. Define dementia and describe the three disorders presented, Alzheimer's, dementia from HIV-1 infection, and vascular dementia, in terms of clinical picture, prevalence, any genetic or environmental aspects, treatment outcomes and effects on caregivers.

7. Explain amnestic syndrome.

8. Explain traumatic brain injury (TBI), describe the clinical picture, and discuss treatment outcomes.

9. Discuss the research on the benefits of dietary supplements on the brain.

AS YOU READ
Answers can be found in the Answer Key at the end of the book.

KEY WORDS
Each of the words below is important in understanding the concepts presented in this chapter. Write the definition next to each word.

Term	Page	Definition
Amnestic syndrome	409	
Amyloidal plaques	401	
Anterograde amnesia	410	
APOE-E4 allele	405	
Delirium	400	
Dementia	401	
Early-onset Alzheimer's	405	

disease		
Functional mental disorders	397	
HIV-associated dementia	408	
Late-onset Alzheimer's disease	405	
Neurofibrillary tangles	402	
Organic mental disorders	397	
Retrograde amnesia	410	
Traumatic brain injury (TBI)	410	
Vascular dementia (VAD)	408	

MATCHING
Who's Who and What's What
Name the brain structures using the terms in bold in the top of the box. Match the term with its proper answer.

Corpus callosum	Limbic system	Reticular formation	Sensory strip	Motor strip
Cerebel-lum	Frontal lobe	Hypothalamus	Parietal lobe	Thalamus
Medulla	Temporal lobe	Occipital lobe		

_____ Learning, abstracting, reasoning, inhibiting
_____ Integration of sensory information from various parts of the body
_____ Somaesthetic and motor discriminations and functions
_____ Major relay station for messages from all parts of the body, important in sensations of pain
_____ Visual discrimination and some aspects of visual memory
_____ Fine motor coordination, posture, and balance
_____ Communication between the brain's right and left

_____ hemispheres
_____ Attention, emotions, "fight or flight," memory
_____ Regulation of voluntary movement
_____ Regulation of metabolism, temperature, emotions
_____ Discrimination of sounds, verbal and speech behavior
_____ Arousal reactions, information screening
_____ Breathing, blood pressure, other vital functions

SHORT ANSWERS
Provide brief answers to the following questions.

1. Why are cognitive disorders discussed in the textbook? (p. 396)

2. What determines the extent and magnitude of behavioral deficits or psychological impairments in persons with damage to brain tissue? (pp. 397–398)

THE DOCTOR IS IN...PSYCHIATRIC HELP—5¢
Read the following scenarios and diagnose the client. Remember to look carefully at the criteria for the disorder before you make a decision as to the diagnosis. Make a list of other information you might need to help you understand the causal factors.

1. Glen is an 82-year-old man who suddenly became very confused, unable to remember things and very agitated. In addition, he was unable to stay on tasks long enough to even complete dressing himself. Glen had been taking several medications and was recently given another.

How would you diagnose Glen and why? Also, what treatment would you recommend?

2. Terry is a 44-year-old man who has a long history of alcohol abuse. He has come to see you at the insistence of his sister with whom he is staying. In your interview with Terry, he is very capable of telling you about his life and past experiences working on oilrigs around the world. You had asked him to look at a picture in a magazine and tell you what he saw. He was able to do this as he looked at the picture. However, when you asked him to recall what the picture was about a few minutes later, he had no idea

what you were talking about and made up a story that seemed to him a reasonable explanation as to why he didn't recall the picture.

How would you diagnose Terry and why?

3. What six factors in the case below suggest that your patient has an unfavorable prognosis?

An 18-year-old male who had several run-ins with the law during high school received a serious head injury in a motorcycle accident. He was in a coma for almost a month. He is currently suffering some paralysis, and is very angry and depressed. He refuses to cooperate with his physical therapist. His parents, who live in a remote rural area where no rehabilitation facilities are available, will take him back home, but are rather unenthusiastic about the prospect.

a.

b.

c.

d.

e.

f.

AFTER YOU READ

PRACTICE TESTS
Take the following three multiple-choice tests to see how much you have comprehended from the chapter. Each represents roughly one third of the chapter. As you study the chapter, use these to check your progress.

Practice Test 1

1. Before the DSM-IV was published, delirium, dementia, and other amnestic and cognitive disorders, were considered (p. 397)

a. functional mental disorders.
b. dysfunctional mental disorders.
c. organic mental disorders.
d. brain injury disorders.

2. When structural defects in the brain occur before birth or at a very early age, the typical result is (p. 397)
a. mental retardation.
b. delirium.
c. dementia.
d. progressive.

3. To distinguish the possibility of a brain disorder from mood disorder, the clinician will look to see if the client has (p. 397)
a. headaches.
b. a major change in behavior.
c. a prior history of psychopathology.
d. All of the above

4. In the past, organic mental disorders were thought to have a _____ cause while functional mental disorders were thought to have a _____ cause. (p. 397)
a. physiological, psychological
b. psychological, physiological
c. internal, external
d. overt, covert

5. The area involved in the regulation of metabolism, temperature, and emotions is the (p. 398)
a. medulla.
b. corpus callosum.
c. hypothalamus.
d. temporal lobe.

6. The _____ hemisphere of the brain is mostly responsible for language and solving mathematical equations. (p. 398)
a. right
b. left
c. center
d. remote

7. This lobe is associated with visual discrimination and some aspects of visual memory. (p. 398)
a. parietal lobe
b. frontal lobe
c. occipital lobe

      d. temporal lobe

8. After a traumatic brain injury caused by an accident or a fall, for example, around _____ percent of patients make a suicide attempt. (p. 399)
      a. 10
      b. 18
      c. 8
      d. 5

9. Which of the following does NOT affect the development of behavioral deficits after a head injury? (p. 397)
      a. the nature and location of the injury
      b. the individual's prior competence and personality
      c. the amount of time since the injury
      d. the person's life situation

10. A rapid and widespread disorganization of complex mental processes caused by a generalized disturbance in brain metabolism is called (p. 400)
      a. amnestic syndrome.
      b. hallucinosis.
      c. dementia.
      d. delirium.

Practice Test 2

1. Delirium is treated with (p. 400)
      a. neuroleptic medications.
      b. benzodiazepines.
      c. Aricept.
      d. a and b

2. Most cases of delirium are reversible, except when the delirium is caused by (p. 400)
      a. terminal illness or by mild brain trauma.
      b. terminal illness or by moderate brain trauma.
      c. terminal illness or by severe brain trauma.
      d. None of the above

3. Children are at high risk of delirium because their brains are not yet fully (p. 400)
      a. organized.
      b. developed.
      c. integrated.
      d. active.

4. The prevalence of AIDS-related dementia has decreased because of (p. 408)
      a. the use of antiretroviral therapy.
      b. psychoimmunological treatments.

c. the use of CBT.

d. high death rates from AIDS.

5. Alzheimer's cannot be absolutely confirmed until the patient's (p. 401)

a. complete physical exam.

b. complete neurological exam.

c. behavior has deteriorated sufficiently.

d. death.

6. Which of the following is the most common behavioral manifestation of Alzheimer's disease? (p. 401)

a. slow mental deterioration

b. jealousy delusions

c. paranoid delusions

d. psychopathological symptoms

7. Since there is no cure for Alzheimer's, _____ care seems to help with diminishing the patient's and caregiver's distress and some of the complications that come with the disorder. (p. 407)

a. family

b. palliative

c. hospital

d. nursing home

8. These drugs have been shown to slow the rate at which patients with Alzheimer's deteriorate. (p. 407)

a. placebos

b. tacrine

c. Donepezil

d. b and c

9. Environmental factors that could contribute to Alzheimer's include (p. 406)

a. diet.

b. aluminum.

c. head trauma.

d. All of the above

10. Most people with Alzheimer's live (p. 408)

a. with family members in the community.

b. in nursing homes.

c. on the streets.

d. on their own.

Practice Test 3

1. Vascular dementia involves a (p. 408)

a. dementia as a result of repeated injury.

b. continuing recurrence of small strokes.

c. breakdown of veins and arteries.

d. b and c

2. Laura has been diagnosed with VAD and AD. As a clinician you would refer to this condition as (p. 409)

a. varied dementia.

b. mixed dementia.

c. undifferentiated dementia.

d. multi dementia.

3. Patients with VAD are more likely to suffer from _____ disorders than patients with Alzheimer's. (p. 409)

a. anxiety

b. cognitive

c. stress

d. mood

4. A person with VAD is vulnerable to sudden death from a (p. 409)

a. stroke.

b. cardiovascular disease.

c. blood disorder.

d. a and b

5. Traumatic brain injury affects more than _____ people each year in the United States. (p. 410)

a. 1 million

b. 2 million

c. 100,000

d. 500,000

6. The general types of TBI recognized by clinicians are (p. 410)

a. closed-head injuries.

b. penetrating head injuries.

c. skull fractures.

d. All of the above

7. If a head injury is sufficiently severe to result in unconsciousness, the person may experience retrograde amnesia or an inability to recall (p. 410)

a. events immediately following the injury.

b. concrete facts, such as names and dates.

c. events immediately preceding the injury.

d. long-past events.

8. In a study of TBI in boxers, it was found that the presence of the _____ genetic-risk factor was associated with more chronic neurological deficits. (p. 411)
      a. 23rd allele
      b. APOE-4
      c. Alzheimer's
      d. neurofibrillary

9. A recent study has shown that older individuals and individuals who have TBI share several changes in (p. 411)
      a. cognitive deterioration.
      b. motor skills.
      c. information-processing speed.
      d. tactile performance.

10. Common after effects of moderate brain injury are (p. 412)
      a. chronic headaches.
      b. anxiety.
      c. impaired memory.
      d. All of the above

COMPREHENSIVE PRACTICE TEST
The following tests are designed to give you an idea of how well you understood the entire chapter. There are three different types of tests: multiple-choice, true/false, and essay.

Multiple Choice

1. The thick outer membrane that protects the brain and literally means "hard mother" is called the (p. 396)
      a. corpus callosum.
      b. medulla.
      c. cerebellum.
      d. dura mater.

2. People with amnesia can have trouble (p. 409)
      a. remembering new information.
      b. remembering events that took place very recently.
      c. only personal information.
      d. in virtually all areas of working and short-term memory.

3. The _____ hemisphere of the brain is mostly responsible for grasping overall meanings in novel situations, reasoning on a nonverbal, intuitive level, and appreciation of spatial relations. (p. 398)
      a. right
      b. left
      c. center

d. remote

4. These are brain disorders that are considered not to have an organic basis and are treated by psychiatrists. (p. 397)
        a. functional mental disorders
        b. organic mental disorders
        c. botanic mental disorders
        d. dysfunctional mental disorders

5. Twenty-four percent of TBI cases overall develop post-traumatic epilepsy, thought to be caused by (p. 412)
        a. scar tissue.
        b. low neurotransmitter levels.
        c. temperature changes.
        d. None of the above

6. The general types of TBI recognized by clinicians are (p. 411)
        a. closed-head injuries.
        b. penetrating head injuries.
        c. skull fractures.
        d. All of the above

7. If a head injury is sufficiently severe to result in unconsciousness, the person may experience retrograde amnesia or an inability to recall (p. 410)
        a. events immediately following the injury.
        b. events immediately preceding and following the injury.
        c. events immediately preceding the injury.
        d. names or faces of friends.

8. In a study of TBI in boxers, it was found that the presence of the _____ genetic-risk factor was associated with more chronic neurological deficits. (p. 411)
        a. granulovacuoles
        b. APOE-4
        c. PS1
        d. PS2

9. In contrast to diffuse damage that results in dementia, focal lesions are _____ areas of abnormal change in brain structure. (p. 397)
        a. deep
        b. circumscribed
        c. large
        d. progressive

10. The most common cause of delirium is (p. 400)
        a. stroke.
        b. HIV/AIDS.

c. drug intoxication.

d. syphilis.

11. The herb ginko biloba has been shown to (p. 414)
a. increase dementia.
b. decrease dementia.
c. increase delirium.
d. decrease delirium.

12. Cases of early-onset AD appear to be caused by rare (p. 405)
a. brain cell mutations.
b. environmental factors.
c. genetic mutations.
d. neurological mutations.

13. Chronic alcoholism combined with vitamin B1 deficiency can cause (p. 409)
a. amnestic syndrome.
b. Alzheimer's disease.
c. epilepsy.
d. depression.

14. Cerebral arteriosclerosis can be medically managed by decreasing the likelihood of further (p. 409)
a. contact with hazardous waste.
b. medical problems.
c. strokes.
d. None of the above

15. Post-trauma epilepsy is common in (p. 410)
a. closed-head injuries.
b. penetrating head injuries.
c. skull fractures.
d. b and c

16. The TBI that could result from a roller coaster ride. (p. 410)
a. closed-head injury
b. penetrating head injury
c. skull fracture
d. subdural hematomas

17. The _____ a child, who has a significant traumatic brain injury, the more likely they are to be adversely affected. (p. 413)
a. older
b. younger
c. more mature

      d. a and c

18. Damage to this area is associated with either behavioral inertia, passivity, apathy, and perseverative thought or impulsiveness and distractibility. (p. 398)
      a. temporal areas
      b. occipital areas
      c. parietal areas
      d. frontal areas

19. Language and solving mathematical equations take place mostly in the (p. 398)
      a. occipital hemisphere
      b. left hemisphere
      c. right hemisphere
      d. frontal hemisphere

20. Jimmy survived a motorcycle accident but sustained severe damage to the back of his head that left him unable to see for two months. Most likely, the damage affected his (p. 398)
      a. temporal lobe
      b. occipital lobe
      c. parietal lobe
      d. frontal lobe

21. Hank was in the Detox Unit for alcohol withdrawal and was experiencing delirium. He was given this type of medication. (p. 401)
      a. a mood stabilizer
      b. an antidepressant
      c. a benzodiazepine
      d. an antipsychotic

22. Winifred began to forget where she placed her keys and had a difficult time remembering places and family members. Her family says that things have begun to slowly worsen over time. Winifred may be showing signs of (p. 401)
      a. delusional disorder.
      b. delirium.
      c. dementia.
      d. Parkinson's disease.

23. Loretta had always been an active and outgoing person. She had seven children, numerous grandchildren, and was a beloved person not only within her family but to everyone she knew. When she reached her sixties, no one noticed that she was somewhat forgetful at times—especially with such a large family, who could remember everyone? However, as the years progressed her memory worsened, she forgot things, stopped cleaning the house, stopped cleaning herself, and laughed inappropriately. Eventually she needed to be placed in a nursing home where, in six years, she past away. Loretta suffered from (pp. 401–402)

    a. Parkinson's disease.
    b. Alzheimer's disease.
    c. delusional disorder.
    d. age progression disorder.

24. The brain starts to decrease in size after about the age of (p. 404)
    a. 25.
    b. 24.
    c. 22.
    d. 18.

25. Bill cannot remember anything for more than one to two minutes. His near-fatal accident on the job last year left him with poor memory and this form of amnesia. (p. 410)
    a. anterograde amnesia
    b. retrograde amnesia
    c. posterograde amnesia
    d. multigrade amnesia

TRUE/FALSE

1. T / F Alzheimer's disease is the most common cause of dementia. (p. 414)

2. T / F Alzheimer's disease usually begins after about age 65. (p. 404)

3. T / F AD is not an inevitable consequence of aging. (p. 404)

4. T / F People who are the caregivers for Alzheimer's patients are at high risk for depression. (p. 408)

5. T / F Brain damage is the root cause of amnestic disorders. (p. 409)

6. T / F Sports injuries are the most common cause of TBI. (p. 410)

7. T / F In a majority of brain injury cases, notable personality changes occur. (p. 410)

8. T/F Both environmental and genetic influences determine an individual's reaction to brain damage. (p. 414)

9. T/F Treating TBI most often focuses on recovery, rather than teaching compensatory strategies. (p. 413)

10. T/F Anterograde amnesia involves the inability to store in memory events that happen after a brain injury. (p. 410)

11. T / F After a traumatic brain injury caused by an accident or a fall, around 18 percent of patients make a suicide attempt. (p. 399)

12. T / F Delirium is very common in the elderly after they have had surgery. (p. 400)

13. T / F It is estimated that the rate of Alzheimer's dementia triples about every five years after a person reaches the age of 40. (p. 404)

14. T/F Men seem to have a slightly higher risk of developing Alzheimer's disease than women. (p. 404)

15. T/F Vascular dementia tends to occur after the age of 50 and affects more men than women. (p. 409)

Essay Questions

1. Discuss the progressively diffuse damage that may occur when a brain disorder has a mainly focal origin but gradually spreads over a greater area to become diffuse. (pp. 397–398)

2. Explain dementia using the DSM-IV-TR criteria (pp. 401–402)

3. Describe the clinical picture of Alzheimer's disease. (pp. 401–405)

4. Explain the difference between early- and late-onset Alzheimer's disease. (pp. 405–406)

5. Explain the three general types of traumatic brain injury (TBI). (p. 410)

WHEN YOU HAVE FINISHED

WEB LINKS TO ITEMS OR CONCEPTS DISCUSSED IN CHAPTER 13

Resources for Care Givers

http://www.caregiver.org/caregiver/jsp/publications.jsp?nodeid=345

The Family Caregiver Alliance has more than one hundred fact sheets at this site as well as numerous links on its home page.

Dealing with Dementia

http://www.ncpamd.com/dementia.htm

This is a wonderful site that is written at an understandable level for relatives, friends, and caregivers of persons with dementia.

Korsakoff's Syndrome

http://www.alzheimers.org.uk/Facts_about_dementia/What_is_dementia/info_kor sakoffs.htm

The Alzheimer's Society provides a detailed explanation of Korsakoff's syndrome and numerous links to other disorders.

Various Types of Agnosia

http://www.psychnet-uk.com/dsm_iv/agnosia.htm

Psychnet-UK provides a detailed description of the various types of agnosia including visual agnosia.

The Alzheimer's Society

http://www.alzheimers.org.uk/index.htm

This is the home page of the Alzheimer's Society. On it you will find a number of excellent articles, up-to-date information, and links to various other dementia-related topics and research.

The International Brain Organization

http://www.ibro.org/Pub_Main_Display.asp?Main_ID=34

The International Brain Organization has put together a well-done synopsis of the man who codiscovered (with Emil Kraepelin) the disease that is named after him, Alzheimer's disesase.

Alzheimer's Disease Education and Referral Center
　　　　http://www.nia.nih.gov/alzheimers
This Web site is managed by the Alzheimer's Disease Education and Referral Center and is part of National Institute on Aging. It has links to many of the institutions involved in working with this disorder, as well as current articles on research findings and clinical trials.

The Journal of Alzheimer's Disease
　　　　http://www.j-alz.com/
This is the Web site of the Journal of Alzheimer's Disease where you can pull up the abstracts of the latest articles as well as some of the archived material.

USE IT OR LOSE IT
Provide an answer to the thought question below, knowing that there is more than one way to respond. Possible answers are presented in the Answer Key.

As the population ages more and more, families will find themselves dealing with a member with Alzheimer's disease. What sorts of support should we be providing for these individuals and their caregivers?

CRISSCROSS
Now that you know all there is to know about this chapter, here's your opportunity to put that knowledge to work.

Across
7. Similar to progressive, but caused by a series of circumscribed cerebral infarcts
9. An acute confusional state lying between normal wakefulness and stupor

Down
1. Dementia producing general deterioration of the brain; observed in AIDS patients
2. A syndrome in which short-term memory is so impaired that the person is unable to recall events from a few minutes previously
3. Gradual, permanent decline from a previously attained level of functioning
4. The man who first described Alzheimer's disease
5. Brain abnormalities characteristic of Alzheimer's disease
6. A form of amnesia where person cannot recall the events preceding the injury
8. A form of amnesia in which a person cannot recall events after an injury

Puzzle created with Puzzlemaker at DiscoverySchool.com

ANSWERS TO TEST QUESTIONS – CHAPTER 13

MATCHING
Frontal lobe - Learning, abstracting, reasoning, inhibiting
Sensory strip - Integration of sensory information from various parts of the body
Parietal lobe - Somaesthetic and motor discriminations and functions
Thalamus - Major relay station for messages from all parts of the body, important in sensations of pain
Occipital lobe - Visual discrimination and some aspects of visual memory
Cerebellum - Fine motor coordination, posture, and balance
Corpus callosum - Communication between the brain's right and left hemispheres
Limbic system - Attention, emotions, "fight or flight," memory
Motor strip - Regulation of voluntary movement
Hypothalamus - Regulation of metabolism, temperature, emotions
Temporal lobe - Discrimination of sounds, verbal and speech behavior
Reticular formation - Arousal reactions, information screening
Medulla - Breathing, blood pressure, other vital functions

SHORT ANSWERS
Your answer should contain the following points.

1. a. these disorders are regarded as psychopathological conditions
b. some brain disorders cause symptoms that look remarkably like other abnormal psychology disorders
c. brain damage can cause changes in behavior, mood, and personality
d. many people who suffer from brain disorders react to the news with depression or anxiety
e. cognitive disorders take a heavy toll on family members in the form of depression and anxiety

2. a. the nature, location, and extent of neural damage
b. the premorbid competence and personality of the individual
c. the individual's life situation
d. the amount of time since the first appearance of the condition

THE DOCTOR IS IN...PSYCHIATRIC HELP—5¢
1. Glen suffers from delirium. The sudden onset, age considerations, and behaviors point to this diagnosis. He has also been given another medication, so the delirium may be brought on by the interactions of the medicines. For treatment: neuroleptics, environmental manipulations, family support, and orienting techniques.

2. Amnestic syndrome. Terry had a long history of alcohol abuse and his memory for remote events is intact as is immediate recall. However, his short-term memory is impaired, as he can't remember events that took place a few minutes before.

3. a. in a coma for a month
b. cognition impairment
c. only graduated from high school (he is young)
d. didn't have well-functioning, promising personality
e. refuses to cooperate with physical therapist
f. not returning to favorable situation

PRACTICE TESTS

Q#	TEST 1	TEST 2	TEST 3
1	C	A	B
2	A	C	B
3	D	B	D
4	A	A	D
5	C	D	B
6	B	A	D
7	C	B	C
8	B	D	B
9	D	D	C
10	D	A	D

COMPREHENSIVE PRACTICE TEST

Q#	M/C	T/F
1	D	T
2	B	F
3	A	T
4	A	T
5	A	T
6	D	F
7	C	F
8	B	T
9	B	F
10	C	T
11	B	T
12	D	T
13	A	F
14	C	F
15	D	T
16	D	
17	B	
18	D	
19	B	
20	B	
21	C	

22	C	
23	B	
24	D	
25	A	

Essay Questions
Your answer should contain the following points.

1. a. Impairment of memory: notable trouble remembering recent events but not necessarily remote past events
b. Impairment of orientation: unable to locate him or herself accurately
c. Impairment of learning, comprehension and judgment: thinking becomes clouded, sluggish, and/or inaccurate
d. Impairment of emotional control or modulation: emotional over reactivity
e. Apathy or emotional blunting: emotional under activity
f. Impairment in the initiation of behavior: lack of self-starting capability and may have to be reminded about what to do next
g. Impairment of controls over matters of propriety and ethical conduct: marked lowering of personal standards in appearance, personal hygiene, etc.
h. Impairment of receptive and expressive communication: inability to comprehend written or spoken language or to express his or her own thoughts
i. Impaired visuospatial ability: difficulty coordinating motor activity with the characteristics of the visual environment

2. a. Senile plaques: made of deformed nerve cell terminals that, at their core, contain beta amyloid, which has been shown to be neurotoxic, causing cell death
b. Neurofibrillary tangles: webs of abnormal filaments within a nerve cell that contain a protein called "tau," thought to be caused by increasing burden of amyloid, thus the presence of tau indicates the disease is progressing
c. Abnormal appearance of small holes in the neuronal tissue: called granulovacuoles and caused from cell degeneration—the earliest and most severely affected structures are a cluster of cell bodies located in the basal forebrain and involved in reducing the release of ACh, a neurotransmitter involved in mediation of memory

3. Alzheimer's disease is associated with a characteristic dementia syndrome that has an imperceptible onset and a usually slow but progressively deteriorating course, terminating in delirium and death. Amyloid plaques and neurofibrillary tangles are distinctive signs of Alzheimer neuropathology. The diagnosis is usually made after all other potential causes of dementia are ruled out. It is impossible to date the onset of the disorder precisely.

4. Early onset appears to be caused by rare genetic mutations of the APP gene on chromosome 21 as well as PS1 and PS2. Late onset is caused by the APOE gene on chromosome 19, which codes for a blood protein that helps carry cholesterol through the bloodstream.

5. Close-head injury, in which the cranium remains intact, penetrating head injury, in which the cranium, as well as the underlying brain, are penetrated by some object such as a bullet, and a skull fracture, with or without compression of the brain by fragmented bone cavity.

USE IT OR LOSE IT

As Alzheimer's disease rates rise we will need to find ways to provide safe, secure care for patients that is affordable, and more support services for their caregivers who are at risk for poor physical and mental health themselves.

CRISSCROSS ANSWERS

Across
7. Vascular
9. Delirium

Down
1. AIDS-related
2. Amnestic
3. Dementia
4. Alzheimer
5. Plaques
6. Retrograde
8. Anterograde

CHAPTER 14: Disorders of Childhood and Adolescence

BEFORE YOU READ

Many of the mental disorders described in previous chapters do not develop until early or middle adulthood. There are some problems that do develop during childhood and adolescence. Most importantly, we must keep in mind that children are not simply small versions of adults, but instead they are dynamic, developing individuals. Children's symptoms of mental illness may vary widely from adults, and even differ in the same child over time. This chapter discusses the types of problems seen in children and adolescents, including attention-deficit hyperactivity disorder, oppositional defiant disorder, conduct disorder, anxiety disorders, and childhood depression. Three disorders that begin in childhood and can persist into adulthood are also discussed including depression, autism, and mental retardation. The chapter concludes with a discussion of the difficulties inherent in developing and testing treatments in children, and how society might better deal with youthful maladaptive and disruptive behaviors.

- **MALADAPTIVE BEHAVIOR IN DIFFERENT LIFE PERIODS**
    Varying Clinical Pictures
    Special Vulnerabilities of Young Children
    The Classification of Childhood and Adolescent Disorders

- **COMMON DISORDERS OF CHILDHOOD**
    Attention-Deficit/Hyperactivity Disorder
    Oppositional Defiant Disorder and Conduct Disorder
    Anxiety Disorders of Childhood and Adolescence
    Childhood Depression
    Pervasive Developmental Disorders
    Autism

- **LEARNING DISORDERS AND MENTAL RETARDATION**
    Learning Disorders
    Causal Factors in Learning Disorders
    Treatments and Outcomes
    Mental Retardation
    Brain Defects in Mental Retardation
    Organic Retardation Syndromes
    Treatment, Outcomes, and Prevention

- **PLANNING BETTER PROGRAMS TO HELP CHILDREN AND ADOLESCENTS**
    Special Factors Associated with Treatment for Children and Adolescents
    Child Advocacy Programs

- **UNRESOLVED ISSUES**
    Can Society Deal with Delinquent Behavior?

OBJECTIVES
After reading this chapter, you should be able to do the following:

1. Discuss how childhood disorders are different from adult disorders, and describe how young children are especially vulnerable to psychological problems.

2. Discuss attention-deficit/hyperactivity disorder.

3. Describe the clinical features, causal factors, and treatment of conduct disorder and oppositional defiant disorder.

4. Describe the clinical features, causal factors, and treatment of the anxiety disorders of childhood.

5. Describe the clinical features, causal factors, and treatment of childhood depression.

6. Describe the clinical features, causal factors, and treatment of autism.

7. Review treatment approaches, outcomes, and prevention with regard to mental retardation.

8. Describe the clinical features, causal factors, and treatment of learning disorders.

9. Explain the four levels of mental retardation and describe the functioning associated with each level.

10. Discuss the types of brain defects associated with mental retardation.

11. List and explain mental retardation stemming from biological causes, especially Down syndrome, PKU, and cranial anomalies.

12. List and explain six special factors that must be considered in relation to treatment for children.

13. Describe the need for mental health services for children, and review the difficulties with recent efforts to increase the available resources.

14. Discuss delinquency as a major societal problem, summarize the many causal factors involved in delinquency, and describe different ways that society deals with delinquency.

AS YOU READ
Answers can be found in the Answer Key at the end of the book.

KEY WORDS
Each of the words below is important in understanding the concepts presented in this chapter. Write the definition next to each word.

Term	Page	Definition
Asperger's disorder	429	
Attention-deficit/hyperactivity disorder (ADHD)	419	
Autism	430	
Conduct disorder	422	
Developmental psychopathology	417	
Down syndrome	439	
Dyslexia	434	
Echolalia	430	
Hydrocephaly	441	
Juvenile delinquency	421	
Learning disabilities	434	
Macrocephaly	440	
Mainstreaming	442	
Mental retardation	435	
Microcephaly	440	
Oppositional defiant disorder	422	
Pervasive developmental disorders	429	
Phenylketonuria	440	
Ritalin	420	
Selective mutism	426	
Separation anxiety disorder	425	

MATCHING
Who's Who and What's What
Match the following with the appropriate description.

Name/Term

_____ ADHD
_____ Oppositional defiant disorder
_____ Dyslexia
_____ Asperger's disorder
_____ Kanner
_____ Autistic-savant
_____ Siegel
_____ "Eden Model"
_____ Integrative strategy instruction
_____ Hypoxia
_____ Langdon Down
_____ Children's Defense Fund

Description/Definition

A. The first to describe autism in infancy and childhood
B. Author of the book *The World of the Autistic Child*
C. An approach to assisting people with autism over the course of their lifespan
D. Difficulties that interfere with effective task-oriented behavior in children
E. A public-interest group based in Washington D.C. that advocates for children
F. A recurring pattern of negativistic, defiant, disobedient, and hostile behaviors toward authority figures
G. Problems in word recognition and reading comprehension
H. A comprehensive intervention model to facilitate learning in LD children offered by Ellis
I. Autistic children who show markedly discrepant and relatively isolated abilities
J. Pervasive developmental disorder that appears later than autism
K. Lack of sufficient oxygen to the brain
L. The first person to describe the best-known clinical conditions associated with moderate and severe mental retardation

SHORT ANSWERS

Provide brief answers to the following questions.

1. What are the three subtypes of ADHD now recognized in the DSM-IV-TR? (pp. 419–420)

2. What are the clinical signs of separation anxiety? (p. 425)

3. Describe the clinical picture of a child with autism. (pp. 430–431)

4. What two groups do children who are institutionalized fall into? (pp. 441–442)

THE DOCTOR IS IN...PSYCHIATRIC HELP—5¢
Read the following scenarios and diagnose the client. Remember to look carefully at the criteria for the disorder before you make a decision as to the diagnosis. Make a list of other information you might need to help you understand the causal factors.

1. Mark, who is seven years old, is referred to your office by his school. He comes to the session with his mother. The school report says that Mark is defiant, disobedient, and has tried to punch his teacher and the principal on more than one occasion. This behavior has been getting worse for the past year. You note that the mother is also hostile and believes that coming to see you is a waste of time. You find out that the household is in turmoil and the parents are having marital problems.

How would you diagnose Mark, and what treatment would you recommend?

2. Gary is an 8-year-old boy who has started withdrawing from school and has been crying both at home and at school for no apparent reason. He has recently lost five pounds and eats once a day. He becomes irritable at times, but usually sits alone in his room for hours. His parents are troubled and don't know what to do.

How would you diagnose Gary, and what would you do to treat him?

AFTER YOU READ

PRACTICE TESTS
Take the following three multiple-choice tests to see how much you have comprehended from the chapter. Each represents roughly one third of the chapter. As you study the chapter, use these to check your progress.

Practice Test 1

1. Until the 20th century, children were seen as being (p. 417)

   a. unique in their psychopathology.
   b. miniature adults.
   c. unable to have any mental illness.
   d. All of the above

2. Clinicians now realize that to understand childhood disorders, they must take into account (p. 417)
   a. developmental processes.
   b. play time.
   c. diblings.
   d. unconscious motivations.

3. Cindy is two years old, has temper tantrums, and puts everything she finds into her mouth. This behavior, for her age, is (p. 417)
   a. appropriate.
   b. inappropriate.
   c. a sign of anxiety.
   d. something to watch as it may lead to future psychopathology.

4. Perhaps because of their behavioral problems, children with ADHD are often lower in intelligence by about _____IQ points. (p. 419)
   a. 12 to 15
   b. 10 to 15
   c. 7 to 15
   d. 5 to 15

5. ADHD is thought to occur in about __ __ percent of school-age children. (p. 419)
   a. 4 to 5
   b. 3 to 5
   c. 3 to 6
   d. 10 to 12

6. Attention-deficit/hyperactivity disorder, conduct disorder, anxiety disorders of childhood, depressive disorders, symptom disorders, and autism are coded on which axis? (p. 418)
   a. Axis I
   b. Axis II
   c. Axis III
   d. Axis IV

7. Learning disabilities and mental retardation are coded on which axis? (p. 418)
   a. Axis I
   b. Axis II
   c. Axis III
   d. Axis IV

8. This disorder is characterized by difficulties that interfere with effective task-oriented behavior in children. (p. 419)
      a. OCD
      b. ODD
      c. ADHD
      d. conduct disorder

9. In ADHD, six or more of the symptoms of inattention or hyperactivity-impulsivity have persisted for at least (p. 420)
      a. 6 months.
      b. 5 months.
      c. 4 months.
      d. 3 months.

10. ADHD is more frequently found in boys before the age of (p. 419)
      a. 10.
      b. 11.
      c. 12.
      d. 8.

Practice Test 2

1. Which of the following is not a characteristic of ADHD? (p. 419)
      a. impulsivity
      b. exaggerated motor activity
      c. sustained attention
      d. decreased IQ

2. Oppositional defiant disorder is apparent by about the age of (p. 421)
      a. 8.
      b. 9.
      c. 15.
      d. 18.

3. Conduct disorder is apparent by about the age of (p. 422)
      a. 8.
      b. 9.
      c. 15.
      d. 18.

4. Risk factors that oppositional defiant and conduct disorders have in common include (p. 423)
a. family discord.
b. socioeconomic disadvantage.
c. antisocial behavior in parents.
d. All of the above

5. Conduct disordered children and adolescents are frequently comorbid for (p. 422)
      a. depressive symptoms.
      b. substance abuse disorder.
      c. conversion disorder.
      d. a and b

6. An effective treatment strategy for conduct disorder is the (p. 424)
      a. juvenile justice system model.
      b. cohesive family model.
      c. punitive model.
      d. IP model.

7. The goal of teaching behavior therapy techniques to the parent or parents of children with conduct disorder is so they can (p. 424)
      a. function as therapists in reinforcing desirable behavior.
      b. function as disciplinarians.
      c. increase their child's behavior.
      d. decrease their interaction with the child.

8. _____ is the most common childhood anxiety disorder. (p. 425)
      a. Selective mutism
      b. Post-traumatic stress
      c. Separation anxiety
      d. OCD

9. Selective mutism is rare in clinical populations and is seen most typically at what age? (p. 426)
      a. within the first year of life
      b. elementary school age
      c. kindergarten
      d. preschool

10. Although childhood and adult depression essentially use the same DSM diagnostic criteria, a recent modification to the childhood diagnosis is (p. 427)
      a. sadness.
      b. loss of appetite.
      c. irritability.
      d. withdrawal.

Practice Test 3

1. Depression in children has been related to depression in (p. 428)
      a. their siblings.
      b. their mothers.
      c. their fathers.
      d. b and c

2. Andrea is ten years old has been diagnosed with childhood depression. She could benefit from what type of therapy? (p. 429)
      a. antidepressants
      b. implosive therapy
      c. cognitive-behavioral therapy
      d. psychoanalytical therapy

3. In childhood depression, this is often found as the major symptom and may be substituted for depressed mood. (p. 427)
      a. poor appetite
      b. suicidality
      c. insomnia
      d. irritability

4. This is the parrot-like repetition of a few words. (p. 430)
      a. deecholalia
      b. echoleia
      c. dyslexia
      d. echolalia

5. _____ was a pioneer in the development of behavioral treatment for autistic children. (p. 433)
      a. Sigmund Freud
      b. Ivar Lovaas
      c. Albert Ellis
      d. Eric Erikson

6. Many famous and successful people have overcome their learning disabilities. Which of the following people had a learning disability? (p. 434)
      a. Sir Winston Churchill
      b. Woodrow Wilson
      c. Nelson Rockefeller
      d. All of the above

7. Ionizing radiation may harm a child by acting directly on the _____ or may damage the sex chromosomes of either parent. (p. 438)
      a. fertilized egg
      b. womb
      c. brain tissue
      d. unfertilized egg

8. Research has shown that a person with Down syndrome will have the greatest deficits in (p. 440)
      a. math skills.
      b. spatial relationships.
      c. verbal and language-related skills.

d. visual-motor coordination.

9. Treatment without parental consent is permitted in all of the following cases, EXCEPT (p. 443)
    a. immature minors.
    b. emancipated minors.
    c. emergency situations.
    d. court-ordered situations.

10. Haney and Gold found that most delinquent acts were committed (p. 447)
    a. alone, without any help.
    b. in association with one or two other persons.
    c. with three or four other persons.
    d. as part of a gang of at least a dozen.

COMPREHENSIVE PRACTICE TEST
The following tests are designed to give you an idea of how well you understood the entire chapter. There are three different types of tests: multiple-choice, true/false, and essay.

Multiple Choice

1. Children are vulnerable to psychological problems because they (p. 417)
    a. have less self-understanding.
    b. haven't developed a stable sense of identity.
    c. haven't a clear understanding of what is expected of them.
    d. All of the above

2. _____ is devoted to studying the origins and course of individual maladaptation in the context of normal growth processes. (p. 417)
    a. Behavioral psychopathology
    b. Cognitive psychopathology
    c. Aging psychopathology
    d. Developmental psychopathology

3. Recent research, although inconclusive, has pointed to ADHD being a result of (p. 420)
    a. biological factors.
    b. social environmental factors.
    c. cognitive behavioral factors.
    d. a and b

4. Side effects of Ritalin include (p. 420)
    a. decreased blood flow to brain.
    b. disruption of growth hormone.
    c. psychotic symptoms.

d. All of the above

5. Which of the following is the most common developmental sequence for conduct disorder (CD), antisocial personality (ASP), delinquency, and/or oppositional defiant disorder (ODD)? (pp. 421–422)
    a. CD, ODD, ASP
    b. ODD, CD, ASP
    c. CD, ASP, ODD
    d. CD, ODD, delinquency

6. Depression is more common in which group? (p. 428)
    a. adolescent boys
    b. adolescent girls
    c. infants
    d. middle-school children

7. Twelve-year-old Jake's parents had had enough of his lying, stealing, and everyday temper tantrums. His teachers were also at a loss for how to control his bullying. So when the judge sentenced Jake to two years in juvenile hall for vandalizing the school computer lab, many were not surprised and some were relieved. Jake would have this disorder. (p. 422)
    a. conduct disorder
    b. oppositional defiant disorder
    c. mental retardation
    d. ADHD

8. Children's exposure to early _____ events can increase their risk for developing depression. (p. 428)
    a. happy
    b. traumatic
    c. unplanned
    d. All of the above

9. Dr. Sims has been studying the same children with ADHD and ODD for the last five years. This type of research is called (p. 421)
    a. longitudinal
    b. cross-sectional
    c. lateral
    d. correlational

10. This is often a precursor of the antisocial behavior seen in children who display negativistic, defiant, disobedient, and hostile behavior toward authority figures. (p. 422)
    a. conduct disorder
    b. OCD
    c. oppositional defiant disorder
    d. ADHD

11. Causal factors in autism include (p. 432)
    a. genetic factors.
    b. disturbance in the central nervous system.
    c. chromosome abnormalities.
    d. All of the above

12. All of the following are true of autism EXCEPT (pp. 432–433)
    a. there have been several effective treatments found, which are awaiting approval by the FDA.
    b. it is usually identified before the child is thirty months old.
    c. self-stimulation is a common symptom in autistic children.
    d. most investigators believe that autism beings with an inborn defect that impairs perceptual-cognitive functioning.

13. The drug(s) used most often in autism is/are _____; however, the effects have not been very impressive. (pp. 432–433)
    a. haloperidol
    b. barbiturates
    c. caffeine
    d. anxiolytics

14. Dana has trouble in school. He has difficulty in spelling and word recognition. Often Dana will omit, add, or distort words. Dana probably has (p. 434)
    a. autism.
    b. dyslexia.
    c. mental retardation.
    d. ADHD.

15. Mental retardation is coded on (p. 448)
    a. Axis I.
    b. Axis II.
    c. Axis III.
    d. Axis IV.

16. Which of the following degrees of retardation is, by far, the most common? (p. 436)
    a. profound
    b. moderate
    c. severe
    d. mild

17. One of the factors that should be considered when studying or treating children is the fact that (pp. 443–444)
    a. children can always seek help on their own.
    b. children are dependent on those around them.
    c. drugs are never warranted to treat children under 12.
    d. children are small adults.

18. The goal of early intervention programs for children is to (p. 445)
      a. reduce the stressors in the child's life.
      b. strengthen the child's coping mechanisms.
      c. not have the problem repeat itself.
      d. a and b

19. Many habitual delinquents share the traits typical of the _____ personality. (p. 446)
      a. antisocial
      b. obsessive-compulsive
      c. narcissistic
      d. passive-aggressive

20. Alienation from family and the broader society causes juveniles to become more vulnerable to (p. 446)
      a. incest and related sexual crimes.
      b. negative influences of TV and other media.
      c. the psychological support afforded by membership in a delinquent gang.
      d. solitary acts of violence.

TRUE/FALSE

1. T / F Children have a complex and realistic view of the world around them. (p. 417)

2. T / F Young children may attempt suicide without any understanding of the finality of death. (p. 417)

3. T / F Hyperactive children are not anxious, in general. (p. 418)

4. T / F Ritalin, when used to treat children with ADHD, has no side effects. (p. 420)

5. T / F Not all children with conduct disorder will go on to become antisocial personalities. (p. 421)

6. T / F Kazdin (1995) said that family and social context factors are not as important causal factors in conduct disorders as genetics. (p. 423)

7. T / F Selective mutism should be diagnosed only if the child actually has the ability to speak and knows the language. (p. 426)

8. T / F Typically, children with anxiety disorders grow up to be adults who don't fit in. (p. 425)

9. T / F Depression in children and adolescents occurs with high frequency. (p. 428)

10. T / F Children can learn to be depressed. (p. 428)

11. T / F Asperger's disorder is a severe and persistent impairment in social interaction that involves marked stereotypic behavior and inflexible adherence to routines. (p. 429)

12 T / F The corresponding IQ range for mild retardation is 35–40 to 50–55. (p. 436)

13. T / F Only about 25 to 40 percent of cases of early-onset conduct disorder go on to develop adult antisocial personality disorder. (p. 421)

14. T / F Microcephaly is a relatively rare condition in which the accumulation of an abnormal amount of cerebrospinal fluid within the cranium causes damage to the brain tissues and enlargement of the skull. (p. 440)

15. T / F ADHD is thought to occur in about 3 to 5 percent of school-age children. (p. 419)

Essay Questions

1. Explain the causal factors in childhood anxiety disorders. (pp. 425–427)

2. Discuss the causal effects of mental retardation. (pp. 437–438)

3. Describe mental retardation and the various levels with IQ ranges. Please be specific in your answer. (pp. 435–437)

4. Explain the causal factors in childhood depression disorders. (pp. 428–429)

WHEN YOU HAVE FINISHED

WEB LINKS TO ITEMS OR CONCEPTS DISCUSSED IN CHAPTER 14

The American Academy of Child and Adolescent Psychiatry
http://aacap.org/index.ww

The home page of the American Academy of Child and Adolescent Psychiatry provides facts for families on child and adolescent mental illness, how to find a child and adolescent psychiatrist in your area, current research, and various other links.

The American Psychological Association
http://www.apa.org/pi/cyf/cmh/

The American Psychological Association provides an entire Web site devoted to children's mental health with various articles, resources, links, and current research in the area.

Oppositional Defiant Disorder
http://www.noah-health.org/

Browsing this site will yield a good overview of many disorders, including oppositional defiant disorder, its treatment and guidelines for recovery and maintenance of a more normal existence.

The Autism Society of America
http://www.autism-society.org/site/PageServer

This is the official Web site of the Autism Society of America, which helps to promote awareness, supports research and advocates for numerous services and programs for the autism community, provides the latest news on legislative and research issues, and is an overall terrific resource on the disorder.

Savant Syndrome
http://www.savantacademy.org/

This is an extremely interesting and heart-warming Web site on Savant syndrome syndrome and the various methods used to teach skills to those with the disorder.

USE IT OR LOSE IT

Provide an answer to the thought question below, knowing that there is more than one way to respond. Possible answers are presented in the Answer Key.

Psychologically, why do you think that membership in a gang appeals to young men from impoverished background?

CRISSCROSS

Now that you know all there is to know about this chapter, here's your opportunity to put that knowledge to work.

Across

2. anxiety-based condition involving persistent failure to speak in certain situations
4. irreversible limitations on survivability, achievement, and competence; 1 in every 1,000 babies
5. damage caused by accumulation of an abnormal amount of cerebrospinal fluid in the cranium
6. a group of severely disabling conditions that are among the most difficult to understand and to treat
8. a liver-based disorder, leading to brain damage if not diagnosed early
9. the parrot-like repetition of a few words
10. a developmental disorder involving a wide range of problematic behaviors

Down

1. medication most administered by school nurses
3. failure of cranium to achieve full size
7. problems in word recognition and reading comprehension; routinely omit, add, and distort words; often resulting in slow reading

Puzzle created with Puzzlemaker at DiscoverySchool.com

ANSWERS TO TEST QUESTIONS – CHAPTER 14

MATCHING
D. ADHD
F. Oppositional defiant disorder
G. Dyslexia
J. Asperger's disorder
A. Kanner
I. Autistic-savant
B. Siegel
C. "Eden Model"
H. Integrative strategy instruction
K. Hypoxia
L. Langdon Down
E. Children's Defense Fund

SHORT ANSWERS
Your answer should contain the following points.

1.　　a. Attention: Deficit/Hyperactivity Disorder, Combined Type
　　　b. Attention: Deficit/Hyperactivity Disorder, Predominantly Inattentive Type
　　　c.　Attention: Deficit/Hyperactivity Disorder, Hyperactive/Impulsive Type

2.　　a. excessive anxiety about separation from major attachment figure
　　　b. lack of self-confidence
　　　c. unrealistic fears
　　　d. oversensitive
　　　e. self-conscious
　　　f. nightmares
　　　g. chronic anxiety

3.　　a. difficulties in relating to others
　　　b. problems with perceptual-cognitive functioning
　　　c. absence of speech
　　　d. lack of development of sense of identity
　　　e. engage in bizarre and repetitive activities
　　　f.　fascinations with unusual objects
　　　g. obsession with maintaining environmental sameness

4.　　a. those who in infancy and childhood manifest severe mental retardation and associated physical impairment and are institutionalized at an early age
　　　b. those who have no physical impairments but show relatively mild mental retardation and a failure to adjust socially in adolescence and are institutionalized because of behavior problems

THE DOCTOR IS IN...PSYCHIATRIC HELP—5¢

1. Diagnosis: oppositional defiant disorder
   Treatment: work on getting the family in for therapy; use the cohesive family model as a treatment strategy, along with behavioral therapy techniques, and possibly remove Mark from his home as a last resort.

2. Diagnosis: major depressive episode
   Treatment: use medication, such as Prozac, an antidepressant; also psychotherapy.

PRACTICE TESTS

Q#	TEST 1	TEST 2	TEST 3
1	B	C	D
2	A	A	A
3	A	B	D
4	C	D	D
5	B	B	B
6	A	B	D
7	B	A	A
8	C	C	C
9	A	D	A
10	D	C	B

COMPREHENSIVE PRACTICE TEST

Q#	M/C	T/F
1	D	F
2	D	T
3	D	T
4	D	F
5	B	T
6	B	F
7	A	T
8	B	F
9	A	T
10	C	T
11	D	T
12	A	F
13	A	F
14	B	F
15	B	T
16	D	
17	B	
18	D	

19	A	
20	C	

Essay Questions

Your answer should contain the following points.

1. a. early illnesses, accidents, or losses that involved pain and discomfort
b. modeling effect of an overanxious and protective parent who sensitizes a child to the dangers and threats of the outside world
c. indifferent, detached, or rejecting parents
d. possibly cultures that favor inhibition, compliance, and obedience
e. exposure to violence leading to a reduced sense of security and psychological well-being

2. a. genetic—chromosomal factors; mental retardation tends to run in families and is in the moderate to severe categories
b. infections and toxic agents
c. trauma (physical injury)—physical injuries at birth
d. ionizing radiation—radiation acting on fertilized egg or parents' eggs and sperm
e. malnutrition and other biological factors—may affect child more indirectly by altering child's responsiveness, curiosity, and motivation

3. Mental retardation is significantly subaverage; general intellectual functioning that is accompanied by significant limitations in adaptive functioning. There are four distinct ranges of severity, mild (50–70), moderate (35–40 to 50–55), severe 20–25 to 35–40), and profound retardation (below 20–25).

4. There are a number of biological factors including parental depression, alcohol intake by the mother during pregnancy, and family history of the disorder. Children also model maladaptive behaviors that they are exposed to such as negative parental behavior or negative emotional states.

USE IT OR LOSE IT

It is believed that young people join gangs when they feel inadequate and rejected by the larger society. Belonging to a gang gives them a sense of belonging and a means of gaining status and approval from others.

CRISSCROSS ANSWERS

Across
2. Selective mutism
4. Down syndrome
5. Hydrocephaly
6. PDD
8. Phenylketonuria

9. Echolalia
10. Autism

Down
1. Ritalin
3. Microcephaly
7. Dyslexia

Chapter 15: Contemporary and Legal Issues in Abnormal Psychology

BEFORE YOU READ

This chapter focuses on the ways in which society deals with abnormal behavior and changes that could be made to optimize these efforts. Chief among these are finding ways to prevent, rather than to treat, mental illness. Another topic addresses the availability of mental health care and the state of mental hospitals, and the role of health management organizations in regulating health care services. Finally, a number of legal issues are raised including the voluntary and involuntary commitment of mentally ill individuals for treatment, the assessment of whether a person is dangerous to themselves or others, the use of the insanity defense in criminal proceedings, and the issue of how best to treat mentally ill patients who commit crimes. As a final challenge, the ways in which people can improve mental health in their communities and on an individual level are discussed in detail.

- **PERSPECTIVES ON PREVENTION**
  Universal Interventions
  Selective Interventions
  Indicated Interventions
  The Mental Hospital as a Therapeutic Community
  Deinstitutionalization

- **CONTROVERSIAL LEGAL ISSUES AND THE MENTALLY DISORDERED**
  The Commitment Process
  Assessment of "Dangerousness"
  The Insanity Defense

- **ORGANIZED EFFORTS FOR MENTAL HEALTH**
  U.S. Efforts for Mental Health
  International Efforts for Mental Health

- **CHALLENGES FOR THE FUTURE**
  The Need for Planning
  The Individual's Contribution

- **UNRESOLVED ISSUES**
  The HMOs and Mental Health Care

OBJECTIVES

After reading this chapter, you should be able to do the following:

1. Define *universal intervention* and explain how it includes biological, psychosocial, and sociocultural efforts.

2. Define *selective intervention*, and describe and illustrate selective intervention programs using the example of teen alcohol and drug abuse prevention.

3. Define *indicated intervention,* describe two types of crisis intervention, and describe and illustrate three types of indicated intervention using the example of an airplane crash or other major disaster.

4. Describe efforts to resocialize patients in mental hospitals and aftercare programs, including methods for making a mental hospital a therapeutic community. Compare the effectiveness of these approaches.

5. Outline the procedures involved in civil commitment and the safeguards for patients' rights and due process in involuntary commitment.

6. Discuss the problems of assessing and predicting "dangerousness" and explain the obligations of the clinician under the "duty-to-warn" legal doctrine.

7. Review the various legal rulings relevant to the insanity defense and discuss the problems and controversies associated with this concept.

AS YOU READ

KEY WORDS
Each of the words below is important in understanding the concepts presented in this chapter. Write the definition next to each word.

Term	Page	Definition
Deinstitutionalization	457	
Forensic psychology (forensic psychiatry)	458	
Guilty but mentally ill (GBMI)	465	
Health maintenance organization (HMO)	469	
Indicated interventions	451	
Insanity defense	462	
Managed health care	469	
Milieu therapy	456	
NGRI plea	462	
Selective interventions	451	
Social-learning programs	456	
Tarasoff decision	462	
Universal interventions	451	

MATCHING
Who's Who and What's What
Alphabet Soup.
The acronyms and abbreviations in column one are all related to mental health. Name these in the second column and describe what each does in the third.

What it means...

Column 1	Column 2 – Name	Column 3 – Function
APA		
NAMI		
NARC		
NIMH		
NIOSH		
NMHA		
WHO		

SHORT ANSWERS
Provide brief answers to the following questions.

1. Briefly discuss the three requirements for psychosocial "health." (p. 452)

a.

b.

c.

2. Our government has approached the drug abuse problem with three broad strategies, all of which have proven insufficient. Name these and discuss. (p. 453)

a.

b.

c.

3. Discuss the three general therapeutic principles that guide the "milieu therapy" approach. (p. 456)

a.

b.

c.

4. Discuss why violent acts are difficult to predict. (p. 461)

THE DOCTOR IS IN...PSYCHIATRIC HELP—5¢
Read the following scenarios and diagnose the client. Remember to look carefully at the criteria for the disorder before you make a decision as to the diagnosis. Make a list of other information you might need to help you understand the causal factors.

1. Stuart, a 26-year-old man you had been seeing for several years, comes into your office demanding to see you immediately even though he doesn't have an appointment. He hasn't seen you for more than a month because he had a job and was trying to go to school. Stuart is diagnosed with schizophrenia and is fine as long as he takes his medications; his behavior indicates he is not taking his medication. You try explaining to him that you have other appointments, but he becomes more and more agitated, talking about the people at work who are out to get him—but that he is going to get them first. Stuart is disheveled and looks like he hasn't bathed in several days. He tells you that you have to help him or he will do something awful.

As Stuart's therapist, what would you do, and why?

2. Jack had been friends with Jennifer for two years. He was madly in love with her although she had made it clear that she liked him only as a friend and didn't want a romantic relationship. About five months ago, Jennifer met Brian and they began dating. Jack felt jealous and left out. He had seen Jennifer go through other "boyfriends" and

always managed to wait them out until Jennifer stopped seeing them. This time is different, and Jennifer is talking about possibly marrying Brian. Jack is beside himself and is consumed with anger and jealousy. He is talking about killing Brian and making it look like an accident. He reasons that Jennifer will then have to seek him out again for comfort, and "she'll have no choice this time." When asked how he would make it look like an accident, Jack replies that he would fix the brakes on Brian's car. Jack is a mechanic and has the knowledge to do such a thing.

As Jack's therapist, how would you respond, and what are your legal responsibilities?

AFTER YOU READ

PRACTICE TESTS
Take the following three multiple-choice tests to see how much you have comprehended from the chapter. Each represents roughly one third of the chapter. As you study the chapter, use these to check your progress.

Practice Test 1

1. Universal interventions are concerned with (p. 451)
    a. altering conditions that can cause or contribute to mental disorders.
    b. establishing conditions that foster positive mental health.
    c. early detection and prompt treatment of maladaptive behavior.
    d. a and b

2. Any effort aimed at improving the human condition, at making life more fulfilling and meaningful, may be considered part of _____ prevention of mental or emotional disturbance. (p. 451)
    a. universal
    b. selective
    c. indicated
    d. secondary

3. All of the following are sociocultural efforts toward universal intervention of mental disorders EXCEPT (p. 452)
    a. economic planning.
    b. penal systems.

    c. public education.
    d. social security.

4. Teenage drug and alcohol use is still viewed as one of today's (p. 453)
    a. biggest money makers for organized crime.
    b. victories over crime.
    c. most significant psychological and community problems.
    d. a and c

5. Through their own drinking or verbalizations about alcohol, parents may (p. 454)
    a. encourage use in their children.
    b. sanction usage by their children.
    c. have little effect in their children's usage.
    d. a and b

6. The most powerful influence on whether a teen begins to use drugs seems to be (p. 454)
    a. peers.
    b. parents.
    c. teachers and schools.
    d. commercials.

7. Programs designed to help youngsters overcome negative pressures from peers focus on (p. 455)
    a. boxing and kung fu.
    b. teaching social skills and assertiveness.
    c. chess.
    d. strengthening family bonds.

8. These programs normally make use of learning principles and techniques such as token economies to shape more socially acceptable behavior. (p. 456)
    a. prosocial learning programs
    b. antisocial learning programs
    c. psychosocial learning programs
    d. social learning programs

9. A persistent concern about hospitalization is that (p. 456)
    a. the mental hospital may become a permanent refuge from the world.
    b. negative feedback is used to encourage appropriate verbalizations and actions by patients.
    c. the environment, or milieu, is a crucial aspect of the therapy.
    d. b and c

10. Milieu therapy is (p.456)
    a. the temporary substitution of one treatment mode by another until adequate resources can be acquired to provide the treatment of choice.

b. a general term for any form of preventive treatment.
c. the use of the hospital environment itself as a crucial part of the therapeutic process.
d. the integration of any two distinct forms of treatment.

Practice Test 2

1. This movement or effort was initiated to prevent the negative effects, for many psychiatric patients, of being confined to a mental hospital for long periods of time as well as to lower health care costs. (p. 457)
        a. reinstitutionalization
        b. deinstitutionalization
        c. preinstitutionalization
        d. institutionalization

2. Studies have shown that in the past, up to _____ percent of schizophrenic patients have been readmitted to the hospital within the first year after their discharge. (p. 457)
        a. 1.732
        b. 12.6
        c. 45
        d. 99

3. Between 1970 and 1992, the number of state mental hospitals dropped from 310 to 273, and the patient population was reduced by 73 percent due to (p. 457)
        a. the AIDS epidemic.
        b. fallout from the Vietnam War.
        c. the introduction of antipsychotic drugs.
        d. deinstitutionalization.

4. Deinstitutionalization has contributed substantially to (p. 458)
        a. mental health and general well-being in the United States.
        b. the number of homeless people.
        c. the number of mentally ill people in prison.
        d. b and c

5. According to recent Justice Department statistics, _____ of the people in prison in the United States (275,000) have a mental disorder. (p. 458)
        a. 1.732 percent
        b. more than 16 percent
        c. about half
        d. almost all

6. Typically, the first step in committing an individual to a mental hospital involuntarily is (p. 459)
        a. appointing a physician and a psychologist to examine the client.
        b. filing a petition for a commitment hearing.

c. holding a commitment hearing.

d. notifying the police.

7. Studies have confirmed that individuals acquitted of crimes by reason of insanity typically spend _____ time in psychiatric hospitals as (than) individuals convicted of crimes spend in prison. (p. 459)

a. less

b. about the same amount of

c. about the same amount or more

d. much more

8. Violent acts are difficult to predict because these are determined as much by _____ circumstances as by the personality traits of the individual. Mental health professionals typically err on the conservative side when assessing violence proneness. (p. 461)

a. territorial

b. behavioral

c. situational

d. hostile

9. Which of the following groups of mentally ill individuals would be the LEAST likely to commit a violent act? (p. 461)

a. schizophrenic individuals

b. manic individuals

c. patients with deeply entrenched delusions

d. patients in a major depressive state

10. Congress passed its first comprehensive mental health bill, the National Mental Health Act in (p. 465)

a. 1789.

b. 1865.

c. 1946.

d. 1993.

Practice Test 3

1. The M'Naghten Rule of 1843 established legal defense for a person (p. 464)

a. if she lacked "substantial capacity" to appreciate the criminal character of her behavior.

b. if he were "unable to appreciate" the criminality of his act and the mental disorder involved must be severe.

c. unless it can be proven that at the time of her act, she did not know what she was doing was wrong, she is assumed to be sane.

d. if an "irresistible impulse" caused him to commit the crime, even though he knew what he was doing was wrong.

2. The Irresistible Impulse Rule of 1887 established legal defense for a person (p. 464)
>   a. if she lacked "substantial capacity" to appreciate the criminal character of her behavior.
>   b. if he were "unable to appreciate" the criminality of his act and the mental disorder involved must be severe.
>   c. unless it can be proven that at the time of her act, she did not know what she was doing was wrong, she is assumed to be sane.
>   d. if an "irresistible impulse" caused him to commit the crime, even though he knew what he was doing was wrong.

3. The American Law Institute (ALI) Standard of 1962 established legal defense for a person (p. 464)
>   a. if she lacked "substantial capacity" to appreciate the criminal character of her behavior.
>   b. if he were "unable to appreciate" the criminality of his act and the mental disorder involved must be severe.
>   c. unless it can be proven that at the time of her act, she did not know what she was doing was wrong, she is assumed to be sane.
>   d. if an "irresistible impulse" caused him to commit the crime, even though he knew what he was doing was wrong.

4. The Federal Insanity Defense Reform Act (IDRA) of 1984 redefined legal defense for a person to be such that (p. 464)
>   a. if she lacked "substantial capacity" to appreciate the criminal character of her behavior.
>   b. if he were "unable to appreciate" the criminality of his act and the mental disorder involved must be severe.
>   c. unless it can be proven that at the time of her act, she did not know what she was doing was wrong, she is assumed to be sane.
>   d. if an "irresistible impulse" caused him to commit the crime, even though he knew what he was doing was wrong.

5. The National Institute of Mental Health (NIMH) was formed in Washington D.C. in (p. 464)
>   a. 1812.
>   b. 1849.
>   c. 1946.
>   d. 1984.

6. The National Institute of Mental Health (NIMH) (p. 464)
>   a. conducts and supports research.
>   b. supports training in the mental health field.
>   c. helps communities plan, establish, and maintain effective mental health programs.
>   d. All of the above

7. The National Mental Health Association (NMHA) (p. 466)
    a. sets and maintains the high professional and ethical standards within the psychological industry.
    b. recognizes psychological disorders as one of the ten leading work-related health problems.
    c. works for the improvement of services in community clinics and mental hospitals.
    d. works to reduce the incidence of mental retardation and carry on a program of education.

8. The American Psychological Association (APA) (p. 466)
    a. sets and maintains the high professional and ethical standards within the psychological industry.
    b. recognizes psychological disorders as one of the ten leading work-related health problems.
    c. works for the improvement of services in community clinics and mental hospitals.
    d. works to reduce the incidence of mental retardation and carry on a program of education.

9. The National Institute for Occupational Safety and Health (NIOSH) (p. 466)
    a. sets and maintains the high professional and ethical standards within the psychological industry.
    b. recognizes psychological disorders as one of the ten leading work-related health problems.
    c. works for the improvement of services in community clinics and mental hospitals.
    d. works to reduce the incidence of mental retardation and carry on a program of education.

10. The National Association for Retarded Citizens (NARC) (p. 466)
    a. sets and maintains the high professional and ethical standards within the psychological industry.
    b. recognizes psychological disorders as one of the ten leading work-related health problems.
    c. works for the improvement of services in community clinics and mental hospitals.
    d. works to reduce the incidence of mental retardation and carry on a program of education.

COMPREHENSIVE PRACTICE TEST
The following tests are designed to give you an idea of how well you understood the entire chapter. There are three different types of tests: multiple-choice, true/false, and essay.

Multiple Choice

1. At high risk for mental disorders are (p. 451)
      a. recently divorced people and the physically disabled.
      b. elderly people and physically abused children.
      c. persons recently uprooted from their homes and victims of severe trauma.
      d. All of the above

2. Adequate preparation for potential problems likely to be encountered by anyone during a given life stage is a requirement for _____ health, at the _____ level of prevention. (p. 451)
      a. biological, universal
      b. psychosocial, universal
      c. biological, selective
      d. psychosocial, selective

3. In addition to mental illness, grounds for commitment require that a person must be judged to be _____ and in need of treatment or care in a hospital. (p. 456)
      a. dangerous to themselves or to others
      b. incapable of providing for their basic physical needs
      c. unable to make responsible decisions about hospitalization
      d. Any of the above

4. Which of the following patient rights was limited, according to a 1990 U.S. Supreme Court ruling? (p. 460)
      a. right to compensation for work
      b. right to refuse ECT and psychosurgery
      c. right to receive treatment
      d. right to refuse psychotropic medication

5. Violence among psychiatric patients is especially prominent for those who (p. 461)
      a. watch television.
      b. drink alcohol.
      c. do not get enough exercise.
      d. All of the above

6. Franklin was unable to care for himself and was seen as a threat to others after his outburst at the local fast food restaurant. The need for _____ _____ was evident. (p. 459)
      a. proactive commitment
      b. active commitment

    c. voluntary commitment
    d. involuntary commitment

7. A man's NGRI plea ("not guilty by reason of insanity") in a court case means (p. 462)
    a. "He couldn't have done it, because that would be an insane thing to do."
    b. "Not Getting Rightful Incarceration."
    c. "While he did do it, he lacked moral blameworthiness, because he was insane."
    d. Whichever reason seems like it might work.

8. The duty-to-warn ruling that spelled out a therapist's responsibility in situations where there has been an explicit threat on a specific person's life is also known as (p. 462)
    a. the Tarasoff decision.
    b. the Korsakoff decision.
    c. the Hasselhoff decision.
    d. the Sarasoff decision.

9. An NGRI plea was more likely to be found to be successful if the defendant was (p. 464)
    a. diagnosed with a major mental disorder, or there had been prior mental hospitalizations.
    b. a female.
    c. accused of a violent crime other than murder.
    d. All of the above

10. Several states have adopted a different mentally ill plea, known as (p. 465)
    a. Please Let Me Go (PLMG)
    b. Guilty But Mentally Ill (GBMI)
    c. Too Drunk To Know (TDTK)
    d. All of the above

11. During World War II, _____ recruits were rejected for military service for psychiatric reasons. (p. 465)
    a. no
    b. 50 percent of
    c. two out of seven
    d. 55,734

12. Most often, in an HMO the gatekeeper who determines which mental health treatments will be offered is a (p. 469)
    a. psychiatric social worker.
    b. psychologist.
    c. medical generalist or business professional.
    d. psychiatrist.

13. The World Health Organization (WHO) estimates that mental disorders affect at least _____ people worldwide. (p. 467)
    a. 42
    b. 3 million
    c. 200 million
    d. 1.732 billion

14. George was arrested on three counts of attempted murder, and two murders in the first degree. He knew exactly what he was doing but did not want to face the legal consequences for his actions. He told the judge that he was hearing voices that told him to do it. George was trying to use (p. 462)
    a. a sobriety defense.
    b. a sanity defense.
    c. a profanity defense.
    d. an insanity defense.

15. Other than accepting some measure of responsibility for the mental health of others through the quality of one's own interpersonal relationships, another constructive course open to each citizen is (p. 468)
    a. serving as a volunteer in a mental or other hospital.
    b. supporting realistic measures for ensuring comprehensive health services for all age groups.
    c. working toward improved public education, responsible government, the alleviation of prejudice, and the establishment of a more sane and harmonious world.
    d. All of the above

TRUE/FALSE

1. T / F For the most part, mental health efforts have been restorative, rather than preventative. (p. 451)

2. T / F Often the most beneficial aspect of a therapeutic community is the interaction among the patients themselves. (p. 456)

3. T / F Today, in most states, the therapist not only can violate confidentiality with impunity, but may be required by law to take action to protect persons from the threat of imminent violence against them. (p. 462)

4. T / F The new "guilty but mentally ill" (GBMI) plea requires a two-part decision. (p. 465)

5. T / F Psychological difficulties among employees may result in absenteeism, accident proneness, poor productivity, and high job turnover. (p. 466)

6. T / F The World Federation for Mental Health was established in 1861. (p. 467)

7. T / F The world's mental health problems are so large and so scattered that there is really nothing that an individual can do to help. (p. 468)

8. T / F Most people will have to deal with severely maladaptive behavior during their lives. (p. 467)

9. T / F Economic considerations have drastically altered the machinations of the mental health field. (p. 470)

10. T / F Prevention of mental illness focuses on universal, selective, and indicated interventions (p. 470)

11. T / F Teenage alcohol and drug use remains one of the most significant psychological community problems. (p. 453)

12. T / F Early alcohol use is NOT a strong predictor of lifetime alcohol abuse and dependence. (p. 454)

13. T / F Some consider deinstitutionalization to be the abandonment of chronic patients to a cruel and harsh existence, which for many includes homelessness, violent victimization, or suicide. (p. 457)

14. T / F Inpatient psychiatric hospitalization may be increasing because of the failures to provide adequate mental health care for patients in need of mental health services in the community. (p. 457)

15. T / F In most states, the therapist is allowed to violate confidentiality of any of his or her clients and may be required by law to take action to protect people from the threat of imminent violence against them. (p. 462)

Essay Questions

1. A relatively new approach in behavioral psychology is in its prevention, as opposed to previous approaches, all aimed at treatment. Name and discuss the three subcategories of these efforts. (pp. 451–457)

2. Deinstitutionalization, the movement to close down mental hospitals and treat persons with severe mental disorder in the community, has been the source of considerable controversy. Discuss the pros and cons of deinstitutionalization. (pp. 457–458)

a.

b.

c.

3. The wake of the Tarasoff decision left many perplexing issues for practitioners. Discuss the decision and its aftermath. (pp. 461–462)

WHEN YOU HAVE FINISHED

WEB LINKS TO ITEMS OR CONCEPTS DISCUSSED IN CHAPTER 15
Web Site of the American Psychology-Law Society Division 41
        http://www.ap-ls.org/
This is the official Web site of the American Psychology-Law Society Division 41 of the American Psychological Association where you will find the latest publications, conferences, and information related to psychology and the law.

The Court TV Crime Library
        http://www.crimelibrary.com/criminal_mind/psychology/insanity/1.html
The Court TV crime library devotes thirteen chapters to the history and present-day use of the insanity plea in the judicial system written by Mark Gado.

Serial Killer – Ted Bundy
http://www.crimelibrary.com/serial_killers/notorious/bundy/index_1.html
This Web page is the starting point that chronicles the beginnings of serial killer Ted Bundy and progresses into his state of mental health and eventual execution.

Serial Killer – Jeffrey Dahmer
http://www.crimelibrary.com/serial_killers/notorious/dahmer/index.html
This Web site chronicles the life and death of Jeffrey Dahmer and describes his mental state during and after his crimes as well as his childhood.

Serial Killer – John Wayne Gacy
http://www.crimelibrary.com/serial_killers/notorious/gacy/gacy_1.html
Quite possibly one of the most dangerous serial killers from the Midwest, John Wayne Gacy's story is told in quite vivid detail.

The Madness of Deinstitutionalization
http://www.psych-health.com/pages/idxredirect.cgi?fn=/idx/PSYCH-HEALTH1/madness.htm
This site discusses the failure of deinstitutionalization.

The Harvard Newsletter
http://www.innovations.harvard.edu/showdoc.html?id=3035
This issue of the *Harvard Newsletter* discusses the reduction in the use of public services with the placement of mentally ill homeless persons in supportive housing.

Rush University Medical Center Psychiatry Services
http://www.rush.edu/rumc/page-1099611552138.html
This Web site provides a description of the types of mental health services provided by Rush University Medical Center, one of largest medical centers in the United States.

Rush Day Hospital
http://www.rush.edu/rumc/page-1134773769347.html
The Rush Day Hospital (RDH) in Chicago provides an intensive group-based program that offers partial hospitalization, intensive outpatient and group therapy during day and evening hours. This site demonstrates a contrast with typical community-based care or hospitalization.

Early Detection of Mental Illness
http://www.preventmentalillness.org/
This Web site is devoted entirely to preventing mental illness by advocating early detention and has links to various organizations that specialize in early detection and screening for mental illness.

USE IT OR LOSE IT

Provide an answer to the thought question below, knowing that there is more than one way to respond. Possible answers are presented in the Answer Key.

Should mentally ill people who commit crimes be put in jail or mental institutions?

CRISSCROSS

Now that you know all there is to know about this chapter, here's your opportunity to put that knowledge to work.

Across

2. Recognizes psychological disorders as one of the leading work-related health problems
3. Agency serving as central research and training center
4. Professional organization for psychologists
9. Total treatment program
12. Volunteer organization working for improvement of services in community clinics
14. Health services company
15. Intervention efforts directed toward high-risk individuals

Down

1. Legal status of the mentally ill
5. NGRI
6. New criminal court plea requiring two-part decision
7. Volunteer organization for the mentally ill
8. Intervention efforts aimed at a specific subgroup
10. Murder victim whose death led to duty-to-warn rule
11. Professional organization that sets standards for U.S. psychiatric industry
13. Intervention efforts aimed at influencing the general population
16. Professional organization for behavioral therapists

Puzzle created with Puzzlemaker at DiscoverySchool.com

ANSWERS TO TEST QUESTIONS – CHAPTER 15

SHORT ANSWERS
Your answer should contain the following points.

1. a. develop the skills needed for effective problem solving, expressing emotions constructively, and engaging in satisfying relationships
b. an accurate frame of reference on which to build his or her identity
c. be prepared for the types of problems likely to be encountered during life

2. a. interdicting and reducing the supply of drugs available
• war on drugs has had little impact on the availability of drugs
b. providing treatment services for those who develop drug problems
• perhaps the least effective way to reduce the problem
c. encouraging prevention
• most desirable; teaching young people ways to avoid use; hasn't worked because efforts have not been powerful enough or been well implemented

3. a. staff expectations are clearly communicated to patients
b. patients are encouraged to become involved in all decisions
c. patients belong to social groups on the ward

4. They are apparently determined as much by situational circumstances (such as whether the person is under the influence of alcohol) as by an individual's personality traits or violent predispositions. One significantly predictive risk factor is a past history of violence.

THE DOCTOR IS IN...PSYCHIATRIC HELP—5¢

1. Call 911 for an ambulance to transport Stuart and have Stuart committed to the hospital as an emergency. There isn't time to get a court order; Stuart is dangerous and a threat to himself and others, incapable of providing for his basic physical needs, unable to make responsible decisions about hospitalization, and is in need of treatment.

2. First, you would discuss the consequences of such behavior and what it could mean to his life and others. If, as the therapist, you believe that Jack is capable of carrying out his threat, you have a duty to warn. Given Jack's statements, unrequited love for Jennifer, and occupation as a mechanic, there is a high likelihood of homicidal ideation. Ultimately, the client/therapist confidentiality can be broken to inform police and to make "reasonable efforts" to inform the potential victim. In this case, both Jennifer and Brian would need to be notified. Jack may need to be committed as well for observation depending on the level of insight and mental status.

PRACTICE TESTS

Q#	Test1	Test 2	Test 3
1	D	B	C
2	A	C	D
3	B	D	A
4	C	D	B
5	D	B	C
6	A	B	D
7	B	A	C
8	D	C	A
9	A	D	B
10	C	C	D

COMPREHENSIVE PRACTICE TEST

Q#	M/C	T/F
1	D	T
2	B	T
3	D	T
4	D	T
5	B	T
6	D	F
7	C	F
8	A	T
9	D	T
10	B	T
11	C	T
12	C	F
13	C	T
14	D	T
15	D	T

Essay Questions
Your answer should contain the following points.
1. a. universal interventions: general population
• biological measures lifestyles, diet, physical exercise, good health habits
• psychosocial measures develop physical, intellectual, emotional, and social competencies
• sociocultural measures relationship between an individual and his or her community
b. selective interventions: specific subgroup
• selective prevention strategies
• education programs for high-risk teens
• parent and family-based intervention
• peer group programs

• increase self-esteem
• mass media
c. indicated interventions: high-risk individuals
• mental hospital as therapeutic community
• aftercare programs

2. a. significant improvement versus "abandonment"
b. seemed a workable plan
c. problems arose
• substandard homes and services
• many became homeless
• lack of follow-up

3. a. decision held therapists responsible to warn authorities if a specific threat emerges during a session with a client
b. calls into question the patient confidentiality
c. ethical dilemmas

USE IT OR LOSE IT

This is a complex question with no clear answer. Most people would agree that the public should be protected from crime and dangerous behavior. However, it is often difficult to determine who constitutes a future threat, or how mental health issues have contributed to a particular crime. In addition, if people are placed in a mental institution instead of prison there are questions about how long they should be held, who will determine their release, and whether this constitutes incarceration without due process of law if they did not receive a trial.

CRISSCROSS ANSWERS

Across
2. NIOSH
3. NIMH
4. APS
9. Milieu therapy
12. NMHA
14. HMO
15. Indicated

Down
1. Forensic psychology
5. Insanity defense
6. GBMI
7. NAMI
8. Selective
10. Tarasoff
11. APA
13. Universal
16. AABT

NOTES

NOTES

NOTES

SRA
Practice Decodable
Stories Takehome
Book

Grade 1
aligned with *Reading Mastery*

McGraw Hill SRA

Columbus, OH

The *McGraw·Hill* Companies

Contents

3

About the Decodable Takehome Books

The *Decodable Takehome Books* provide opportunities for your students to apply the skills and vocabulary they learn in the **Reading Mastery** program as they read independently. The stories also use the orthography used at this level of the **Reading Mastery** program. The vocabulary in these stories is ten lessons behind the vocabulary in the corresponding **Reading Mastery** lessons so students will have had many opportunities to practice reading the words before reading the *Decodable Takehome Books*.

Students can fold and staple the pages of each *Decodable Takehome Book* to make books of their own to keep and read. We suggest you keep extra sets of the stories in your classroom for the students to reread.

Directions for preparing the books are on pages 6 and 7.

How to Make a Takehome Book

1. Tear out the pages you need.
2. Place pages 4 and 5 and pages 2 and 7 face up.

3. Place pages 4 and 5 on top of pages 2 and 7.

4. Fold along the center line.

5. Check to make sure the pages are in order.

mom is mad at him now. nō dog digs a lot. hē digs in thē mud.

sēē thōs. traccs on thē rug? nō dog mād. thōs. traccs. mom got mad. mom said, "nō, dog, nō." nō dog had to gō to his hut.

6. Staple the pages along the fold.

nō dog digs

by Art Little
Illustrated by Timothy Pack
Decodable Book Lesson 127

For you and your child . . .

You can share the joy of independent reading with your child. From time to time your child will bring home his or her own *Decodable Takehome Books* to read with you. With your help, these stories can give your child important reading practice and a joyful shared reading experience.

The Reading Mastery System

In these stories there is an unusual way to represent the sounds of English. This is the way students begin reading in the ***Reading Mastery*** program, and it is surprisingly easy. The unusual elements give students clues to the sounds. For example, when a letter stands for a long vowel sound there is a straight line above it, and a "silent *e*" is represented by a small *e* (cāke).

Also, the only capital letter taught in Grade K is the pronoun *I*. This allows students to focus on learning the relationships of sounds and symbols and on comprehension without other concerns.

This system is used throughout Grade K and into Grade 1. It "fades" to our conventional system beginning in Lesson 81 of Grade 1.

Reading with Your Child

You might want to set aside a few minutes each evening to read these stories together. Here are some suggestions you might find helpful:

- Do not expect your child to read each story perfectly. Concentrate on sharing the book together.
- Participate by doing some of the reading.
- If your child gets stuck on a word, just say the word and ask the child to reread the sentence.
- Talk about the stories as you read, give lots of encouragement, and watch your child become more fluent.

Learning to read takes lots of practice. Sharing these stories is one way that your child can gain that valuable experience. Encourage your child to keep the books in a special place. This collection will become a library of books that your child can read and reread. Take the time to listen to your child read. Just a few moments of shared reading each day can give your child the interest, enthusiasm, and confidence needed to excel in reading.

A message from _____

Para Usted y su Hijo(a) . . . . .

Se puede compartir el placer de leer independientemente con su hijo(a). De cuando en cuando su hijo(a) traerá a casa su propio *Decodable Books* para leer con usted. Con su ayuda, estos cuentos le pueden dar a su hijo(a) práctica importante en la lectura y una experiencia agradable.

El Sistema Reading Mastery

En estos cuentos se usa un alfabeto especial para representar los sonidos de inglés. De esta manera los estudiantes empiezan a leer en el programa *Reading Mastery* y es bastante fácil. El alfabeto especial les da a los estudiantes las pistas a los sonidos. Por ejemplo, cuando una letra representa el sonido de un vocal larga hay una línea recta sobre la letra y una "e mudo" que se representa con una "e" pequeña (**cāke**).

También la única letra mayúscula que se enseña en Grado K es el pronombre *"I"*. Esto les permite a los estudiantes enfocar en el aprendizaje de las relaciones entre los sonidos y los símbolos, y en la comprensión de los textos, sin otras preocupaciones.

Este sistema se usa a lo largo del Grado K y en la primera parte del Grado 1. Se introduce el sistema convencional gradualmente, empezando con la Lección 81 del Grado 1.

Leyendo con su Hijo(a)

Si usted quiere reservar algunos minutos por la tarde para leer juntos los cuentos, aquí hay algunas sugerencias interesantes:

- No espere que su hijo(a) sepa leer perfectamente cada cuento. Concéntrese en leer el libro juntos.
- Participe usted leyendo parte del cuento.
- Si su hijo(a) no conoce alguna palabra, dígale la palabra y pídale que la pronuncie. Entonces vuelva a leer la frase otra vez.
- Discuta los cuentos, dé mucho ánimo y verá como su hijo(a) llegará a ser más fluente.

Aprender a leer exige mucha práctica. Compartir los cuentos es una manera de ganar experiencia. Esta colección será una biblioteca de libros que su hijo(a) podrá leer muchas veces. Escuche a su hijo(a) leer. Unos pocos minutos leyendo juntos cada día pueden proveer el interés, el entusiasmo, y la confianza que le hace falta para sobresalir en la lectura.

Un mensaje de _____

don't jump on the bed

Illustrated by Brad Mancuso

Decodable Book Lesson 4

Mc Graw Hill SRA

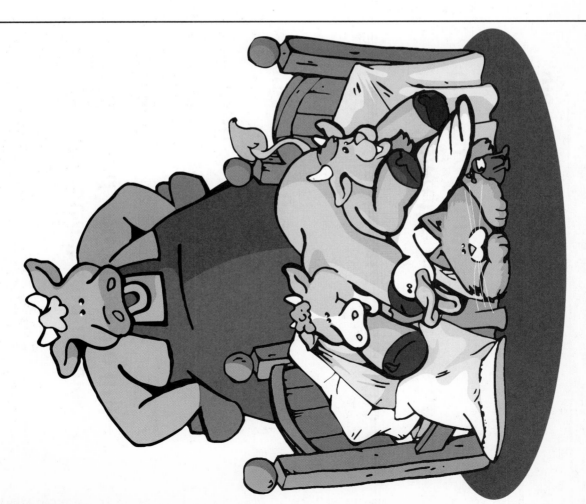

2

"the littлe bug," said mother.
"what did you do to the littлe bug?"

"wherе is the bug?" said the kitten.

"wherе is the bug?" said the duck.

"wherе is the bug?" said the goat.

"Ōh," said the cow. "hērе hē is. that bug bit mȳ ēar."

"sēē, I tōld you not to jump on the bed," said mother.

7

© SRA/McGraw-Hill

the cow jumpₑd on the bed.

"dōn't jump on the bed," mother said.

the gōat jumpₑd on the cow that jumpₑd on the bed.

"dōn't jump on the bed," mother said.

"Ōh, nō, bug. you brōkₑ the bed," they said.

the bug fell on the rug.

the kitten fell on the bug that fell on the rug.

the ducₖ fell on the kitten that fell on the bug that fell on the rug.

the gōat fell on the ducₖ that fell on the kitten that fell on the bug that fell on the rug.

the cow fell on the gōat that fell on the ducₖ that fell on the kitten that fell on the bug that fell on the rug.

the duck jumped on the goat that jumped on the cow that jumped on the bed.

"dōn't jump on the bed," mother said.

the kitten jumped on the duck that jumped on the goat that jumped on the cow that jumped on the bed.

"dōn't jump on the bed," mother said.

the bug jumped on the kitten that jumped on the duck that jumped on the goat that jumped on the cow that jumped on the bed.

"dōn't jump on the bed," mother said.

the yarn shop part I

Illustrated by Timothy Pack

Decodable Book Lesson 9

McGraw Hill SRA

15

8

2

miss tan and her chicks cāme into the shop. the chicks werₑ slēēpiñg in a box. miss tan got lots of yarn fōr hats and socₖs. miss tan and slīder werₑ talkiñg when the chicₖs jumpₑd from the box.

sam is a duck. hē runs the farm. Well, wē let him think hē runs the farm. wē līke sam.

sam and dan and I went to the yarn shop. wē were wet from the rāin. there was a lot of mud on us. slīder yelled, "wīpe your fēēt. dōn't get mud on the yarn. come give mē a hug. you nēēd to bē fatter. hēre, ēat a cōrn tart." wē līke slīder. shē is fun.

sam has lots of nãmₑs: sam ron will macₖ moon chip. when his mother gets mad, shē says, "sam ron will macₖ moon chip, wherₑ arₑ you?" then sam runs as fast as hē can to the pond.

his mother is slīder moon chip. shē has a yarn shop. shē has lots and lots of yarn. shē can not walk fast in her shop. shē can not run in her shop. shē has red socₖs sō shē can slīdₑ. slīding is faster than walking.

the yarn shop part 2

Illustrated by Timothy Pack

Decodable Book Lesson 14

Mc Graw Hill SRA

after miss tan went, slīder sat down on the rug. "mȳ, mȳ, mȳ," shē said. "look at this shop."

"wē will fix it," said sam. "it will bē fīne."

and wē did fix it, and the shop was fīne.

2

sam and dan and I took the chicks fōr a littlᵉ walk. the chicks went to slēēp in the box. then wē went bacк to the shop.

dan took the yarn fōr miss tan.
miss tan took the box of chicкs.
then dan walked hōmᵉ with miss tan and the chicкs.

miss tan and slīder did not sēē the chicks flȳ up into the yarn. they did not sēē the chicks digging in a big pīle of yarn. they did not sēē the chicks dīve into a box of red yarn.

miss tan and slīder yelled, "stop, chicks. get back into the box now."

"I must get mȳ yarn. then wē must gō hōme," said miss tan. "boys, I nēēd help. will you tāke the chicks sō I can shop?"

yarn went every wher_e. hēr_e. ther_e. every wher_e. red yarn. whīt_e yarn. thōs_e chick_s. they wer_e having fun.

sam and dan and ī hid under a pīl_e of hats.

socks and rocks

Illustrated by Brad Manscuso

Decodable Book Lesson 19

SRA

2

"arf. arf. arf," said Jāne.

mother said to tiger, "Jāne says you rock. so rocks is the nāme for you. now you are socks and rocks."

then mother said, "socks you can tēach rocks to talk dog talk. rocks, you can tēach socks to talk tiger talk. you will have fun."

"arf."

"arf? what do you mēan? arf? whȳ do you talk līke that?" said little tiger.

"hē is a dog. hē is barking," said mother tiger.

"is that what a dog looks līke? hē looks līke a mop to mē," said little tiger.

"a dog can look līke that," said her mother.

"arf. arf. arf," said the little dog.

mother tiger smiled. "hē is not a hē, little tiger. hē is a dog. her nāme is Jāne. but shē says the nāme socks is better."

littlₑ tiger walkₑd ōver to the littlₑ dog. shē lookₑd at the dog fr̄om nōsₑ to tāil.

"can I pet him?" littlₑ tiger said to her mother.

"can littlₑ tiger pet you?" mother said to the littlₑ dog.

"arf. arf," littlₑ dog barkₑd.

"hē said yes, littlₑ tiger."

littlₑ tiger smilₑd at the littlₑ dog. then littlₑ dog jumpₑd up and kissₑd littlₑ tiger on the nōsₑ.

"hē kissₑd mē. hē kissₑd mē. I līkₑ him. what is his nāmₑ? look at his f̄eet. his f̄eet look līkₑ hē has socₖs. is his nāmₑ socₖs?"

socks and rocks gō swimming

Illustrated by Brad Mancuso

Decodable Book Lesson 24

Mc Graw Hill SRA

---

when the sun started to gō down, mom said, "wē must gō now, rocks. it is tīme to gō hōme."

rocks started to crȳ. "don't crȳ, rocks. big girls don't crȳ ōver things līke that. wē will plāy another tīme."

then rocks ran hōme with her mother. and socks went into her hōme.

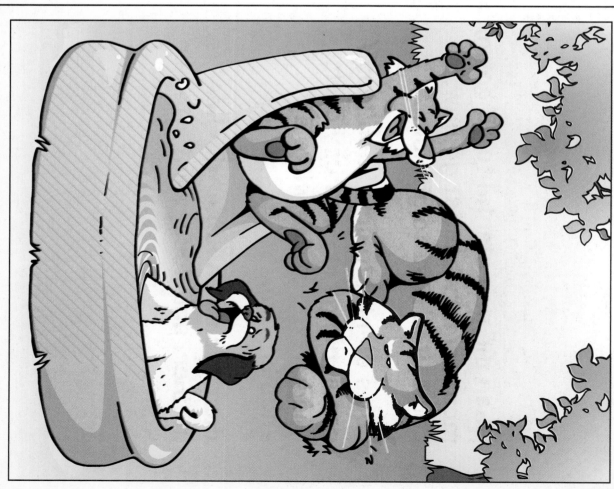

© SRA/McGraw-Hill

"it is a hot, hot dāy. come to mȳ hōme and plāy in the water. wē can jump and slῙde in the pool," said socks.

"let's ask mom," said rocks. "she will gō with us."

soon socks yelled, "there is mȳ hōme. there is mȳ pool."

they ran to the pool. rocks and socks jumped in. mom sat bȳ the pool.

rocks and socks plāyed in the pool. they went up and down the slῙde.

mother tiger was under a tree. it looked like she was sleeping. but she was not really sleeping.

"sh-sh-sh," said rocks. "mother is sleeping. let's jump on her."

rocks and socks ran and jumped on mom. mom and rocks and socks played and played. mom licked them and gave them hugs. mom after a little bit, they stopped and went to sleep in the sun.

when they got up from sleeping, rocks said to her mom, "let's go swimming. we can go home with socks. we can swim in her pool."

so mom and rocks and socks started walking. when they got to a stream, rocks said, "mom, let us ride on your back, and you can swim."

"you girls can swim. but you think it is fun to ride on my back. you are funny. hold on. here we go," said mom.

macₖ is pāinₜed

Illustrated by Brad Mancuso

Decodable Book Lesson 29

Mc Graw Hill SRA

sam pāinted. pāint was flȳing every wher_e. pāint got on sam. pāint got on the trēē. pāint got on the pad. pāint got on mac_k, but don't tell him.

"ther_e. do you want to sēē what you look līk_e?" ask_ed sam.

"what? that is not mē. I don't look līk_e that. I don't hav_e a red tāil. I don't hav_e a whīt_e nōs_e. I don't hav_e pāint on mȳ ēar_s," mac_k yell_ed.

"you do now," said sam.

sam and mack are not brothers. sam is a duck. mack is a dog. but they are like brothers. they like each other. they are with each other every day.

the other day, mack and sam were walking. sam had a big box. sam had on a funny hat and top and pants. there was a lot of paint on the hat and the top and the pants.

"I am going to paint you," answered sam.

"no," said mack. "no. no. I let you do some funny things, sam. but you are not going to paint me. I don't want paint on me because I will have to take a bath."

"I am not going to get paint on you. I am going to paint on this pad. I will paint what you look like. I will not get paint on you, but I will get some more paint on me," said sam.

"you had better not get paint on me," said mack.

"then hold still and let me paint," said sam.

"wher_e are you gōīng?" ask_ed mac_k.

"come with mē. you will sēē," said sam.

"whȳ is ther_e pāint on your hat and top and pants?" ask_ed mac_k.

"come with mē. you will sēē," said sam.

"what is in the box?" ask_ed mac_k.

"come with mē. you will sēē," said sam.

"come with mē. you will sēē," said sam.

sō mac_k went with sam.

---

when they got to the park, sam went to a spot in the sun. it was nēar a trēē and a pond.

"stand hēr_e, mac_k," said sam.

"whȳ?" ask_ed mac_k.

"you will sēē," answered sam.

sam got a brush. hē got pāint. hē got a pad.

"now stand still," said sam.

"whȳ?" ask_ed mac_k. "it is tīm_e to tell mē."

sam and the gōₐt cart

Illustrated by Brad Mancuso

Decodable Book Lesson 34

"let's gō, ron. let's gō to the stōr₂," said sam.

"I have to do lots of shopping. the pig and the chicks need feed. miles, the rabbit, must have beans. mack must have bones. jill must have rope, and I need corn," said sam. "I need a ride to the store. I am going to make a goat cart. then I can take the goat cart to the store. A goat cart will hold lots of things."

"now I will get the old bikes from the barn. they will be good for the cart," said sam. "then I will get the goat."

sam got a big box. "I will help you," said jill. "I can pãint the box red and yellow. I can pãint your nãme on the box."

"I must fīnd a sēat fōr the cart," said sam.

"did you look in the barn?" asked jill. "fīnd a littᴸe box and nãil it to the big box."

"that is good. yes, I will do that," said sam.

sam got a littᴸe box. he sat on it. "this is a hard sēat," said sam. if I takᴇ the cart on the rōad, I will nēēd a pad."

"I will help you," said mīles. "I can get a pad fōr the sēat. the pad will be red and the sēat will be yellōw."

4

5

38

down
the rōad

Illustrated by Brad Mancuso

Decodable Book Lesson 39

Mc Graw Hill **SRA**

SRA

www.sraonline.com

Copyright © 2008 SRA/McGraw-Hill.

All rights reserved. Permission is granted to reproduce the material contained herein on the condition that such material be reproduced only for classroom use; be provided to students, teachers, or families without charge; and be used solely in conjunction with *Reading Mastery Signature Edition*. Any other reproduction, for use of sale, is prohibited without prior written permission of the publisher.

Printed in the United States of America.

Send all inquiries to:
SRA/McGraw-Hill
4400 Easton Commons
Columbus, OH 43219

---

sam saw the stōrₑ. "wē will bē therₑ sŏŏn, ron. you can slōw down now."

ron walkₑd up to the stōrₑ. then sam got down from the cart. hē ran to the stōrₑ and trīₑd to get in. "oh, nō, nō," said sam. "wē are lātₑ. wē can't shop."

sam sat down on the steps and crīₑd, "wē are lātₑ. it is getting dark. what will wē do?"

"do not crȳ, sam. wē can slēēp in the park. it will bē fun."

sam and the gōat cart started down the rōad. "yes, this is very good," said sam to ron. "don't you think wē will have fun, ron?"

"wē will have fun if you don't trȳ to tell mē what to do," said ron.

"wē are a tēam, ron. I will not tell you what to do. now gō faster. At this rāte, wē will not get to the stōre in tīme to shop," said sam.

"hōld on you silly duck. if you want mē to run, I will run." ron started running. hē ran faster and faster. ēach tīme hē hit a rock, the cart went up and down. ēach tīme the cart went up and down, sam went up and down.

"stop, ron, stop," sam yelled.

"I can't hēar you," ron answered.

"mȳ tāil, mȳ tāil is sore," sam crīed, and ron ran down the rōad.

"faster? if I gō faster you will
gō flȳing. you hōld on and don't
tell mē to gō faster."

ron walked and walked. sam went
to slēep in his sēat. the cart went
slōwer and slōwer. ron stopped
in the rōad and dropped his head.
ron was slēeping.

at last a big bug bit ron on the
ēar. ron jumped and yelled, "what
was that? whȳ did you bīte
mē, sam? I was having a good
drēam."

"I did not bīte you, you silly
gōat. you were slēeping. wē will
not get to the stōre if you slēep.
now you must run. run to the
stōre."

jāne's hōme

Illustrated by Brad Mancuso

Decodable Book Lesson 44

Mc Graw Hill SRA

Mc Graw Hill

SRA

www.sraonline.com

Send all inquiries to:
SRA/McGraw-Hill
4400 Easton Commons
Columbus, OH 43219

sō jāne and sam and ron went dōwn the rōad. when they got to her hōme, jāne said, "let's ēat dinner. then you can slēep. wē have lots of fun hēre, but there is one thing you can't do."

"what is that?" ron asked.

"you can't jump on the bed. nō jumping on the bed."

"Oh, wē never jump on the bed," said sam.

"never," said ron. "wē never jump on the bed."

sam told himself to stop crying.

sam said, "sam, you and ron are fine. you will have fun. get back on the cart and go to the park."

they started for the park. then sam saw a big, big thing walking down the road. "wow. ron, look. what is that big thing? it has a big nose and a little tail. look at that big head. look at those ears. have you ever seen anything like that? wouldn't you love to be that big?"

"I have a big home," said jane. "you could have dinner and stay at my home. I would be happy to have you."

"thank you so much," said ron. "it would be good to have dinner and a good sleep. we like to sleep."

"Oh, sam, it is so big. what if it can't see us? what if it steps on us?"

a big foot came near ron. sam yelled, "stop. stop. don't step on us."

"what was that," said the big thing. "I can't see anything. but I can feel something with my foot. I must get my glasses."

the big thing stopped. she got her glasses so she could see.

"my, oh, my," she said. "who are you?"

"I am ron," said the goat. "and this is sam the duck. who are you?"

"I am jane. I am an elephant," jane answered.

"do you live here?" asked ron.

"yes, I live down the road. you don't live here. where are you from?" asked jane.

"we live on a farm. we came to shop, but it got late. the shops are shut," answered sam.

not sō good

Illustrated by Brad Mancuso

Decodable Book Lesson 49

Mc Graw Hill SRA

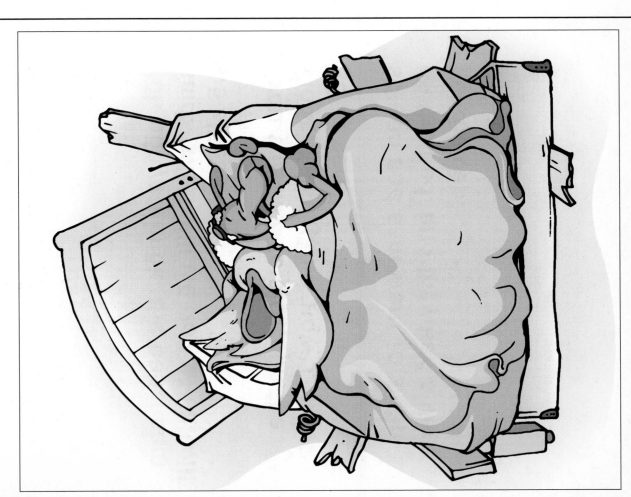

www.sraonline.com

SRA

Copyright © 2008 SRA/McGraw-Hill.

All rights reserved. Permission is granted to reproduce the material contained herein on the condition that such material be reproduced only for classroom use; be provided to students, teachers, or families without charge; and be used solely in conjunction with *Reading Mastery Signature Edition*. Any other reproduction, for use of sale, is prohibited without prior written permission of the publisher.

Printed in the United States of America.

Send all inquiries to:
SRA/McGraw-Hill
4400 Easton Commons
Columbus, OH 43219

"ōh nō, you brōke the bed," sam said. "what will wē do? where will wē slēep?"

"you will have to slēep on the flōor," said Jāne. "now I must gō to bed."

sō ron and sam went to slēep on the bed. and they had a very good slēep.

ron and sam went to bed. the bedroom was big. there was one big bed. sam sat on the bed. it felt like a cloud. it felt like a big pile of clouds.

"oh-h-h-h," said sam. "this will be like sleeping on a cloud."

"let me see," said ron. ron sat on the bed.

"oh-h-h-h," said ron. "this will be like sleeping on a cloud."

STOP!!! yelled jane. no more jumping on the bed.

ron and sam stopped.

"boys. boys. didn't I say, don't jump on the bed?" asked jane.

"yes," they answered. "but why? jumping on this bed is so much fun."

"yes, it is," said jane. "I'll tell you why you shouldn't jump on the bed. because then I want to jump on the bed." So jane jumped on the bed.

sam sat very still. then hē jumped just a little jump.

"stop, sam," ron said. "wē can't jump on the bed."

"just a little, little jump," said sam. "then I'll stop."

sō ron said, "then I'll do just a little jump."

and they did very little jumps on the bed.

then they did not do little jumps. soon they werₑ doing big jumps. and they kept jumping.

jumping. jumping. ōh-h-h-h.

the hound is around

Illustrated by Brad Mancuso

Decodable Book Lesson 54

SRA
Mc Graw Hill

51

SRA

www.sraonline.com

Copyright © 2008 SRA/McGraw-Hill.

All rights reserved. Permission is granted to reproduce the material contained herein on the condition that such material be reproduced only for classroom use; be provided to students, teachers, or families without charge; and be used solely in conjunction with *Reading Mastery Signature Edition*. Any other reproduction, for use of sale, is prohibited without prior written permission of the publisher.

Printed in the United States of America.

Send all inquiries to:
SRA/McGraw-Hill
4400 Easton Commons
Columbus, OH 43219

"well, don't scrēam around mē. you silly thin͞gs, g͞o awāy."

s͞o the cow and the hound and the kitten went bacₖ to the barn.

"do you all want to g͞o for a bῙkₑ rῙdₑ?" askₑd the kittens.

"wē can rῙdₑ down the r͞oad and scrēam," said the cow.

what is that sound?

the hound is around.

whereₑ?

ōver bȳ the barn.

what is he doiñg?

hē is slēēping.

sh-sh-sh. let's trȳ to slip past him.

"STOP!" shouted the gōat.

bam. bam. bam. the cow stoppₑd. the kittens ran into the cow. the hound ran into the kittens.

"what is goiñg on?" askₑd the gōat.

"the cow scrēamₑd," said the hound and the kittens. "shē mādₑ us scrēam."

"whȳ did you scrēam, cow?" askₑd the gōat.

"bēcausₑ I felt līkₑ it. somₑtīmₑs I just fēēl līkₑ scrēamiñg," said the cow.

the little kittens got down on the ground. they slipped around the hound. the hound smīled in his slēēp. just as the kittens got past the hound, a cow scrēamed, "MOOOOOOOOOOOOOOOOOO."

the kittens jumped and scrēamed, "OOOOOOOOOOOOOOW."
the hound jumped and scrēamed, "WOOOOOOOOOOOW."
the cow ran. the kittens ran after the cow. the hound ran after the kittens. they all ran and scrēamed.

shē'll bē coming around the mountain

Folksong
Illustrated by Brad Mancuso

Decodable Book Lesson 59

Mc Graw Hill **SRA**

ōh, wē'll all gō out to grēēt her,
ōh, wē'll all gō out to grēēt her,
ōh, wē'll all gō out to grēēt her,
when shē comₑs,
(when shē comₑs.)

Ōh, wē'll all gō out to grēēt her

when shē comes,

(when shē comes.)

Ōh, wē'll all gō out to grēēt her

when shē comes,

(when shē comes.)

shē'll bē coming around the
mountain

when shē comₑs,

(when shē comₑs.)

shē'll bē coming around the
mountain

when shē comₑs,

(when shē comₑs.)

shē'll bē drīvⁱng six whītₑ
hōrses,

shē'll bē drīvⁱng six whītₑ
hōrses,

shē'll bē drīvⁱng six whītₑ
hōrses,

when shē comₑs,

(when shē comₑs.)

shē'll bē coming around the
mountain,

shē'll bē coming around the
mountain,

shē'll bē coming around the
mountain,

when shē comes,

(when shē comes.)

shē'll bē drīving six whīte
hōrses

when shē comes,

(when shē comes.)

shē'll bē drīving six whīte
hōrses

when shē comes,

(when shē comes.)

ten in
a bed

folk rhyme
Illustrated by Artifact Group

Decodable Book Lesson 64

there wer‍ₑ 2 in a bed and the littl‍ₑ one said, "rōll ōver, rōll ōver."

sō they all rōll‍ₑd ōver and one fell out.

there was 1 in the bed and the littl‍ₑ one said, "good nīght."

ther₍ₑ₎ were 10 in a bed and the littlₑ one said, "rōll ōver, rōll ōver."

sō they all rōllₑd ōver and one fell out.

ther₍ₑ₎ wer₍ₑ₎ 9 in a bed and the littlₑ one said, "rōll ōver, rōll ōver."

sō they all rōllₑd ōver and one fell out.

ther₍ₑ₎ wer₍ₑ₎ 4 in a bed and the littlₑ one said, "rōll ōver, rōll ōver."

sō they all rōllₑd ōver and one fell out.

ther₍ₑ₎ wer₍ₑ₎ 3 in a bed and the littlₑ one said, "rōll ōver, rōll ōver."

sō they all rōllₑd ōver and one fell out.

ther_e wer_e 8 in a bed and the littl_e one said, "rōll ōver, rōll ōver."

sō they all rōll_ed ōver and one fell out.

ther_e wer_e 7 in a bed and the littl_e one said, "rōll ōver, rōll ōver."

sō they all rōll_ed ōver and one fell out.

ther_e wer_e 6 in a bed and the littl_e one said, "rōll ōver, rōll ōver."

sō they all rōll_ed ōver and one fell out.

ther_e wer_e 5 in a bed and the littl_e one said, "rōll ōver, rōll ōver."

sō they all rōll_ed ōver and one fell out.

silly
songs

folk rhymes

Decodable Book Lesson 69

keep gōing. drop a word
ēach versē.

same song, next verse.

a littlᵉ bit faster and a littlᵉ bit worse.

Ōh, the hōrsᵉ went around with his foot off . . .

Ōh, the hōrsᵉ went around with his foot off . . .

Ōh, the hōrsᵉ went around with his foot off . . .

Ōh, the hōrsᵉ went around with his foot off . . .

Ōh, the hōrsᵉ went around with his foot off . . .

the bear went ōver the mountain

the bear went ōver the mountain,
the bear went ōver the mountain,
the bear went ōver the mountain,
to sēē what hē could sēē
to sēē what hē could sēē,
to sēē what hē could sēē.

same song, next verse.

a little bit faster and a little bit worse.

Ōh, the hōrse went around with his foot off the . . . .

Ōh, the hōrse went around with his foot off the . . . .

Ōh, the hōrse went around with his foot off the . . . .

Ōh, the hōrse went around with his foot off the . . . .

the other side of the
mountain,
the other side of the
mountain,
the other side of the
mountain,
was all that he could see

was all that he could see,
was all that he could see,
the other side of the
mountain,
was all that he could see!

---

the horse went around

Oh, the horse went around
with his foot off the
ground.
Oh, the horse went around
with his foot off the
ground.
Oh, the horse went around
with his foot off the
ground.
Oh, the horse went around
with his foot off the
ground.

66

the little red hen

folk tale

Illustrated by Artifact Group

Decodable Book Lesson 74

McGraw Hill **SRA**

"nō, you won't," said the little red hen. "you would not plant the whēat. you would not tāke it to the mill. you would not māke it into brеad. so you will not ēat the brеad. I will ēat it."

and shē callеd her chicks to help her.

the little red hen was in the farm yard with her chicks, when she found a wheat seed.

"who will plant this wheat?" she said.

"not I," said the cat.

"not I," said the duck.

"then I will," said the little red hen, and she planted the wheat seed.

---

when the bread was baked, she said, "who will eat this bread?"

"I will," said the cat.

"I will," said the duck.

when the wheat was rīpe shē said, "who will take this wheat to the mill?"

"not I," said the cat.

"not I," said the duck.

"then I will," said the little red hen, and shē took the wheat to the mill and had it ground into flour.

when shē got the flour hōme shē said, "who will māke bread with this flour?"

"not I," said the cat.

"not I," said the duck.

"then I will," said the little red hen.

the sun and the wind

by Aesop
illustrated by Timothy Pack

Decodable Book Lesson 79

SRA

Mc Graw Hill

then it was the sun's turn. hē shōne with all his bēams on the man. as it got hotter and hotter, the man ōpened his cāpe. then hē brushed it back. at last hē took it off! the sun was the winner.

the sun and the wind wanted to see who was stronger. one day they saw a man walking down the road. he was wearing a big cape.

but the colder it got and the more it rained, the tighter the man held his cape around himself. the wind could not get it off.

"now we can find out which is stronger," said the wind. "let us sēē which of us can māke that man tāke off his cāpe. the one who can do that will be called stronger."

"that's what we will do," said the sun.

sō the wind began to blow. hē puffed and tugged at the man's cāpe. hē māde rāin bēat the man.

chicken little

retold

Decodable Book Lesson 84

Mc Graw Hill   SRA

"stop, you silly things," said a rabbit who had been following them. "fox is trying to trick you. let me see your tail, chicken little."

The rabbit reached into chicken little's tail and took out an acorn.

"chicken little, the sky is not falling. this acorn fell from a tree and landed on your tail."

"oh," said chicken little. "Well, let's just go on home and have some dinner." and they did.

www.sraonline.com

SRA
McGraw Hill

Copyright © 2008 SRA/McGraw-Hill.

Send all inquiries to:
SRA/McGraw-Hill
4400 Easton Commons
Columbus, OH 43219

They met foxy loxy. goosey loosey said, "The sky is falling, foxy loxy."

"how do you know, goosey loosey?"

"ducky lucky told me."

"how do you know, ducky lucky?"

"Turkey lurkey told me."

"how do you know, turkey lurkey?"

"henny penny told me."

"how do you know, henny penny?"

"chicken little told me."

"how do you know, chicken little?"

"I saw it. I heard it. some of it fell on my tail."

foxy loxy said, "go into my den, and I will tell the king."

chicken little was in the woods when an acorn fell on his tail. chicken little said, "The sky is falling. I must go and tell the king."

chicken little met henny penny. chicken little said, "The sky is falling, henny penny."

henny penny said, "how do you know, chicken little?"

"I saw it. I heard it. some of it fell on my tail."

"We must go and tell the king," said henny penny.

They met goosey loosey. ducky lucky said, "The sky is falling, goosey loosey."

"how do you know, ducky lucky?"

"Turkey lurkey told me."

"how do you know, turkey lurkey?"

"henny penny told me."

"how do you know, henny penny?"

"chicken little told me."

"how do you know, chicken little?"

"I saw it. I heard it. some of it fell on my tail."

"We must go and tell the king," goosey loosey said.

They met turkey lurkey. henny penny said, "The sky is falling, turkey lurkey."

"how do you know, henny penny?"

"chicken little told me."

"how do you know, chicken little?"

"I saw it. I heard it. some of it fell on my tail."

"We must go and tell the king," said turkey lurkey.

They met ducky lucky. turkey lurkey said, "The sky is falling, ducky lucky."

"how do you know, turkey lurkey?"

"henny penny told me."

"how do you know, henny penny?"

"chicken little told me."

"how do you know, chicken little?"

"I saw it. I heard it. some of it fell on my tail."

"We must go and tell the king," ducky lucky said.

This old man

folksong

Decodable Book Lesson 89

Mc Graw Hill SRA

This old man, he played 10,
he played knick knack once again,
With a knick knack, paddy whack,
give the dog a bone;
This old man came rolling home.

This old man, he played 8,
he played knick knack on my gate,
With a knick knack, paddy whack,
give the dog a bone;
This old man came rolling home.

This old man, he played 9,
he played knick knack, rise and shine,
With a knick knack, paddy whack,
give the dog a bone;
This old man came rolling home.

www.sraonline.com

SRA
Mc Graw Hill

Copyright © 2008 SRA/McGraw-Hill.

All rights reserved. Permission is granted to reproduce the material contained herein on the condition that such material be reproduced only for classroom use; be provided to students, teachers, or families without charge; and be used solely in conjunction with *Reading Mastery Signature Edition*. Any other reproduction, for use of sale, is prohibited without prior written permission of the publisher.

Printed in the United States of America.

Send all inquiries to:
SRA/McGraw-Hill
4400 Easton Commons
Columbus, OH 43219

This old man, he played 1,
he played knick knack with his thumb,
With a knick knack, paddy whack,
give the dog a bone;
This old man came rolling home.

This old man, he played 6,
he played knick knack with his sticks,
With a knick knack, paddy whack,
give the dog a bone;
This old man came rolling home.

This old man, he played 7,
he played knick knack with his pen,
With a knick knack, paddy whack,
give the dog a bone;
This old man came rolling home.

This old man, he played 2,
he played knick knack on my shoe,
With a knick knack, paddy whack,
give the dog a bone;
This old man came rolling home.

This old man, he played 3,
he played knick knack on my knee,
With a knick knack, paddy whack,
give the dog a bone;
This old man came rolling home.

This old man, he played 4,
he played knick knack at my door,
With a knick knack, paddy whack,
give the dog a bone;
This old man came rolling home.

This old man, he played 5,
he played knick knack on a hive,
With a knick knack, paddy whack,
give the dog a bone;
This old man came rolling home.

The Hat Seller and the Monkeys

folktale

Decodable Book Lesson 94

SRA

One monkey jumped down from the tree, walked over to Habib, tapped him on the head and said, "Do you think only you had a grandfather?"

SRA

www.sraonline.com

Copyright © 2008 SRA/McGraw-Hill.

All rights reserved. Permission is granted to reproduce the material contained herein on the condition that such material be reproduced only for classroom use; be provided to students, teachers, or families without charge; and be used solely in conjunction with *Reading Mastery Signature Edition.* Any other reproduction, for use of sale, is prohibited without prior written permission of the publisher.

Printed in the United States of America.

Send all inquiries to:
SRA/McGraw-Hill
4400 Easton Commons
Columbus, OH 43219

"Oh, I can trick these monkeys!" said Habib. "I will make them do what I do, and I will get all my hats back!"

Habib waved at the monkeys, and the monkeys waved back at him. He rubbed his head, and the monkeys rubbed their heads. He jumped, and the monkeys jumped. Then, he tossed his hat on the ground.

84

Once upon a time there was a hat seller named Ozan. He went from town to town selling hats.

One day, Ozan felt tired and wanted to take a nap in the woods. He found a tree with lots of leaves and cool shade. He put his bag of hats beside himself and went to sleep.

When Habib woke up, he could not see any of his hats. He started looking for them and found some monkeys sitting in the tree with his hats on. He was upset and did not know what to do. Then he remembered a story his grandfather told him.

When he woke up from his nap, he found that there were no hats in his bag! "Oh, no!" he said to himself and shook his head, "Who took my hats?"

Then he looked up and saw that the tree was full of monkeys with hats on. He yelled at the monkeys. They screamed back. He hopped. They hopped. He tossed a rock at them. They tossed nuts at him.

"Oh, how do I get my hats back?" Ozan asked himself. Upset, he took off his hat and tossed it on the ground. The monkeys tossed their hats also! Ozan did not take any time. He grabbed the hats and went on his way to the next town.

Fifty years later, Habib, grandson of the hat seller Ozan, was walking in the same woods. Habib felt tired and wanted to take a nap in the woods. He found a tree with lots of leaves and cool shade. He put his bag of hats beside him and went to sleep.

The Gingerbread Man

retold

Illustrated by Timothy Pack

Decodable Book Lesson 99

8

Well, the fox had a trick or two. He called out to the gingerbread man, "Run, run as fast as you can. You have run away from a little old woman, a little old man, farmers working, and a cow, but you'll not run away from me. I'm the best runner in the land."

And the fox did catch that gingerbread man and ate him for supper.

© SRA/McGraw-Hill

Once upon a time there were a little old man and a little old woman who lived in the woods. One day while the woman baked, she made a gingerbread cake and cut it into the shape of a man. She put frosting on the cake and popped it into the oven.

After a while, she opened the oven door to see how her gingerbread cake was doing. As soon as the oven door was open, the gingerbread man jumped out and ran out the door and down the road. The little old man and the little old woman called after him, but he just kept running.

Not long after that the gingerbread man came upon a fox. The fox saw him. "Run, run as fast as you can. You can't catch me, I'm the gingerbread man. I've run away from a little old woman, a little old man, farmers working, and a cow, and I'll run away from you," he shouted as he ran on.

"Run, run as fast as you can. You can't catch me, I'm the gingerbread man," he shouted as he ran on.

Soon the gingerbread man ran past farmers working. The farmers saw him and tried to catch him.

"Run, run as fast as you can. You can't catch me, I'm the gingerbread man. I've run away from a little old woman and a little old man, and I'll run away from you," he shouted as he ran on.

The gingerbread man ran on till he saw a cow eating grass along the road. The cow saw him and tried to catch him.

"Run, run as fast as you can. You can't catch me, I'm the gingerbread man. I've run away from a little old woman, a little old man, and farmers working, and I'll run away from you," he shouted as he ran on.

90

The Green Grass Grew All Around

folksong

Decodable Book Lesson 104

Mc Graw Hill **SRA**

And in that egg
(And in that egg)
There was a bird
(There was a bird)
The prettiest bird
(The prettiest bird)
That you ever did see
(That you ever did see)

Oh, the bird in the egg
And the egg in the nest
And the nest on the branch
And the branch on the limb
And the limb on the tree
And the tree in a hole
And the hole in the ground
And the green grass grew all around
all around
The green grass grew all around

SRA

www.sraonline.com

Copyright © 2008 SRA/McGraw-Hill.

All rights reserved. Permission is granted to reproduce the material contained herein on the condition that such material be reproduced only for classroom use; be provided to students, teachers, or families without charge; and be used solely in conjunction with *Reading Mastery Signature Edition*. Any other reproduction, for use of sale, is prohibited without prior written permission of the publisher.

Printed in the United States of America.

Send all inquiries to:
SRA/McGraw-Hill
4400 Easton Commons
Columbus, OH 43219

And in that nest
(And in that nest)
There was an egg
(There was an egg)
The prettiest egg
(The prettiest egg)
That you ever did see
(That you ever did see)

Oh, the egg in the nest
And the nest on the branch
And the branch on the limb
And the limb on the tree
And the tree in a hole
And the hole in the ground
And the green grass grew all around
    all around
The green grass grew all around

There was a tree
(There was a tree)
All in the wood
(All in the wood)
The prettiest little tree
(The prettiest little tree)
That you ever did see
(That you ever did see)

The tree in a hole and the hole in the
ground
And the green grass grew all around
all around
And the green grass grew all around

And on that branch
(And on that branch)
There was a nest
(There was a nest)
The prettiest nest
(The prettiest nest)
That you ever did see
(That you ever did see)

Oh, the nest on the branch
And the branch on the limb
And the limb on the tree
And the tree in a hole
And the hole in the ground
And the green grass grew all around
all around
The green grass grew all around

Oh, the tree in a hole
And the hole in the ground
And the green grass grew all around
all around
The green grass grew all around

And on that tree
(And on that tree)
There was a limb
(There was a limb)
The prettiest limb
(The prettiest limb)
That you ever did see
(That you ever did see)

Oh, the limb on the tree
And the tree in a hole
And the hole in the ground
And the green grass grew all around
all around
The green grass grew all around

And on that limb
(And on that limb)
There was a branch
(There was a branch)
The prettiest branch
(The prettiest branch)
That you ever did see
(That you ever did see)

Oh, the branch on the limb
And the limb on the tree
And the tree in a hole
And the hole in the ground
And the green grass grew all around
all around
The green grass grew all around

The Boy Who Cried "Wolf"

by Aesop

Decodable Book Lesson 109

The wolf growled again and got closer and closer. The little boy screamed again, "Wolf! Wolf!" He kept screaming, but no one came to help him.

So the little boy took off running back to the house, all the time telling himself, "I'll never lie again. I'll never lie again." And he didn't.

2

The brother who was dressed as a wolf sneaked out from behind the bush and growled. The little boy looked around. His brother dressed as the wolf growled again and walked closer to the little boy and his sheep. The little boy screamed, "Wolf! Wolf! Wolf! Wolf!"

7

96

Once upon a time, there was a little boy who liked to tell lies. Of course, this made people sad.

To help his father, the little boy sometimes watched the sheep. It was his job to keep the wolf away from the sheep. If he saw a wolf, he was to yell as loud as he could, "Wolf! Wolf!" Then anyone who could hear him would help him chase the wolf away.

When everyone was back at the farmer's house, they talked about the little boy and his lying. They decided that someone should teach him a thing or two.

A day or so later, one of the brothers dressed up as a wolf. Then people went out where the boy was watching the sheep. They hid behind a bush to watch.

One sunny afternoon, the little boy decided to have some fun. He cried, "Wolf! Wolf!" as loud as he could. Everyone who could hear him grabbed big sticks and ran to chase away the wolf.

When they found the little boy and the sheep, the little boy was rolling around on the ground laughing. He liked to see all those people leave their work and run to help him.

The next afternoon, the little boy decided to have fun again, so what do you think he did? He cried, "Wolf! Wolf!" as loud as he could. Everyone who could hear him grabbed big sticks and ran to chase away the wolf.

When they found the little boy and the sheep, the little boy was rolling around on the ground laughing. This time the people got mad, and his father hold him, "Lying is not right. One day the wolf will come, and you really will need help, and no one will come to help you." The little boy just laughed.

Rip Van Winkle Part 1

by Washington Irving
retold

Decodable Book Lesson 114

Rip awoke with the hot sun shining on him. He was not in the clearing, and there were no little men playing long pins. He was back beside the river where he first saw the little old man. "Oh, my. Oh, my," he said. "I've stayed out all night. My wife will be mad, and she'll never believe my story. What will I tell her?"

Rip and the old man took dinner from the sack. As the other men played, Rip gave them dinner. Then Rip sat down with his dinner. He was so tired that he soon fell asleep.

A long time ago, Rip Van Winkle lived in a little town. Everyone loved Rip. He was a kind man who loved to laugh and play with the children. He always had time to help others or tell stories.

They walked a long time. At last, the two men got to a clearing. The moon shone down on little men playing long pins. The men had long hair and long beards. They wore big hats, long coats, and short pants.

The game stopped. The men looked at Rip. Then they went back to their long pins. There was no sound but the rolling balls crashing into the pins, like thunder in the mountains.

One day, Rip and Wolf, his dog, were walking along the river in the mountains. Late in the afternoon, they stopped under a tree to watch the river.

Clouds piled up over the mountains and the sky turned gray. Rip turned to head home. Then someone called, "Rip Van Winkle. Rip Van Winkle." Rip stopped. He looked around. Maybe it was the wind.

A little man carrying a big sack walked slowly to Rip. He asked Rip to help him carry the sack. As they went along, Rip could hear a strange sound, like thunder in the mountains. He grew more afraid.

Rip Van Winkle Part 2

by Washington Irving
retold

Decodable Book Lesson 119

McGraw Hill SRA

Judith took Rip home. Soon Rip was back to his old ways. And to this day when the thunder rolls, people say, "Rip's little friends are bowling again."

"Rip Van Winkle. But he left over 20 years ago."

"And who is that under the tree?"

"That is my brother, Rip Van Winkle."

Then Rip told his story, and most people didn't believe it. But it didn't matter because it was a good story.

104

Rip tried to get up, but he was sore so he got up very slowly. He called for Wolf, but Wolf didn't come. And what had happened to the path that led to the town? It was overgrown with grass and trees. Slowly, Rip worked his way to the town. He couldn't understand why he felt so old.

"I don't know who I am," answered Rip. "I believe I am Rip Van Winkle, but you tell me that Rip Van Winkle is sleeping under that tree."

Just then a woman and her baby passed. "Hush, Rip," she said to her baby.

Rip turned to her. He said, "What is your name?"

"Judith," she answered.

"And your father? What is his name?" asked Rip.

As Rip got near town, he met many people, but they just looked at him. He didn't know them, and they didn't know him. Rip stopped and looked and rubbed his chin. His chin? On his chin was a long, white beard. Rip was scared. What was the matter? How could this be the town he just left?

In fear, Rip walked to his farm. He hoped to hear his children playing in the yard. He hoped to hear his wife yelling at him to get to work. There was nothing but an old house.

Rip ran back to town. People stood around him. At last, Rip asked, "Does anyone here know Rip Van Winkle?"

"Yes, we do," someone said. "There he is sitting under that tree in the park."

The man under the tree looked just as Rip had when he went to the mountains. The man turned back to Rip and asked, "Who are you, old man? Where did you come from?"

106

The Silly Monkeys

A Jataka story

Decodable Book Lesson 124

SRA

When the gardener came back the next day, the little trees were all dead.

2

Then those silly monkeys pulled up all the little trees to see which trees had long roots and which had short roots.

7

108

Once upon a time a king gave a holiday to all the people in one of his cities.

The king's gardener said to himself: "All my friends are having a holiday in the city. I could go into the city and have fun with them if I did not have to water the little trees in this garden. I know what I'll do. I'll get the monkeys to water the trees for me." In those days, monkeys lived in the king's garden.

When the sun went down, the monkeys took the watering cans and began to water the little trees. "See that each little tree has enough water," said the boss monkey.

"How will we know when each little tree has enough?" they asked. The boss of the monkeys had no good answer, so he said, "Pull up each little tree and look at its roots. Give a lot of water to those with long roots, but only a little to those trees with short roots."

So the gardener went to the boss monkey, and said: "You are lucky monkeys to be living in the king's garden. You have a fine place to play in. You have the best food. You have no work at all to do. You can play all day, every day. Today my friends are having a holiday in the city, and I want to have fun with them. Will you water the little trees so that I can go away?"

"Oh, yes!" said the boss monkey. "We will be glad to do that."

"Don't forget to water the trees when the sun goes down. See they have enough water, but not more than enough," said the gardener. Then he showed them where the watering cans were kept, and he went away.

Two Tales

The Ant and the Grasshopper

&

The Lion and the Mouse

by Aesop

Decodable Book Lesson 129

The other animals could hear the lion, and they ran to him. But no one could think of what to do.

The little mouse ran to him. She ran up the tree and out onto the net. She chewed on the ropes. In no time, she chewed the ropes, and the lion was free.

The lion was very happy. He told the mouse, "You're a very brave mouse. Thank you for helping me. I will never laugh at you again."

"Wait!" she shouted. "Don't eat me, please. If you will let me go, I will help you."

The lion laughed. How could a mouse help a lion? Well, he was not hungry, so he let her go and went back to sleep.

The little mouse ran away as fast as her legs would carry her.

Many days later the lion fell into a net and was trapped. No matter how hard he tried, he couldn't get out. The lion began to roar. He roared and he roared and he roared.

The Ant and the Grasshopper

Once upon a time, a grasshopper was hopping around, chirping and singing, singing and chirping. An ant passed by, carrying a big seed of corn.

"Ant," said the grasshopper, "rest a minute. Let's talk a while."

"No time for chit-chat," said the ant as she rushed on. "No time at all. I must get food put away for the winter. You should do the same."

"Oh, winter is a long way off, and there is lots of food," said the grasshopper.

The Lion and the Mouse

A long time ago, there was a mean lion. One day, he ate a big lunch. Then he went to his den to take a nap.

As the lion was sleeping, a little mouse was looking for seeds. She ran smack into the lion's nose and woke him. The mouse tried to run away, but the lion got her by the tail.

The next day as the grasshopper was hopping around, chirping and singing, singing and chirping, the ant passed by again. This time she was carrying a grain of wheat.

"Ant," said the grasshopper, "rest a minute. Let's talk a while."

"No time for chit-chat," said the ant as she rushed on. "No time at all. I must get food put away for the winter. You should do the same."

"Oh, winter is a long way off, and there is lots of food," said the grasshopper.

And so it went, day after day. The ant worked. The grasshopper played.

Winter came, as it always does. The plants died, and the grasshopper could not find any food.

The ant was snug in her home with a lot to eat. And the grasshopper? Well, the grasshopper got colder and colder because it was not ready for winter.

The Wind in the Willows

Chapter 1
THE RIVER BANK
Part 1

by Kenneth Grahame
retold
illustrated by Artifact Group

Decodable Book Lesson 134

Rat said nothing. He bent down and grabbed a rope and pulled on it. Then he stepped into a little boat which Mole had not seen. It was painted blue outside and white inside. And it was just the size for two animals. Mole's heart went out to it at once, even if he didn't know what it was for.

Rat rowed across and made fast. Then he held up a paw as the Mole stepped down. "Lean on me!" he said. "Now then, step carefully!" Mole found himself seated in the rear of a real boat.

Mole had been working very hard all morning. He was cleaning his little home. Spring was moving in the air and in the ground and all around him. Suddenly he flung his brush to the floor. He said "O blow!" and also "Hang spring cleaning!" Then he ran out of the house without putting on his coat. Something was calling him. So he dug and dug till at last, pop! His snout came out into the sunshine. He found himself rolling in the warm grass.

"This is fine!" he said to himself. The sunshine struck hot on his fur. A soft wind touched his face. After a long, long winter in the ground, he ran across the grass to the road.

A brown little face, with whiskers. A round face, with a twinkle in its eye. Small neat ears and thick soft hair.

It was Water Rat!

Then the two animals stood and looked at each other.

"Hello, Mole!" said Water Rat.

"Hello, Rat!" said Mole.

"Would you like to come over?" asked Rat.

"Oh, well, that's easy for you to say," said Mole.

"Hold up!" said an old rabbit. "One dime to pass on this road!" "Onion-sauce! Onion-sauce! Onion-sauce!" Mole said. He was off before the rabbits could think what to say. Then they said to each other: "How silly you are! Why didn't you tell him—" and so on. But, of course, it was much too late.

Suddenly Mole stood beside a river. Never in his life had he seen a river. By the side of the river he ran. And when he was tired at last, he sat on the bank, while the river still chattered to him.

He saw a dark hole in the bank on the other side of the river. "What a nice home that hole would be," he said to himself. Something small seemed to twinkle down in the hole. It went away. Then it twinkled once more like a little star. Then, as he looked, it winked at him. An eye. A small face grew up around it, like a frame around a window.

The Wind in the Willows

Chapter 1
THE RIVER BANK
Part 2

by Kenneth Grahame
retold
illustrated by Artifact Group

Decodable Book Lesson 139

2

Mole never heard a word he was saying. He trailed a paw in the water and dreamed long waking dreams. Water Rat, like the good little fellow he was, rowed on and let Mole dream.

"This is a wonderful day!" said Mole, as Rat started rowing again. "Do you know, I've never been in a boat before in all my life."

"What?" cried Rat. "Never been in a—you never—well, what have you been doing, then?"

"Is it so nice as all that?" asked Mole.

"Nice? It's the only thing," said Water Rat. "Believe me, my friend, there is nothing as much fun as messing about in boats."

"Look ahead, Rat!" cried Mole.

"Put that under your feet," he said to Mole. Then he untied the rope and rowed off again.

"What's inside it?" asked Mole.

"There is cold chicken inside it," answered Rat. "Cold ham, cold beef, pickles, rolls, water—"

"O stop, stop," cried Mole. "This is too much!"

"Do you really think so?" asked Rat. "It's only what I always take on these little trips."

121

It was too late. The boat struck the bank. Rat lay on his back at the bottom of the boat, his heels in the air.

Rat went on, picking himself up with a laugh. "In or out of them, it doesn't matter. Nothing seems really to matter. Whether you get away or whether you don't; whether you reach your goal or whether you reach somewhere else, or whether you never get anywhere at all, you're always doing something. But you never really do anything. And when you've done it, there's always something else to do. And you can do it if you like, but you are better off not doing it. Look here! If you've really nothing else to do this morning we can go down the river and have a long day of it?"

Mole leaned back into the soft pillows. "What a day I'm having!" he said. "Let us start at once!"

"Hold on a minute, then!" said Rat. He tied the rope through a ring in his dock. Then he disappeared into his home. After a time, he came out carrying a big basket.

The Wind in the Willows

Chapter 1
THE OPEN ROAD
Part 3

by Kenneth Grahame
retold
illustrated by Artifact Group

Decodable Book Lesson 142

"And on past the Wild Wood?" he asked.

"On past the Wild Wood comes the Wide World," said Rat. "And that's something that doesn't matter, either to you or me. I've never been there, and I'm never going. You won't either if you've got any brains at all. Don't ever speak of it again, please. Now then! Here is our backwater at last, where we are going to lunch."

"I like your coat, old chap," Rat said after some time had passed. "I'm going to get a black coat myself some day."

"I'm sorry," said Mole. "But all this is so new to me. So—this—is—a—River!"

"The River," said Rat.

"And you really live by the river? What a happy life!"

"By it and with it and on it and in it," said Rat. "It's brother and sister to me. And food and drink and washing. It's my world, and I don't want any other. Oh! The times we have had! Any time of the year, the river is fun."

"Why, who should mess with him?" asked Mole.

"Well, of course—there—are others," answered Rat. "Foxes and so on. They are all right in a way. I'm very good friends with them. Pass the time of day when we meet. But they act out sometimes, and then you can't really trust them, and that's the fact."

"But is it a bit boring at times?" Mole asked. "Just you and the river, and no one else to pass a word with?"

"No one else to—well, I must not be hard on you," said Rat. "You're new to it, and you don't know. The bank is so crowded now days that many people are moving away. Oh no, it is not what it used to be, at all. Always someone wanting you to do something. As if a fellow had nothing else to do!"

"What lies over there?" asked Mole, waving a paw at a woodland on one side of the river.

"That? Oh, that's just the Wild Wood," said Rat. "We don't go there very much, we river-bankers."

"Are the people in there not very nice?" said Mole.

"W....e...ll," answered Rat, "let me see. Most of them are all right. And the rabbits—some of them. But rabbits are a mixed lot. And then there is Badger, of course. He lives right in the middle of it; wouldn't live anywhere else, either, if you paid him to do it. Dear old Badger! Nobody messes with him. They had better not," he added.

The Wind in the Willows

Chapter 1
THE OPEN ROAD
Part 4

by Kenneth Grahame
retold
illustrated by Artifact Group

Decodable Book Lesson 144

"That's just the sort of fellow he is!" said Rat. "Hates to be around others! Now we won't see any more of him today. Well, tell us, who is out on the river?"

"Toad's out, for one," answered Otter. "In his brand new racing boat!"

The two animals looked at each other and laughed.

"Once, it was nothing but sailing," said Rat. "And a nice mess he made of it. Last year it was house-boating. We all had to go and stay with him in his house-boat. He was going to spend the rest of his life in a house-boat. It's all the same, whatever he takes up; he gets tired of it, and starts on something new."

Leaving the main stream, they now passed into what seemed like a little lake. Green grass sloped down on each side, brown tree roots showed under the still water. Ahead of them was a dripping mill wheel and mill house and little clear chattering voices. It was so very pretty that Mole could only hold up his front paws and say, "Oh my! Oh my! Oh my!"

"Proud to meet you," said Otter, and the two animals were friends.

"So much going on!" said Otter. "All the world seems to be out on the river today. I came up this backwater to try and get a little peace. Then I met you fellows."

There was a sound behind them. Coming from a bush a striped head and a big neck, stared at them.

"Come on, old Badger!" shouted Rat.

The Badger trotted turned his back and disappeared.

Rat took the boat to the bank, tied it, helped Mole safely on shore, and swung out the lunch basket. Mole begged to take it out all by himself. Rat was very pleased to let him and to lie on the grass and rest.

When all was ready, Rat said, "Now, give me a hand, old fellow!" Mole was very glad to obey, for he had started his spring-cleaning very early that morning. And he had not had a bite to eat from that time that seemed to be so many days ago.

"What are you looking at?" said Rat after they had had a bit to eat.

"I am looking," said Mole, "at a streak of bubbles that I see along the top of the water. That is a thing that strikes me as funny."

"Bubbles? Oh, oh!" said Rat, and chirped.

A wide shining nose showed over the bank. Then Otter pulled himself out and shook the water from his coat.

"Did you eat all the food?" he said, going for the food. "Why didn't you ask me to come, Ratty?"

"We didn't know we were going to do it," answered Rat. "By the way, this is my friend Mr. Mole."

The Wind in the Willows

Chapter 1
THE OPEN ROAD
Part 5

by Kenneth Grahame
retold
illustrated by Artifact Group

Decodable Book Lesson 147

2

Mole was still for a minute or two. But he began to feel more and more jealous of Rat. His pride began to think that he could do it every bit as well. He jumped up and grabbed the oars. Rat was taken by surprise and fell back off his seat with his legs in the air. And Mole took his place and grabbed the oars. He knew that he could row the boat.

"Stop it, you silly thing!" cried Rat, from the bottom of the boat. "You can't do it! You'll turn us over!"

7

From where they sat, Mole and Rat could just see the main stream across the land. Just then a racing boat appeared. The rower was splashing badly and rolling a good deal, but working his hardest. Rat stood up and called him, but Toad shook his head and got to his work.

"He'll be out of the boat in a minute if he rolls like that," said Rat, sitting down again.

"Of course he will," laughed Otter.

The afternoon sun was getting low as Rat rowed home. He was day dreaming and not watching Mole. But Mole was very full of lunch, and pride. And he was already at home in a boat. Soon he said, "Ratty! Please, I want to row, now!"

Rat shook his head with a smile. "Not yet, my friend," he said. "Wait till you've had a few lessons. It's not so easy as it looks."

A Mayfly flashed over the river. A swirl of water and a "cloop!" and the Mayfly was gone.

So was Otter.

Mole looked down. The voice was still in his ears, but Otter was not to be seen.

But again there was a streak of bubbles on the river.

"Well, well," said Rat, "I think we should be moving. I wonder which of us had better pack the lunch basket."

"O, please let me," said Mole. So, of course, Rat let him.

Putting things back into the basket was not such fun as taking them out. It never is. But Mole liked everything. Just when he had got the basket packed and strapped up, he saw a plate staring up at him from the grass. And when the job had been done again, Rat showed the Mole a spoon that anybody should have seen. And last of all, the jam pot, which he had been sitting on without knowing it. Still, somehow, the thing got finished at last, without anyone getting mad.

The Wind in the Willows

Chapter 1
THE OPEN ROAD
Part 6

by Kenneth Grahame
retold

Illustrated by Artifact Group

Decodable Book Lesson 149

McGraw Hill SRA

This day was only the first of many for Mole. Each of them longer and full of fun as summer moved on.

Mc Graw Hill

SRA

www.sraonline.com

Copyright © 2008 SRA/McGraw-Hill.

All rights reserved. Permission is granted to reproduce the material contained herein on the condition that such material be reproduced only for classroom use; be provided to students, teachers, or families without charge; and be used solely in conjunction with *Reading Mastery Signature Edition*. Any other reproduction, for use of sale, is prohibited without prior written permission of the publisher.

Printed in the United States of America.

Send all inquiries to:
SRA/McGraw-Hill
4400 Easton Commons
Columbus, OH 43219

Mole was so touched by his kind manner of speaking that he could not answer him. He had to brush away a tear or two with the back of his paw. But Rat looked the other way. Soon Mole felt better again. He was even able to give some backtalk to some hens who were laughing to each other about the way he looked.

When they got home, Rat made a fire in the den, and planted the Mole in an armchair in front of it. He gave him a robe and slippers and told him river stories until dinner time. They were very thrilling stories, too. Stories about leaping fish and about flights down drains and night fishing with Otter or trips with Badger. Dinner was a most cheerful meal; but very shortly after that a sleepy Mole had to be taken upstairs to the best bedroom. He soon laid his head on his pillow in peace, knowing that his new friend the river was lapping at his window.

Mole flung his oars back with a grand show and made a dig at the water. He missed the water. His legs flew up over his head, and he found himself lying on top of the Rat. Very upset, he made a grab at the side of the boat, and then—Sploosh!

Over went the boat, and he found himself fighting in the river.

When all was ready for a start once more, Mole, sagging and wet, took his seat in the rear of the boat. As they set off, he said in a low voice, "Ratty, my good friend! I am very sorry for the way I acted. My heart stops when I think how we might not have found that lunch basket. I have been a silly thing, and I know it. Will you overlook it this once and forgive me, and let things go on as before?"

"That's all right!" answered Rat. "What's a little wet to a Water Rat? I'm more in the water than out of it most days. Don't you think anymore about it. I really think you had better come and stay with me for a little time. It's very plain, you know—not like Toad's house at all—but you haven't seen that yet. Still, I can make you feel at home. And I'll teach you to row and to swim, and you'll soon be as good on the water as any of us."

Oh my, how cold the water was, and oh, how very wet it felt. How it sang in his ears as he went down, down, down! How bright the sun looked as he rose to the top, gagging! How he lost hope when he felt himself sinking again! Then a strong paw gripped him by the back of his neck. It was Rat, and Rat was laughing. Mole could feel him laughing, right down his arm and through his paw, and so into his—Mole's—neck.

Rat got hold of an oar and put it under Mole's arm. Then he did the same to the other side of him. Then swimming behind Mole, Rat got Mole to shore. He pulled him out and set him down on the bank, a lump of gloom.

Rat rubbed him down a bit and got some of the wet out of him. Then he said, "Now old fellow! Trot up and down the path as hard as you can, till you're warm and dry again. I'll dive for the lunch basket."

So Mole trotted about until he was fairly dry, while Rat dived into the water again. He got the boat, turned it right side up, and tied it up. Then he little by little he got his floating things to shore. At last, he got the lunch basket and got to land with it.

The Wind in the Willows

Chapter 2
THE OPEN ROAD
Part 1

by Kenneth Grahame
retold

Decodable Book Lesson 152

Rounding a bend in the river, they came in sight of a handsome, old house of old red brick, with well-kept yards reaching down to the water.

"There is Toad Hall," said Rat; "and that creek on the left, where the sign says, "Keep out. No landing," leads to his boat house. We'll leave the boat there. The barns are over there to the right. That's the dinner hall. Very old, that is. Toad is rather rich, you know. This is really one of the nicest houses in these parts, but we never say so to Toad."

"Why, of course," said Rat, jumping to his feet. His song was gone from his mind for the day. "Get the boat out, and we'll row up there at once. It's always the right time to call on Toad. Early or late he is always the same fellow. Always glad to see you, always sorry when you go!"

"He must be a very nice animal," said Mole. He got into the boat and took the oars, while Rat seated himself in the rear.

"He is the best of animals," answered Rat. "So simple, so good, and so kind. Maybe he is not very smart—we can't all be smart. And maybe that he brags a lot. But he is a good friend."

"Ratty," said Mole suddenly, one bright summer morning. "If you please, I want to ask you to do something for me."

Rat was sitting on the river bank, singing a little song he had just made up. He was singing and not listening to Mole or anything else. From early morning he had been swimming in the river with the ducks. And when the ducks stood on their heads suddenly, as ducks will, he would dive down and tickle their necks, just under where their chins would be if ducks had chins. Then the ducks had to come up again fast. They were mad and shaking their feathers at him, for it is impossible to say all you feel when your head is under water. At last they begged him to go away and leave them alone. So Rat went away and sat on the river bank in the sun. He made up a song about them, which he called "DUCKS' DITTY."

"I don't know that I think so very much of that little song, Rat," said Mole.

"The ducks don't either," answered Rat cheerfully. "They think I should leave them alone to do what they want. They think I shouldn't make fun of them. That's what the ducks think."

"That's true. That's true," said Mole.

"No, it's not!" cried Rat.

"Well then, it's not, it's not, it's not," answered Mole. "But what I wanted to ask you was, won't you take me to call on Mr. Toad? Everyone has said so much about him, and I do so want to meet him."

All along the backwater,
Through the rushes tall,
Ducks are a-dabbling,
Up tails all!
Ducks' tails, drakes' tails,
Yellow feet a-quiver,
Yellow bills all out of sight
Feeding in the river!
Soft green weeds
Where the roach swim
Here we keep our store,
Cool and full and dim.

Everyone for what he likes!
We like to be
Heads down, tails up,
Dabbling free!
Up in the blue sky
Birds swirl and call—
We are down a-dabbling
Up tails all!

The Wind in the Willows

Chapter 2
THE OPEN ROAD
Part 2

by Kenneth Grahame
retold
Illustrated by Artifact Group

Decodable Book Lesson 154

Mc Graw Hill SRA

He led the way to the barn yard. And there, they saw a cart, painted yellow and green with red wheels.

"There you are!" cried Toad. "There is real life for you in that little cart. The open road, the dusty paths, camps, towns, cities! Here today, up and off to somewhere else the next day! The whole world before you. And mind you, this is the very finest cart of its sort that was ever built. Come inside and look at it. Planned it all myself, I did!"

They rowed up the creek, and Mole slipped his oars as they passed near the boat house. Here they saw many handsome boats, hung from the cross beams, but none in the water. It seemed the no one used the place anymore.

Rat looked around him. "I understand," said Rat. "Boating is played out. He is tired of it and done with it. I wonder what new fad he has taken up now? Come along and let's look him up. We will hear all about it soon."

"It's about your rowing, I think," said Rat. "You're getting on fairly well, though you splash a good bit still. With a lot of work, and a lot of teaching, you may . . . ."

"O, pooh! Boating!" said Toad. "I gave that up long ago. A bad way to use time, that's what it is. It makes me downright sorry to see you fellows, who should know better, spending all your time in that way. No, I've found the real thing. I plan to give the rest of life to it. Come with me, dear Ratty, and your friend also, just as far as the barn yard. You will see what you will see!"

They got out and walked across the yard looking for Toad. They found him resting in a wicker garden chair, with a strange look on his face, and a big map spread out on his lap.

"Hooray!" he cried, jumping up on seeing them. "This is wonderful!" He shook their paws. "How kind of you!" He went on, dancing round them. "I was just going to send a boat down the river for you, Ratty. I want you badly—you and your friend. Now what will you take? Come inside and have something! You don't know how lucky it is, your turning up just now!"

"Let's sit a bit, Toady!" said Rat, throwing himself into an easy chair. Mole took another by the side of him and said something about Toad's home.

"Finest house on the whole river," cried Toad. "Or anywhere else, for that matter," he could not help adding.

Here Rat bumped Mole. Toad saw him do it, and turned very red. He said nothing. Then Toad started laughing. "All right, Ratty," he said. "It's only my way, you know. And it's not such a very bad house, is it? You know you rather like it yourself. Now, look here. You are the very animals I wanted. You've got to help me!"

The Wind in the Willows

Chapter 2
THE OPEN ROAD
Part 3

by Kenneth Grahame
retold

Decodable Book Lesson 157

 SRA

"No, no, we'll see it out," answered Rat. "Thanks, but I should stick by Toad till this trip is ended. It wouldn't be safe for him to be left to himself. It won't take very long. His fads never do. Good night!"

The end was nearer than even Rat thought.

Late in the evening, they stopped and turned the horse out to eat. They ate their simple dinner sitting on the grass beside the cart. Toad talked big about all he was going to do in the days to come. The stars grew bigger all around them. A yellow moon appeared suddenly to listen to their talk. At last they turned in to their little bunks in the cart. Toad, kicking out his legs, said, "Well, good night, you fellows! This is the real life! Talk about your old river!"

"I don't talk about my river," answered Rat. "You know I don't," Toad. But I think about it," he added. "I think about it all the time!"

Mole reached out for Rat's paw and gave it a squeeze. "I'll do whatever you like, Ratty," he said. "Should we run away in the morning and go back to our dear old hole on the river?"

148

Mole was thrilled, and followed Toad up the steps and inside the cart. Rat only sniffed and put his hands deep into his pockets, staying where he was.

It was very handsome. Little sleeping bunks—a little table that folded up by the wall. A cooking-stove, lockers, books, a birdcage with a bird in it, and pots, pans, and jugs of every size and kind.

"All done!" said Toad, pulling open a locker. "You see, everything you can want. Soda-water here—note paper, jam, cards," he said, as they went down the steps again. "You'll find that I didn't forget anything, when we start this afternoon."

When they were ready, Toad led his friends to the barn yard to get the old horse. The horse did not want the dusty job of pulling the cart. So it took a lot of chasing to get him. Meantime Toad packed the boxes with things they needed, and hung feed bags, nets of onions, hay, and baskets from the bottom of the cart. At last the horse was ready, and they set off. They were all talking at once. Each animal either walking by the side of the cart or sitting on the seat. It was a golden afternoon. The smell of the dust they kicked up was rich. Birds called to them. Other animals waved or stopped to say nice things about their cart. Rabbits, sitting at their front doors, held up their paws, and said, "O my! O my! O my!"

"I'm sorry," said Rat slowly, "but did I overhear you say something about 'we' and 'start' and 'this afternoon'?"

"Now, you dear good old Ratty," said Toad. "Don't begin talking in that way, because you know you've got to come. I can't do it without you. You really don't mean to stick to your old river all your life, and just live in a hole in a bank, and boat? I want to show you the world! I'm going to make an animal of you, my boy!"

"I don't care," said Rat. "I'm not coming, and that's flat. And I am going to stick to my old river, and live in a hole, and boat, as I've always done. And what's more, Mole will stick me and do as I do, won't you, Mole?"

"Of course I will," said Mole. "I'll always stick with you, Rat, and what you say is to be. All the same, it sounds as if it might have been fun, you know!" he added. Oh, Mole! This life was so new to him, and so thrilling. And he did fall in love at first sight with the yellow cart.

Rat saw what was going on in Mole's mind. He hated upsetting people. He really liked Mole and would do almost anything for him. Toad was watching them.

"Come along in, and have some lunch," he said. "We'll talk it over. You don't have to make up your mind right now. Of course, I don't really care. I only want to please you fellows."

While they ate lunch, Toad let himself go. He talked about living on the road in such glowing colors that Mole could hardly sit still. Soon it seemed that they would take the trip. Rat didn't want to upset his two friends. Toad and Mole were already planning out each day in the weeks to come.

150

The Wind in the Willows

Chapter 2
THE OPEN ROAD
Part 4

by Kenneth Grahame
retold

Decodable Book Lesson 159

 **SRA**

"You see what it is?" Rat said to Mole. "I give up. When we get to the town, we'll get a train to take us back to the river tonight."

The following evening, Mole was sitting on the bank fishing, when Rat came along. "Did you hear the news?" he asked. "There is nothing else being talked about all along the river bank. Toad went up to town this morning. And he is buying a big motor-car."

www.sraonline.com

SRA

Copyright © 2008 SRA/McGraw-Hill.

All rights reserved. Permission is granted to reproduce the material contained herein on the condition that such material be reproduced only for classroom use; be provided to students, teachers, or families without charge; and be used solely in conjunction with *Reading Mastery Signature Edition*. Any other reproduction, for use of sale, is prohibited without prior written permission of the publisher.

Printed in the United States of America.

Send all inquiries to:
SRA/McGraw-Hill
4400 Easton Commons
Columbus, OH 43219

"But what about Toad?" asked Mole. "We can't leave him here, sitting in the middle of the road by himself. It's not safe. What if another Thing comes along?"

"Oh, forget Toad," said Rat. "I've done with him!"

They had not gone very far when there was a tapping of feet behind them.

"Now, look here, Toad!" said Rat. "As soon as we get to the town, you'll have to go to the police. See if they know anything about that motor-car. And then you'll have to find someone to get the cart and fix it. It will take time, but it can be fixed. Mole and I will go find rooms where we can stay till the cart's ready."

"Police! Police!" said Toad. "Fix the cart! I'm done with carts forever. I never want to see the cart, or to hear of it, again. Oh, Ratty! You can't think how happy I am that you came on this trip! I wouldn't have gone without you, and then I might never have seen that that motor-car!"

Rat shook him. "Are you coming to help us, Toad?" he asked.

"Wonderful sight!" said Toad. "The real way to travel! The only way to travel! Oh poop-poop! Oh my! Oh my!"

"Oh stop being so silly, Toad!" cried Mole.

"And to think I never knew!" went on Toad. "All these years, I never knew! But now that I know. Oh what a road lies before me! What dust clouds will spring up behind me as I speed on my way!"

"What are we to do with him?" Mole asked Water Rat.

"Nothing at all," answered Rat. "Because there is really nothing to be done. You see, I know him from of old. He has a new fad, and it always takes him that way at first. He'll continue like that for days now. Never mind him. Let's see what we can do about the cart."

The cart would go no longer. Rat took the horse. "Come on!" he said to the Mole. "It's five or six miles to town. We will just have to walk it."

Nothing could get Toad out of bed the next morning. So Mole and Rat got to work. Rat saw to the horse and started a fire and cleaned the cups and plates. Mole went to the nearest town for milk and eggs and other things Toad forgot. The two animals were resting by the time Toad woke up.

They had a nice ride that day and camped as before. This time Mole and Rat saw that Toad did his part of work. When the time came to travel next morning, Toad wanted to stay in his bunk, but Rat and Mole pulled him out.

Toad and Water Rat walked behind the cart talking. Well, Toad was talking. Then far behind them they could hear a faint hum, like a faraway bee. Looking back, they saw a small cloud of dust. From the dust a faint "Pop-pop!" cry, like an animal in pain.

The animals went back to talking. Then a gust of wind and a swirl of sound made them jump for the nearest ditch. It was on them! The "Pop-pop" shouted in their ears. They had a look at glass and metal. Then the motor-car, with its driver hugging his wheel, flung a cloud of dust at them.

The old horse had been dreaming as he walked along. The motor-car sent him rearing. He drove the cart back into the deep ditch at the side of the road. It shook, and then it crashed. The yellow cart lay on its side in the ditch.

Rat danced up and down in the road. "You monster!" he shouted, shaking his paws, "You—you—road hogs! I'll have the law after you!"

Toad sat down in the middle of the dusty road, his legs out before him, and stared at the disappearing motor-car. At times he smiled and said, "Pop-pop!"

Mole tried to help the horse. Then he went to look at the cart on its side in the ditch. It was a sorry sight.

Rat went to help him, but they could not right the cart. "Toad!" they cried. "Come and give us a hand, can't you!"

The Toad never answered or moved from his seat in the road. They went to see what was the matter with him. They found him with a happy smile on his face. His eyes on the dust of the motor-car. From time to time they could still hear him say "Pop-pop!"